# EXTREME CIVIL WAR

## CONFLICTING WORLDS

NEW DIMENSIONS OF THE AMERICAN CIVIL WAR

T. Michael Parrish, Series Editor

# EXTREME CIVIL WAR

## GUERRILLA WARFARE, ENVIRONMENT, AND RACE ON THE TRANS-MISSISSIPPI FRONTIER

MATTHEW M. STITH

LOUISIANA STATE UNIVERSITY PRESS

BATON ROUGE

Published with the assistance of the V. Ray Cardozier Fund

Published by Louisiana State University Press
Copyright © 2016 by Louisiana State University Press
Manufactured in the United States of America
First printing

Designer: Barbara Neely Bourgoyne
Typeface: Quadraat
Printer and binder: Maple Press

Library of Congress Cataloging-in-Publication Data

Names: Stith, Matthew M., author.
Title: Extreme Civil War : guerrilla warfare, environment, and race on the trans-Mississippi
frontier / Matthew M. Stith.
Description: Baton Rouge : Louisiana State University Press, 2016. | Series: Conflicting worlds:
new dimensions of the American Civil War | Includes bibliographical references and index.
Identifiers: LCCN 2015042804| ISBN 978-0-8071-6314-6 (cloth : alk. paper) | ISBN
978-0-8071-6315-3 (pdf) | ISBN 978-0-8071-6316-0 (epub) | ISBN 978-0-8071-6317-7 (mobi)
Subjects: LCSH: Southwest, Old—History—Civil War, 1861–1865—Underground movements.
| Southwest, Old—History—Civil War, 1861–1865—Commando operations. | Southwest,
Old—History—Civil War, 1861–1865—Campaigns. | United States—History—Civil War,
1861–1865—Underground movements. | United States—History—Civil War, 1861–1865—
Commando operations. | United States—History—Civil War, 1861–1865—Campaigns. |
Guerrilla warfare—Southwest, Old—History—19th century. | Guerrilla warfare—United
States—History—19th century.
Classification: LCC E470.45 .S75 2016 | DDC 979/.02—dc23 LC record available at
http://lccn.loc.gov/2015042804

Part of this book was previously published as "The Deplorable Condition of the Country: Nature,
Society, and War on the Trans-Mississippi Frontier," Civil War History 58:3 (September 2012).
Copyright 2012 by The Kent State University Press. Reprinted with permission.

The paper in this book meets the guidelines for permanence and durability
of the Committee on Production Guidelines for Book Longevity
of the Council on Library Resources. ∞

# CONTENTS

Illustrations follow page 84

# ACKNOWLEDGMENTS

I owe a lot to many people, and I will try my best to thank them properly.

The genesis of *Extreme Civil War* can be traced back to Virginia J. Laas's Missouri history class at Missouri Southern State University. Laas taught me how to be a historian and encouraged my work on the guerrilla war. She also took the class on a trip to the Jasper County Records Center in Carthage, Missouri, to dig around in original primary-source material. There I found boxes of post–Civil War court records full of civilian lawsuits against alleged guerrillas. This discovery, together with Laas's mentorship and the wonderful records-center staff, started me on the path to explore the complex story of irregular warfare on the border. Records-center director Steve Weldon helped refine my earliest ideas and provided countless hours of excellent conversation. I also owe a great deal to local-records archivist Linda Myers and Wilson's Creek National Battlefield historian Connie Langum, both of whom I was fortunate to work with (and learn from) early in my academic career.

Although the book idea started in southwest Missouri, it came far closer to reality in northwest Arkansas. First and foremost, Daniel E. Sutherland at the University of Arkansas proved unerringly helpful as I struggled to make sense of my research and ideas. His patient advice and encouragement serves as yet more proof that he is one of the top scholars thinking and writing about the past today. Any student or scholar who has been fortunate enough to work with Sutherland knows he is *also* among the finest advisors and mentors in the field. Elliott West influenced my thinking significantly, especially in terms of the environment and its direct and ubiquitous role in shaping the war. West's humor and knack for making a good story out of the complex past is inspirational, and his advice and encouragement for this project proved invaluable. Thanks also to Patrick G. Williams. Anyone who knows him will know that he is the epitome of a careful, patient, and exacting scholar. Williams has served as a model not only for my thinking as a historian but also for that of multiple generations of graduate students at the University of Arkansas.

Many other scholars have directly or indirectly shaped this book. Thanks to Lisa M. Brady and Megan Kate Nelson for their advice at different stages of this project and for their own important work on Civil War environmental history. Thanks also to my good friend and colleague Alan Thompson at Prairie Grove Battlefield State Park. Thompson is one of the best scholars I know and, thanks to an ongoing decade-long conversation, has helped shape my thinking about the guerrilla war and the Civil War generally. I am also indebted to great friends from the University of Arkansas, including Geoffrey Jensen and Jeremy Taylor, who are top-notch scholars and have shown enthusiasm and support from the earliest stages, and especially Scott Cashion and David Schieffler, who have spent countless hours over the years talking history and other things; this work has benefitted enormously from those conversations.

Several people helped shepherd the manuscript into book form over the past year. I am thrilled and honored to have this project published as part of T. Michael Parrish's exceptional Conflicting Worlds series. Parrish proved patient, supportive, and incredibly helpful at every step of the process, reading multiple drafts and helping me refine, clarify, and strengthen my ideas and contentions. Kevin Brock used his superb copyediting ability to help clarify those contentions; I see now why so many call him one of the best in the business. Finally, Rand Dotson at Louisiana State University Press patiently walked me through the publication process and helped make the experience positive and rewarding.

On the research trail I received a great deal of generous support. At the University of Arkansas I benefited enormously from the advice and encouragement of the late Willard B. Gatewood and was fortunate to receive the Gatewood Fellowship in Southern History and the James J. Hudson Fellowship for Research Support. Thanks to the Missouri State Archives in Jefferson

City, which funded a week of fruitful research through the William E. Foley Fellowship. Librarians and archivists at a number of libraries and research facilities made research an even-more-enjoyable and rewarding experience. Thanks to the staff at the Rare Book, Manuscript, and Special Collections at Duke University; the Southern Historical Collection at the University of North Carolina, Chapel Hill; the National Archives and Records Administration in Washington, D.C.; the Kansas State Historical Society in Topeka; the Missouri State Archives in Jefferson City; the Arkansas History Commission in Little Rock; and the Missouri Historical Society in Saint Louis. Geoffrey Starks of the Special Collections at the University of Arkansas Libraries proved that the university's research support is among the finest in the country. Thanks also to Alan Chilton at Wilson's Creek, formerly at Fort Scott National Historic Site, who provided a plethora of valuable research material. Finally, Howard Rockwell and the Interlibrary Loan staff at the University of Texas at Tyler's Muntz Library helped bring copious amounts of material to my doorstep—or at least very close to it.

I appreciate the support and friendship provided by my friends and colleagues at the University of Texas at Tyler. Thanks to my fellow historians Melissa Dotson, Pat Gajda, Mickie Koster, James Newsom, Colin Snider, and Ed Tabri. Other friends and colleagues have made working at the university great fun, particularly Tom Guderjan, Randy LeBlanc, Eric Lopez, Cory Sills, Bob Sterken, and Amentahru Wahlrab. My appreciation extends to Marcus Stadelmann for his support and encouragement as department chair and colleague. Finally, thanks to Vicki Betts at the university's Muntz Library for her help, encouragement, and infectious enthusiasm for uncovering and understanding the past. The faculty and staff in Tyler are incredibly fortunate to have such a top-notch librarian on campus, and Civil War historians everywhere benefit from her thorough and exhaustive research.

Finally, my friends and family outside of academia have been enormously supportive. Jim Beien has provided encouragement and good conversation over the years. My mom and sister gave me their good-natured support even when they were probably tired of hearing about the project. But most of all, thanks to Melissa Ann, Lorelei, and Wyatt, who together have made my nonscholarly life the best anyone could possibly ask for. They have made it all worthwhile.

# EXTREME CIVIL WAR

# Introduction

On a cold day in the early spring of 1864, Union cavalry captain Ozias Ruark and his men rode through a wasteland. Directing his small force through Missouri's extreme southwestern corner, Ruark reported the local mills torched and the region mostly uninhabited. The only human life the tired and harried Federal cavalryman had seen consisted of "a small number of indigent women and children, who [had] no forage at all except a very little corn." Worse, he noted, the pitiable civilians probably did not have enough "to bread them more than two months." Those who did have corn guarded it carefully by meticulously shelling and storing it in their bedrooms inside drawers and under floorboards. In a style of warfare that required combatants to live off the land, and with little food remaining in the fields, Ruark and his men had little choice but to keep riding. Even if he had stolen every bit of food from the impoverished locals, the young captain observed, he could not have sustained his force for more than a few days. Three years of hard warfare in tandem with an unforgiving winter and a persistent drought had turned an already difficult countryside into a no-man's land.[1]

One year before Ruark's stark observations, Thomas Alexander's family had felt the full brunt of the irregular war that consumed the western Trans-Mississippi frontier. In October 1863 a small band of guerrillas rode up to Alexander's house in southwest Missouri. In typical fashion the men, led by Rice and Hugh Challas, dismounted and demanded that the family immediately evacuate their home. The guerrillas took what they wanted and then torched the structure, but the trauma did not stop there. In all the excitement one of Alexander's daughters ran back inside in an attempt to rescue "various articles" from the blaze. As she desperately tried to save what she could, her dress caught fire; the girl burned to death in front of her family. In a court case following the war, Alexander was not clear how his daughter's dress had caught fire, at one point suggesting that the guerrillas had "set her clothes on fire." But the details of exactly how she died are immaterial. What is relevant is that the girl perished as a direct result of the violence and terror that had inundated the region since the first year of the war. Now two years after the horrific incident, as people began to filter back into the region and rebuild physically and emotionally, Alexander testified that the raid had ruined his family. It was "such a shock as to seriously impair the mind of his wife. . . . [T]he burning of his house and everything in it . . . [had] made him very poor [and] caused him to suffer great distress of mind." In the vicious frenzy of this indiscriminate action, the guerrillas went far beyond even their common practice of only burning homes and killing men thought to be Union sympathizers. The Challases' men and their unknown accomplices had escalated beyond simply "hard" guerrilla tactics. The girl and her family had become *directly* entangled in the war. Like their neighbors in the region—Unionist or Confederate—they had become active participants, however unwillingly, in a severe and unyielding conflict.[2]

Ruark's and Alexander's experiences are hardly anecdotal. They exemplify irregular warfare on the western edge of the Trans-Mississippi theater—a region where Arkansas, Indian Territory, Missouri, and Kansas met and formed a cultural, racial, and environmental borderland. This war in the margins was experienced by women and children as much as by soldiers and guerrillas. Nobody was immune to its immediate and long-term effects, to the foraging of Union soldiers or Confederate guerrillas, or to the consequences of the environment's extremes. Harsh winters, drought, and a continual struggle to control both crops and livestock indelibly shaped how civilians experienced, and at times succumbed, to the war on the border. When such environmental factors mixed with a conflict defined by the breakdown of society, a different kind of warfare emerged—one that occurred not only in the geographical margins of the Trans-Mississippi but also on the extreme margins of what many scholars have termed "hard war."

This book explores the complexity and brutality of the civilian-centered conflict that occurred in a region that soldiers then and scholars now call the border, with a more specific focus on the area between Fort Scott, Kansas, and Fort Smith, Arkansas. This study, however, stops short of the more robustly examined region around Lawrence, Kansas, and Jackson County, Missouri, a part of the border that has heretofore received the preponderance of scholarly attention.[3] For soldiers and civilians alike, this was the frontier in 1860s America, California and Oregon notwithstanding. Although thousands had crossed the Great Plains for destinations on the West Coast, the Civil War–era "frontier" existed where Kansas met Missouri and where Indian Territory met Arkansas. Here was the edge of Anglo western settlement. In addition to being a geographical frontier that coincided with several political boundaries, this region was also a cultural borderland. More than 130,000 people lived there at the outbreak of the war, including over 21,000 Cherokee Indians, 5,000 slaves in southwest Missouri and northwest Arkansas, and over 4,000 slaves in the Cherokee Nation. African Americans and Native Americans thus comprised more than 30 percent of the wartime population on the western Trans-Mississippi border. By midwar, hundreds of former slaves had joined the Federal ranks in the region, and according to one estimate, at least 1,500 Cherokee men also had joined the fighting.[4] With the outbreak of hostilities, Native Americans, Iowa farm boys, Texans, African American slaves and soldiers, German immigrants, and a host of others, military and civilian, from across the South and North clashed in what became a literal and symbolic war in the margins. It rapidly evolved into a conflict that stretched beyond a fight for nationhood into a destructive and protracted guerrilla warfare typified by civilian involvement and racial animosity amid a challenging and volatile natural environment.

Within this culturally and naturally diverse region, the contest rapidly devolved into what Michael Fellman has called the "nihilist edge." To be sure, as experienced by the Alexander family, this brand of fighting often went well over that edge. Several factors tipped the conflict on the border beyond the relatively limited, or even hard, war raging throughout much of the South. On the western Trans-Mississippi frontier, small bands of men—Union and Confederate—waged war on their own terms. Antebellum rivalries turned bloody, and although regular units from both sides roamed the region, the majority of fighting took place in relative isolation—in random thickets, rugged roadways, and most importantly in front yards and living rooms. Indeed, Confederate guerrillas and Union militiamen were scarcely concerned with military discipline and law. From the first year of the war, they terrorized civilians as much as they fought each other.[5]

The war on the border was both savage and diverse. It was a separate struggle within the wider conflict not only connected through campaigns and battles but also, importantly, overwhelmingly disconnected in terms of civilian-centered violence. The guerrilla fighting there mirrored the worst pockets of irregular warfare across the South. According to historian William L. Shea, the brand of combat in the region "was appalling, so appalling that we have largely eliminated it from our collective memory." In the end, he declares, "the intensity, the brutality of irregular warfare in the Trans-Mississippi was unmatched anywhere else." Shea is right. Combatants and victims from all sides struggled to come to terms with a largely guerrilla style of warfare within a region defined by incredible cultural and environmental diversity. Soldiers and civilians from the North or the South and who were white, black, or Indian found themselves in an unyielding contest within an environment underscored by a rugged landscape, unpredictable waterways, and harsh weather prone to extreme conditions.[6]

The conflict on the western Trans-Mississippi frontier occurred in one of the most difficult environments in the American South. Steep terrain, volatile rivers, and climatic extremes formed the foundation atop which varying cultures and ethnicities suffered guerrilla warfare. Before 1861, Americans had worked diligently to control nature, deeming this an important part of civilization and the American character. With the onset of hostilities, people on the frontier found the accepted paradigm destroyed. Civilians and soldiers alike found themselves once again at odds with the natural world. Rivers, hills, forests, livestock, and crops became tools of war. The environment they had tried so hard to control now reverted to an volatile and harsh obstacle in the medium of the brutal guerrilla struggle. Agricultural products shifted from an important but predictable staple in society to a fulcrum point for the fighting. Countless microbattles occurred throughout the region, and these were centered on corn, hogs, and cows. For civilians, defending their livestock and crops became tantamount to defending their lives. Indeed, to lose such important food sources was to threaten their own health and livelihood. Noncombatants and combatants fought as much with the environment as they did guerrilla bands or Union patrols.[7]

Engaging in war beyond their cultural comfort zone against people outside their "cultural net," as one historian calls it, led to a devastating experience for both civilians and soldiers. Wisconsin farm boys could hardly reconcile their distrust and at times sheer loathing of residents in southwest Missouri. Confederate guerrillas terrorized African American soldiers every chance they had. Native Americans imparted their style of combat—what some American tacticians called a "skulking way of war"—in the greater military effort and incited suspiciousness and often hatred from both Union and Confederate soldiers. The nature of the conflict for soldiers and civilians from different cultures and ethnicities was often deadly and always confusing. According to a historian of the Indian Wars in colonial America, combatants "suffered from muddled convictions and uncertainties about the war's boundaries and divisions." And so it was on the western frontier of the Trans-Mississippi in the middle nineteenth century. War there was a messy, confusing, and altogether brutal affair, blurring the lines of what had been deemed honorable or civilized warfare—the stuff for regular armies fighting regular battles in regular campaigns. The intense racial and political hatred that helped fuel the conflict became its very centerpiece in the western margins of Missouri and Arkansas and in the figurative margins of the Civil War itself.[8]

Racial and cultural struggles therefore emerged as an integral part of the conflict. Union Indians, blacks, and whites often fought together in a unified front against Confederate whites and Indians. Rebel guerrillas sought especially savage retribution against black troops, and white Federal commanders increasingly came to question whether to grant guerrillas even the smallest level of mercy. Native American civilians suffered immeasurably within the first months of the conflict, which had nullified their control over the environment. Recent scholarship has reflected Indian Territory's important role in the regular and, more importantly, irregular war. Clarissa Confer, Mary Jane Warde, and others have laid bare the devastating warfare that occurred in Indian Territory by illustrating its violent and destructive consequences in that region. There Native American combatants and civilians blended with white and African American soldiers and civilians to form an ethnic, cultural, and racial middle ground. No matter their allegiance, Indian residents suffered immeasurably from the very start. Thousands died or became refugees; all were exposed to especially harsh environmental extremes; and they all became directly involved in the fighting. Their war was relentless, ubiquitous, and devastating. For historian Mark Lause, such racial diversity on the frontier exemplified the radical nature of the conflict. The war in the region, he says, had soon become one influenced largely by the "heirs of John Brown." Indeed, the racial tension and violence that had so indelibly marked the antebellum Kansas-Missouri border grew into a complex, terror-driven conflict that spilled over into Indian Territory and Arkansas.[9]

If major battles dictated the *course* of the Civil War, hundreds of much smaller battles redefined its *nature*. Civilians on the border repeatedly fought against Federal patrols and rebel guerrillas over their stored corn, hog pens, houses, and livelihood. For women and children, victory was tied to survival, not an abstract notion of Confederate or Union nationalism. Saving hogs for the winter meant more than nationalistic grandeur emanating from Richmond or Washington, both over a thousand miles to the east. While civilians on the border were hardly disinterested in the larger and more traditional battles and campaigns, unlike most of their counterparts in other parts of the South (or North), they were *part* of the battle in their region. Fighting happened atop hearths and in front yards between civilians and soldiers or guerrillas just as it did in open fields between large armies. Although these engagements taken individually might have had only a very small role in determining Confederate defeat or victory, ignoring them in favor of a singular nationalistic view of the Civil War risks missing the most complex and troubling parts of the conflict.[10] Further, Confederate irregulars, not regular soldiers, were the chief cause for the exceedingly harsh Union countermeasures on the border. By its very nature, guerrilla warfare predisposes civilians as direct players in the combat—willingly or not—becoming targets for both guerrillas and Union troops. As historian Daniel E. Sutherland has argued, the civilian-centered dynamic of this irregular conflict led Union forces to undermine the local core of support for the Confederacy. Taken as a whole, the thousands of microbattles that featured civilians as key players serve to cast the Civil War in a new light, one that refocuses our understanding through a lens tinged not just by army-fueled nationalistic sentiment but also by civilian-centered fighting highlighted by cultural, racial, and environmental brutality.[11]

The western Trans-Mississippi border did not hold a monopoly on racial, cultural, and geographic diversity in the South. In many ways this frontier reflects other pockets of the Confederate home front, especially in the Border States, where difficult terrain melded with a culturally and politically divided population to produce particularly brutal regional guerrilla conflicts. It is imperative to place the western Trans-Mississippi border fighting in the context of this kind of irregular warfare that occurred elsewhere in the South. A strikingly similar contest affected geographically and politically diverse regions in Kentucky, Tennessee, Virginia, and North Carolina. In his important work on the Appalachian region of Kentucky and Virginia, Brian D. McKnight shows that rugged terrain had funneled the regular war into certain pathways, while those geographically isolated regions suffered from a nearly constant guerrilla conflict. This "no-man's land," McKnight contends, was "where the war was most dangerous for nonparticipants." In his community-level study of wartime violence in northeastern North Carolina, Barton A. Myers shows how political dynamics and guerrilla fighting "created a world where irregular military activity could thrive and where murder and execution could hold hostage a southern community on the periphery of the major Confederate war effort." For McKnight and Myers alike, the conflict along the margins of the regular combat raging elsewhere—one that directly enveloped not just soldiers and guerrillas but civilians as well—represents a critically important window through which to understand the wider Civil War.[12]

Evidence of terror, destruction, and death is more than just circumstantial. In a recent study based on census data, J. David Hacker finds that between 50,000 and 100,000 civilians died as a direct result of the war, more than 9,000 of them probably women. Of these, a higher percentage died in the Border States. As even Hacker admits, to calculate specific numbers in any given area remains difficult. But taken on the whole, his findings illustrate a greater mortality among civilians than previously thought. With residents in Missouri, Kansas, Arkansas, and Indian Territory having endured the most destructive war, Hacker's numbers suggest an extreme loss of life among the region's noncombatants in addition to personal terror and property destruction. Other scholars estimate that between 10,000 and 27,000 people died in Missouri alone. Moreover, nearly 300,000 men, women, and children left their homes for refuge farther north or south. In Arkansas most counties lost nearly half of their population, and a good majority of those who remained moved into or near Union or Confederate strongholds for protection. Civilians in Indian Territory suffered even more. By some estimates the Cherokee Nation in northeastern Indian Territory lost over 30 percent of its population, nearly 14,000 people having died or become refugees. In the end, though, coming to any truly reliable number for casualties, deaths, and refugees on the western Trans-Mississippi border is futile. Outside of national census data, local and even state records are dubious if they exist at all.[13]

After more than two decades of important scholarship, historians have come to recognize the guerrilla war's decisive role in shaping the Civil War. This topic has emerged as a thriving and important historiographical field.[14] The first major study to examine a society during the war, Philip Shaw Paludan's Victims, published in 1981, places civilians at the center of the story of the bloody Laurel Valley massacre in western North Carolina. By analyzing the lives of ordinary people amid one of the conflict's more tragic episodes, Paludan strips away the persistent historiographical focus on commanders and armies. After this work, popular guerrilla and partisan leaders and the regions in which they operated were not ignored but rather viewed within the context of civilian-centered warfare.[15]

Almost a decade after Paludan's work appeared, Michael Fellman's Inside War emerged as the most influential study of the civilian conflict. Fellman sought to understand how civilians responded to an environment in which they were at once victims and combatants. His effort, more than any other preceding it, helped turn the attention of scholars toward the social conflict inside the larger Civil War. A generation of scholars since has debated both the confines and severity of the kind of war illuminated in this landmark work. But historians have yet to fully define the war fought along the Trans-Mississippi's western fringes, and such difficulties only underscore the complexities inherent in the conflict that raged there.[16]

Energized by Fellman's social and psychological study, historians have taken similar approaches to expose the brutality of irregular warfare elsewhere. In the last decade McKnight, Robert R. Mackey, Barton A. Myers,

Jonathan Dean Sarris, Jeremy Neely, and Clay Mountcastle have provided excellent looks into specific pockets of such activity throughout the South. Sutherland's A Savage Conflict finally has tied these regionally disparate stories into a unified narrative of irregular warfare fueled by strategy, politics, rage, and greed across the South. Sutherland argues that this particularly nasty guerrilla activity led Federal authorities to alter their military strategy against the Confederacy, including the rebel home front. Because irregulars fought beyond the conventional battlefield, harassing Union soldiers, disrupting supply lines, and equally important, intimidating Unionist civilians, the army allotted enormous amounts of manpower and resources to the enemy home front to destroy the will and morale of the rebel citizenry. Such alterations in the climate and location of war, Sutherland makes clear, "produced a more brutal and destructive war that led to Confederate defeat." And nowhere did this counterguerrilla strategy occur more intensely than along the Trans-Mississippi border.[17]

Historians have long debated the merits of irregular warfare on behalf of the Confederacy—especially as a means of continuing the fight after Appomattox in 1865—but most agree that its skulking nature was not in line with Southern identity and honor. Although Confederate guerrillas occupied Union troops who otherwise might have helped on other fronts, they rarely did much good for the overall war effort. For historian Max Boot, this is where the discussion ends. Instead, he argues, the guerrillas' significance lies not within the war but on its chronological edges. Bleeding Kansas and Reconstruction-era violence, Boot contends, were altogether "far more significant" than any guerrilla actions during the war. Indeed, he maintains, "their strategic importance was negligible." While pre- and postwar violence, or terrorism as Boot calls it, was indisputably brutal, violence on the border during the conflict should not be lost in the shadows of events before and afterward. Irregular combat led to a steady intensification of Federal violence toward both guerrillas and local civilians. Such harsh counterinsurgency measures were especially pronounced on the western Trans-Mississippi frontier, and their effects on the civilian population and the overall conflict in the region were anything but negligible.[18]

Even with a host of important regional studies and a larger narrative illuminating the decisive role played by guerrilla warfare, defining and understanding that role remains at the leading edge of the most recent histo-riographical debates. In a useful and provocative essay, historians Gary W. Gallagher and Kathryn Shively Meier contend that the "current lavishing of attention" on civilian-centered guerrilla warfare is mostly a product of a generational influence from the nature of the Vietnam War and the small, often-irregular conflicts that have followed. The Civil War, then, has received a disproportionate amount of scholarly attention regarding irregular warfare than it merits. In the end, Gallagher and Meier conclude, guerrillas were "ancillary, disruptive, and deemed unacceptable" during the conflict, but their role was neither decisive nor central to its course or nature. While the irregular struggle that raged on the border had only a small effect on the larger strategies and campaigns across the South, it directly influenced the broader nature of the Civil War just as had those in Louisiana, Tennessee, and North Carolina. Taken together, regional pockets of intense, civilian-centered guerrilla warfare might not have heavily influenced the grander machinations of wartime strategy, but they *did* influence the fundamental civilian experience on the Southern home front. Furthermore, if it is import-ant for historians to assess what really mattered to people living through the crisis, as Gallagher and Meier appropriately explain, coming to terms not just with traditional military history but also—and especially—with how thousands of civilians became immersed in a series of confused, lawless, and altogether brutal regional guerrilla contests becomes essential. *Extreme Civil War* explores this dynamic in the context of racial and environmental forces.[19]

According to historian William L. Shea, Americans had suffered "mass amnesia" after the Civil War concerning the reality of the conflict in the Trans-Mississippi. Participants—soldiers and civilians—who had endured the experience made a "collective decision . . . to disremember the breakdown of civilization in the Trans-Mississippi during the Civil War." It was far more comforting to dampen tortured memories of torched homes, murdered spouses, and ruined lives with a celebration of regular armies that fought in conventional battles. Until recently, Civil War historiography had suffered from the very same amnesia.[20] Such an atmosphere of instability, terror, and desolation makes the region a critically important window into a struggle that engulfed everyone, regardless of age or sex. Historians have yet to fully define the war experienced in the Trans-Mississippi theater's fringes, and such difficulties only underscore the complexities inherent in the fighting that raged there. Indeed, for all the advancement in a field once considered a "sideshow," there remains little inquiry concerning certain regional and conceptual frameworks for guerrilla warfare, especially the brand of combat that occurred on the western margins of Missouri and Arkansas. This territory was far more than a simple regional border, however. The area between Fort Scott, Kansas, and Fort Smith, Arkansas, witnessed some of the most pronounced hardship throughout the South during the Civil War. Proslave and antislave white Americans, Native Americans, and African Americans intermingled in a racial and cultural middle ground. When war broke out in 1861, a variety of cultures clashed, creating a war-torn borderland.[21] Traditionally rigid gender roles and social values became distorted when women and children increasingly became responsible for their own survival, unwilling participants in the war. Although some important work exists concerning the Civil War in this region and about civilians caught up in it, the areas of study are framed by political boundaries and largely focus on regular or guerrilla warfare alone. This book seeks to transcend those boundaries in hopes of gaining a more robust understanding of the dynamic nature of the Civil War in its margins.[22]

Just as guerrilla-war scholarship has varied remarkably over space and time, so too has our understanding of exactly who the combatants were. By the very nature of their often enigmatic existence, Confederate guerrillas remain difficult to fully define, though a Union newspaper editor tried to do just that in 1864. "[The guerrilla] is a good judge of a horse, and has one superior in speed . . . to those of his pursuers," he claimed in the Kansas Daily Tribune. The irregular preferred to fight, the editorial continued, "when the leaves are on the trees" for concealment and to more effectively carry out surprise attacks on civilians and soldiers alike. "His arms are a big knife, and one or two navy revolvers, and a rifle or a shotgun," said the writer, and "his original uniform is . . . a ragged suit of butternut." In the most revelatory, accurate, and damning part of the description, the author makes clear that the guerrilla "owes allegiance to no Government; is bound by no laws." Another Union publication exclaimed that such men "take up arms and lay them down at intervals, and carry on petty war chiefly by raids, extortion, destruction, and massacre." Moreover, they were "peculiarly dangerous, because they easily evade pursuit, and by laying down their arms become insidious enemies; because they cannot otherwise subsist than by rapine, and almost always degenerate into simple robbers or brigands."[23]

This style of warfare had complex dimensions. Most Confederate guerrillas sought adventure, and the self-employed nature of irregular activity also served their goal of local defense. They enjoyed the freedom to fight, run, or loot at will. Whether seeking to help the Confederate war effort or not, such men were attracted to the unstructured, self-serving aspect of being an irregular. "There was practically no attempt at discipline," one guerrilla wrote, "every man went and came at his own sweet will." With some exceptions, if a fight looked too dangerous, guerrillas could scatter or sit it out. If they thought it best to leave the area for a while, they did. When they deemed it desirable to burn a house or shoot a suspected Union supporter, they need only get permission from their chieftain, if at all. From a broader military outlook, guerrilla leaders sought cursory acceptance from Confederate commanders. Perhaps they wrote "battle reports" to generals in the conventional army, as William Clarke Quantrill and Thomas Livingston would do, but they did so rarely, never wanting to get too drawn into the structured regular service. In the end, guerrillas were well-armed and well-supplied civilians who sought to fight the war on their own authority.[24]

Historians have long defined guerrillas in broader terms, agreeing that they nearly all used unconventional tactics and did so as much as possible very near their homes. Beyond these general descriptions, recent scholarship illuminates more-specific motivations. Irregulars were a mixed lot. Popular stereotypes perpetuated by Union authorities and newspapers held that these men emerged from the margins of society and had a prewar propensity toward theft and violence. Certainly some fit that bill, but most irregulars were quite socioeconomically connected to their communities. They were often older, wealthier, and therefore less willing to leave their homes to fight on distant battlefields. At the same time, as reflected in the anecdotal description provided by Union newspapermen and embodied in many of their own actions, guerrillas were typically independent operators who celebrated and often abused their relative freedom from the regular army.[25]

Reasoning the strategy of guerrillas is therefore complicated. They brought war to Unionist civilians and their military counterparts for a variety of reasons. Confederate irregulars attempted to aid what they viewed as their new nation's struggle for independence, conducted "community control" to ferret out Unionists on the home front, and as the war dragged on often delved into sheer outlawry. In addition, "blood sport," as one scholar argues, played a significant motivating role among these combatants. Operating in such a state of mind, irregular bands sought to kill, damage, and generally inflict pain and suffering for no practical reason—from shooting men in their doorways to terrorizing widows and children.[26] Psychologically, guerrillas faced a dilemma when fighting their war. In the middle of the nineteenth century, when traditional combat was considered noble, irregulars sought to justify their actions through a rough code of honor, providing them an excuse for gratuitous violence against innocent and often unarmed men. This code also limited violence against white women and children. Yet the guerrillas' self-subscribed "ethics" restrained only their murderous impulses. While they did generally refrain from killing women and children, most had few qualms about burning these civilians' houses and stealing or destroying everything they owned. Even then, women and children died as a direct result of such actions. Men, older boys, and African Americans were rarely exempt from the guerrillas' death code on the Trans-Mississippi border.[27]

Irregular warfare soon became a mainstay of Confederate resistance and a persistent problem for the occupying Union army. Ideally, guerrillas would thwart Federal troops, disrupt their supply and communication lines, and generally force them and pro-Union citizens to consider the viability of continuing the war. In reality, they kept troops distracted and effectively incited terror among civilians. The growing perception of these men as "knights of the brush" who carried out brutal and often uninhibited actions and then melted back into the landscape created an image of invincibility. To be sure, Federal patrols became increasingly frustrated as they chased (and mostly lost) guerrillas through the difficult physical and social landscape along the border.[28]

The potential strategic benefits of irregular warfare as outlined by famed Prussian military theorist Carl von Clausewitz and other strategic thinkers were negated by an unstable war effort and irrational violence that led to increasingly harsh retribution not only against the guerrillas but also those civilians thought to be supporting them. Traditional irregular activities, such as compromising enemy supply and communication routes and harassing enemy soldiers behind the lines, failed to reach their full potential due to the lack of a coherent overall Confederate strategy and, of equal importance, the guerrillas' particularly nasty, profit-driven violence against soldiers and civilians alike.[29]

For most of the war, the clear majority of affected civilians were women and children. It would be easy to say that they were simply in the wrong place at a bad time. By 1863–64, Federal forces would strike at suspected pro-Confederate civilians as a strategy to counter guerrillas in an area. While they often took their retaliatory measures to extremes, their reasoning remained solid: by reducing the number of safe havens, they could reduce the irregular population.[30] Guerrillas and Federals often perpetuated the myth that women (at least those on their own side) were innocent victims caught helplessly in the masculine environment of war. In reality, women were *active* players in the guerrilla war—their war. Regardless of which side they supported, if any at all, women often manipulated whomever happened to be at their doorstep, ensuring that, regardless of their true political loyalty, they would have the best chance to protect their property and, oftentimes, male relatives. Civilians were not mere passive victims of the theft, destruction, and violence dealt them. Women on the border actively and directly fought to survive.[31]

Their war was complex, and although women took an active role in their own survival, the act of surviving often meant fleeing. Despite their fortuitous distinction of being outside the guerrilla death code, women were still subjected to terror. Federals and Confederate irregulars were proud of their policy to generally spare women and children from murder and rape. Still, they pressed the lines of prewar moral boundaries. Though guerrillas and Union militiamen treated women with a kind of gentlemanly respect, even to the extent of tipping their hats after killing a woman's husband, they brutalized them psychologically and emotionally. Combatants from both sides gained a sense of godlike power when dealing with their victims, for they alone determined whether people would live or die. Commonly, they let women and children live, but in doing so they reserved a sense of pride for their acts of calculated kindness. Women endured the same ordeals as most in guerrilla-stricken areas—their husbands and sons killed, their houses burned, all usually right in front of them. Most claimed that the guerrillas, after stealing what they wanted and burning what was left, rendered them destitute refugees caught in a desolated region until they could find shelter in an often crowded and dirty Federal refugee camp.[32]

Neither the Union nor the Confederate armies ever explicitly or officially declared a physical war on civilians, and there are plenty of orders like the 1863 "Lieber Code," officially known as General Order No. 100, to attest to that. Unfortunately, as even Union strategist and advisor Francis Lieber acknowledged, soldiers in the field made their own rules. There is no question that the cycle of retaliation and counterretaliation between the Union army, rebel guerrillas, and noncombatants was a brutal business. Indeed, guerrilla-chasing Federals often loosely interpreted Lieber's Code, which as John Fabian Witt shows, "authorized any measure necessary to secure the ends of war and defend the country." For increasingly frustrated Yankees who could not seem to catch guerrillas or discern exactly who had aided them, any policy intent on refocusing the war away from noncombatants might well have not existed.[33] A clear line between combatant and civilian simply did not exist, at least not in the wilderness. For Michael Fellman, the "deep haze" of guerrilla warfare had blinded most Union commanders, and "the torch and immediate capital vengeance were the norm." On the western Trans-Mississippi border, it became ever more difficult for increasingly frustrated Union patrols—local militia, Unionist "Jayhawkers," and regular cavalry and infantry—to clearly distinguish between real and perceived threats. According to Carl H. Moneyhon, in such an operational environment "military and personal violence were undifferentiable." On the border, civilians were brutalized as a consequence.[34]

Confederate guerrillas did not have a monopoly on terror, however. Union cavalry and militia, from Charles Jennison's Jayhawkers and Jim Lane's "Red Legs" to county-level units, matched the destructive violence of even the worst rebel irregulars. Regular soldiers relied on food and supplies from local civilians, often proving at least as destructive as the guerrillas they were chasing. The Union army and militia also made war against the civilian population. A mere suspicion of a resident aiding guerrillas or having Confederate leanings often resulted in destruction of property and expulsion or imprisonment. Indeed, most civilians on the border, regardless of their political loyalties, consistently saw Union and Confederate combatants as potential enemies to their livelihood.[35]

In addition to guerrillas and civilians, regular soldiers also played a prominent role in this story. Their letters, diaries, and reports add a great deal to our understanding of the conflict on the western Trans-Mississippi frontier. For troops from the upper Midwest, this border region was a foreign land filled with often strange and remarkable physical and cultural attributes. These men wrote with keen interest about the human and geographic terrain, and they regularly lamented the frustratingly effective "bushwhackers" who plagued their every step. They were fighting in a different world against a mostly invisible foe among a dwindling civilian population who remained ambivalent at best. At worst, these residents supplied and protected the guerrillas while maintaining an exasperating deniability. Within such an unfamiliar atmosphere marked by distrust and uncertainty, Union soldiers confided a candid, if somewhat prejudiced, portrait of the war on the western edges. These interpretations together with civilian accounts, newspapers, court documents, and a host of other records form a clearer picture of an otherwise muddled, confused, and altogether brutal conflict.[36]

To fully define the Civil War on the western Trans-Mississippi frontier requires first and foremost the recognition that it was above all else multifaceted and unrelenting. Although scholars debate the war's severity generally, the all-encompassing violence on the frontier during this time came as close to total war as any action.[37] Large battles always have smaller, noteworthy engagements within them. Such was the case on the Trans-Mississippi borderlands. Where the region as a whole was one enormous battlefield, hundreds of smaller engagements—microbattles—occurred on a daily basis. Those who fought them included the usual culprits: Union and Confederate soldiers and irregulars. But the violence also overwhelmingly involved "combatants" who have yet to be fully recognized as such: civilians. The conflict on this frontier was a civilian-centered guerrilla war underscored by environmental, racial, and cultural extremes. And although it occurred in the geographical margins and proved exceptional to the broader prosecution of the war, the guerrilla conflict in the Trans-Mississippi serves to help redefine the nature of the Civil War on the whole.

At its core, what follows is a story about regular people caught in an extra-

The western Trans-Mississippi frontier represents the fifty-mile radius on each side of the political boundary between Fort Scott, Kansas, and Fort Smith, Arkansas. Here a Union state, Border State, and Confederate state met with a divided Indian Territory in a region that had been inundated by heated, slave-based violence, and political rhetoric since the mid-1850s. *Map courtesy of Donald S. Frazier*

ordinary situation in a region—and within a war—directly and irrevocably shaped by race, culture, and the environment. The cast of characters include civilians, irregulars, and soldiers from both sides and from a variety of cultural and ethnic backgrounds. Women, children, and the elderly composed the majority of civilians in the region, especially after the first year of war. Although most were Southern sympathizers, all suffered dearly from both Union and Confederate actions. Guerrillas, a term used here to indicate Confederate irregulars, created an inordinate amount of pressure on the civilian population, though balanced with often equal pressure by the Union army and militia. Both guerrillas and Federal troops vowed to protect civilians but did far more harm than good by directly incorporating them into the conflict. The *regular* Confederate army played the smallest role in the region, having maintained only an occasional presence on the border following the first year of the war. After Southern defeats at the Battles of Pea Ridge and Prairie Grove in 1862, guerrillas more than took their place.

Today dozens of wonderfully manicured Civil War battlefields are maintained across the country. Each has its own monuments, interpretive panels, and well-designed tour routes. Visitors can travel on pristine tour roads through the battlefields at Wilson's Creek and Pea Ridge or walk the one-mile paved loop at Prairie Grove. But there are no such monuments or interpretive trails for the irregular war that ravaged the western Trans-Mississippi frontier. Here a different kind of combat took place, one that destroyed its own markers. Homes and towns were torched. Courthouses and record depositories were destroyed. Nearly every person living and working on this massive battlefield had fled or been killed. The casualties, destruction of property, and sheer level of brutality here, if not *directly* critical to the overall war effort, far outweighed the sum of death and destruction of the largest set-piece battles. In essence, this is a story of the "battle" that raged along the borderland that connected Missouri, Arkansas, Kansas, and Indian Territory.[38]

# 1

## "Ripe for the Harvest"

### THE BORDER BEFORE THE WAR, 1860–1861

To fully understand the Civil War's impact on the western Trans-Mississippi frontier, it is important to acknowledge the prewar social, economic, political, and cultural tapestry that exemplified the region. Although Bleeding Kansas had inaugurated an already violent localized internecine conflict, much of the *southern* Trans-Mississippi border had thrived in the 1850s. Native Americans in Indian Territory had finally begun to emerge from the economic and political vestiges of removal; the white population increased where Kansas, Missouri, and Arkansas met; and a thriving market economy had begun to transform the region. Within a year after the onset of hostilities, however, towns and farms that had once bustled with activity and growth had rapidly been transformed into a war-torn wilderness. The once-strong economic system collapsed. More than simply stunting growth and prosperity, the war had dramatically reversed all that had been gained.

The western Trans-Mississippi frontier lay at the intersection of cultural and environmental diversity. Here there emerged an intricate web of cultural, natural, and military contours. Native Americans, African Americans, anti- and pro-slave whites, Missouri "pukes," and tobacco-chewing Arkansans formed an interesting, if not bizarre, mix of civilians. Such a combination developed into the most unique and complex societies extant during the Civil War. The mountains, prairies, clear highland streams, and big muddy rivers formed a diverse terrain that would only complicate military and civilian life. Harsh weather extremes and the war-induced interruption of agriculture combined to make the region one often beset by starvation. With certain exceptions, the land provided a bountiful crop, but one always threatened by regular and irregular combatants. The conflict that would emerge there challenged traditional definitions of warfare. Civilians witnessed both large-scale, regular battles (which themselves wrought hardship and terror) as well as perpetual irregular fighting that plagued, and eventually ruined, nearly everyone.

The region was developing steadily in 1860. Thousands of recent settlers in western Missouri and Arkansas engaged in small-scale farming and ranching to scratch out a semisubsistence life in a very difficult place. In good agricultural years, when drought, cold snaps, and floods remained absent, residents enjoyed some prosperity. As much as demography, location, and troublesome weather, the region's terrain—largely mountainous with occasional open areas, rough roads, and rivers navigable only part of the year—helped shape the style of war that would develop by 1861.[1]

Drought had plagued the western border since the mid-1850s. Settlers throughout the eastern half of Kansas and Indian Territory and the western half of Missouri and Arkansas had suffered dearly from low crop yields and the consequent economic problems. Especially dry weather led not only to poor harvests and bad water but also to occasional locust swarms that thoroughly destroyed any crops that might have survived. The harsh climatic conditions of the prewar era, embodied by what some called "Starving Kansas," did not relent for war. Frigid winters and wide fluctuations in rainfall would continue to plague civilians, Confederate guerrillas, and Union forces during the nascent conflict.[2]

Although the populations of California and Oregon were growing rapidly too by the late 1850s, the western reaches of Missouri and Arkansas remained the principal frontier of Anglo civilization in 1860. People here lived on the very edge of westward socioeconomic expansion, far removed from the political and economic centers to the east. The majority of residents along the frontier border were first-generation settlers from both slave and nonslave states, having immigrated to the region within the past two or three decades, and thus formed a potentially flammable population. They had brought with them potentially antagonistic cultures from regions as disparate as Ohio and Alabama, a combustible cultural mix further enhanced by the Native Americans in Indian Territory. In the end, the bitter feuds of neighborly conflict led directly to the environment of terror that saturated the area through four years of war.[3]

Expectations of imminent growth and economic expansion abounded on this western border in the late 1850s. Indeed, the area was in the beginning stages of a marked economic transition, rapidly following what had occurred in the upper Midwest in the preceding decades. Although beset by difficult terrain, towns such as Carthage, Missouri; Fayetteville, Arkansas; Tahlequah, Cherokee Nation; and Fort Scott, Kansas Territory, were thriving centers of economic, political, and social activity by 1861. Indeed, much of northwest Arkansas and northeastern Indian Territory had boomed just over a decade earlier after the discovery of gold in far-off California's American River. Thousands used the region as a jumping-off point for the goldfields, significantly spurring local economies. Through the 1850s, this region continued to grow, even in the face of the Kansas crisis just to the north. As much as anywhere in the South, the Trans-Mississippi border embodied agricultural and economic progress by 1860.[4]

Population centers and military forts in tandem with a rough but growing transportation infrastructure and agricultural base proved a solid foundation for a budding market economy. Communities such as Carthage, Tahlequah, Fayetteville, and Van Buren and Fort Smith, Arkansas, provided business and cultural outlets for thousands of civilians working as small-scale farmers in outlying areas. Forts Scott, Gibson (in Indian Territory), and Smith formed a triangle that encompassed much of the region. Although not especially productive in the 1850s, these posts served as anchors for the population and became key military and civilian points after 1861. The military road that connected Fort Scott with Forts Gibson and Smith formed one of the region's primary transportation routes. The Butterfield Stage Road coursed through southwest Missouri and northwest Arkansas and funneled commerce from Springfield and Saint Louis, Missouri. Finally, the Arkansas River connected the Cherokee Nation and western Arkansas with Little Rock and points east, fostering considerable commerce and growth.[5]

Corn, oats, and wheat proved to be the most successful crops in the moderate climate and mixed terrain. Near the bustling town of Cane Hill, Arkansas, farmers found success with apple orchards, which accounted for over one thousand dollars' worth of annual production. In 1860 the frontier

Trans-Mississippi boasted well over half a million bushels of both oats and wheat, and farmers grew more than five million bushels of corn. In addition to crops, large numbers of hogs and cattle had kept the burgeoning population well fed. In the western reaches of Missouri and Arkansas alone, livestock was valued in 1860 at over four million dollars. Cattle, especially in Indian Territory, proved an invaluable meat source for local citizens. An estimated 240,000 beeves roamed the Cherokee Nation in 1860. Due to rugged terrain carpeted by dense forest and interspersed with dozens of creeks and rivers, wild animals flourished in the region, supplementing pork and beef as meat sources.[6] The environment in both its wild and domesticated spheres indelibly shaped society along the lower border area. And such prosperous natural foundations would prove an essential consideration—both helpful and detrimental—in Union and Confederate strategy during the ensuing conflict.

Contemporary descriptions of the social atmosphere along the Trans-Mississippi border are necessarily more subjective. Yet even the most one-sided descriptions yield valuable insights for understanding the place and the people. According to one editor in prewar Van Buren, area civilians were generally seen as living "in a semi-barbaric state, half alligator, half horse." People along the border were perceived to be "armed to the teeth, bristling with knives and pistols, a rollicking daredevil type of personage, made up of coarseness, ignorance and bombast." They were unkempt, rugged, and altogether fitting of the borderlands. Residents of the Ozarks, at least in the eyes of the rest of the country, represented what many had come to expect of them from popular cultural stories about the region. Frederick Gerstae-cker's *Wild Sports of the Far West*, Charles "Fent" Noland's letters in the *Spirit of the Times*, and Thomas Bangs Thorpe's *The Big Bear of Arkansas* colorfully illuminated the raucous bear-hunting personalities of this border society. For most Americans, including many Union soldiers who would chase guerrillas in this region, such a "bear state image" would only intensify.[7]

Another narrative provides an intriguing glimpse into the region's physical and social environment. Writing during the war, Union colonel and Chicago native A. C. Ellithorpe complained in late 1862 that the border was "not prairie country, but one everlasting jungle of dwarf brush, unfit for anything but firewood." He continued: "The farms are generally small and

poorly tilled. Corn is the principal crop, except children, and such children!—
sallow, puny things!" For Ellithorpe, the most shocking features were the
women and their habits. "You have heard of snuff suckers and clay eaters
but here you find them in all their ancient glory," he expounded, "the ladies
mostly are addicted to the filthy habit." Using snuff was quite a process,
according to the shocked Illinoisan. "The snuff is generally contained in a
square four ounce glass bottle," he explained, and a "small stick two or three
inches long with one end chewed in the condition of a small broom is then
adjusted protruding from the corner of the mouth . . . the happy lady sucks
away at the precious thing with all the vigor of [a] three months baby at its
'sugared rag.'" In general, the women presented a pitiable sight, at least to
his Northern sensibilities: "Their teeth are black, eyes sunken, and all look
as though [they] were enjoying a ripe condition of yellow jaundice."[8]

Readers in Chicago and throughout the upper Midwest were told that
women along the lower Trans-Mississippi border did "nothing, apparently,
but lick their snuff, chew and smoke, eat hog and hominy, and raise an inferior quality of stupid, sallow babies." Another Union onlooker admired
the Ozark scenery but was equally shocked by women who would "pick their
teeth and smoke and spit like old tobacco chewers." An Illinois soldier, happy
to find some Ozark women with whom to visit, was nonetheless shocked by
their appearance. They looked, he said, as though they had crawled "through
the brush-fence after the pigs." Another Federal complained that the country
was full of "indolent, go-easy, do-nothing squatters." A Northern newspaper
editor with the Union army concurred, diagnosing the region as being in a
"semi-barbarous condition." He believed that few people had "any just idea
of the ignorance and immorality that prevail[ed] there."[9] But these jaundiced-
looking women with snuff-stained mouths and pallid, scrawny children had
been left to fend for themselves through much of the war.

For Wiley Britton, by contrast, the region held tremendous promise and
natural splendor. On a trip from southwest Missouri to Texas before the war,
Britton commented on the simple circumstances of people who had been
devoted to carving a successful life from the unpolished landscape—and
were succeeding. On his leg through the Ozarks, Britton commented both
on the rugged beauty and the agricultural progress. Descending into the
Arkansas River valley, he noted that "there were many good farms on which

were being raised crops of corn, cotton, oats and different kinds of fruit." Corn and cotton fields covered much of the lowlands along the river and spurred the area's economy. Unfortunately, Britton noted, the fields were "cultivated mostly by slave labor." Farmers sold their crops in Fort Smith, where shallow-draft steamboats took on and transported the goods down the Arkansas toward Little Rock and points farther south and east. All of this would change drastically by 1861.[10]

Farther west in Indian Territory, Cherokee citizens overwhelmingly practiced subsistence farming throughout their lands. Corn cultivation and cattle ranching proved most productive. As elsewhere along the border, creeks and rivers blanketed by dense forest proved an excellent habitat for a wide range of wildlife that enabled Cherokees to supplement their crops and domestic animals with wild game. By 1860 they fostered and thrived in a subsistence-based economy with an eye toward the larger market system slowly infiltrating Missouri and Arkansas as railroad tracks were built west. Soon, so it seemed, the Cherokee Nation could begin to move beyond subsistence and sell excess produce and livestock to rail-connected markets farther east. Indeed, by most accounts northeast Indian Territory, like much of western Arkansas and Missouri, flourished with growth and economic progress in the decades before the Civil War. But when conflict erupted in 1861, the railroads stopped expanding and growth was put on hold.[11]

Slavery played a minor role in the larger Cherokee economic structure. Yet as in western Missouri and Arkansas, the institution remained strong. The Cherokees had long accepted slavery as a key part of their society, and despite the relatively small role it played in the Cherokee Nation, it nevertheless proved a key issue in the region by 1861. Even with a climate and soil less than conducive for successful large-scale cotton plantations, Southerners looked to places like Indian Territory—and the Cherokee Nation specifically—for expansion of the peculiar institution. In a somewhat misleading assessment that insisted on more similarities between his state and Indian Territory than the facts allowed, Arkansas governor Henry Rector declared, "[The Cherokee Nation] is salubrious and fertile, and possesses the highest capacity for future progress and development by the application of slave labor."[12] Although off target, Rector's more general assessment that the two regions were inexorably connected appealed to the Cherokee leadership.

Finally, the Cherokee Nation's social and economic foundations were tied inextricably to the U.S. military presence in Indian Territory. From the first days of tribal resettlement, U.S. soldiers were a visible presence at Forts Smith and Gibson. Roadways and bridges connecting each post provided trade routes for Indians and white Arkansans alike. Moreover, construction and maintenance of the military road connecting them to Fort Scott further established a regional social, cultural, and economic infrastructure.

While small-scale agricultural and manufacturing pursuits drove the economy in Arkansas and Indian Territory, lead mines increased economic development in southwest Missouri and southeast Kansas Territory in the 1850s. With the arrival of miners came a significant influx of support services. Although not approaching the scale of operations after the war, which drew thousands of miners and support personnel to the West, antebellum lead mines in the region proved a vital source of economic and social development. As one prewar resident remembered, those in southwest Missouri "started new life for quite a radius around them, for the mining population had to be supported and supplied with farm products and timbers." As much as any other economic force, lead mines laid the foundation within the region for a market economy before the Civil War.[13]

Citizens in southwest Missouri and northwest Arkansas, as well as those living in Indian Territory, were largely sympathetic toward slavery, even if it played a relatively small role in the larger machinations of their economy. Even people who remained firmly pro-Union during the secession crisis bristled at the thought of emancipation or any vestige of racial equality. As elsewhere in the South, harsh treatment of slaves and rabid racism remained firmly entrenched along the Trans-Mississippi border. In one particularly brutal instance in 1855, two Missouri slaves were accused of killing a local doctor and his family. Apprehended shortly after the bodies were found, the men were publicly burned alive without a trial.[14]

The national slave debate dominated local news and politics, at times devolving from verbal and written arguments to physical violence. In a small town in southwest Missouri, a local schoolteacher allegedly read Harriet Beecher Stowe's Uncle Tom's Cabin aloud to his class. In the mass public outcry that followed, residents demanded that the educator resign and leave the area. He refused. Enraged, a mob awaited his departure from the schoolhouse one evening and tarred and feathered him in the nearby woods. Such violence was relatively rare, but with the majority of citizens along the western Trans-Mississippi border being proslavery, antebellum divisions undoubtedly created discord among neighbors. These tensions would turn more decidedly violent, with reprisal and the settling of old scores, during the war.[15]

The slave issue also played a significant role in shaping area politics. Southwest Missouri and northwest Arkansas voted overwhelmingly in 1860 for the Southern Democrat candidate, John C. Breckenridge, with scattered votes for Northern Democrat Stephen A. Douglas and Constitutional Unionist John Bell; Republican Abraham Lincoln received little support. One of the few residents in the region who supported Lincoln received the full brunt of his neighbors' politically driven animosity. After hearing him bellow his support near a polling place in southwest Missouri, residents warned the man that "he would be ridden on a rail" if he continued to promote the Republican candidate. Tempers were high, and they soared higher with the secession crisis and impending war. Many of the Douglas Democrats (and the few Lincoln supporters) remained loyal to the Union, but the rest supported secession.[16]

While heated rhetoric abounded in local newspapers and political debates, and some unlucky people like the small-town schoolteacher were brutalized because of it, the peculiar institution did not ignite the degree of brutality experienced farther north in Kansas, where Free-Soil and proslavery rhetoric turned to violence. Much of this was due to the lack of antislavery sentiment along the Trans-Mississippi borderlands. Southeast Kansas's marginal population had neither the desire nor the ability to wage antislavery campaigns like those that occurred in west central Kansas. In addition, Missouri governor Robert M. Stewart had ordered state militia to southwest Missouri at the height of the border conflict to keep peace there. Although intimidation and violence certainly occurred over the issue in southwest Missouri and northwest Arkansas, such violence was muted.[17]

The majority of people in southwest Missouri and western Arkansas sympathized with the Confederacy, but those living within the Cherokee Nation held more divisive and complex allegiances. At first, Cherokee chief John Ross proclaimed his allegiance with Missouri and Arkansas as states within the Union. With such a diplomatic stance, Ross was able to both reinforce relations with his nation's neighbors while, at least for a time, not abrogating its allegiance to the United States. Cherokee leadership at first hoped to avoid any entanglements with either side. "We do not wish our soil to become the battleground between the States, and our homes to be rendered desolate and miserable by the horrors of a civil war," Ross made clear. But by early 1861, neutrality had become increasingly difficult as Confederate and Union officials contended for Cherokee support. In a passionate letter to Ross in late January 1861, Governor Rector warned that the United States would soon be altered irrevocably. Six states had seceded from the Union due to Lincoln's presidential victory, and more states, including Arkansas, would surely follow. "It may now be regarded as almost certain," wrote Rector, "that the States having slave property within their borders will, in consequence of repeated Northern aggression, separate themselves and withdraw from the Federal government." To the governor, it only made sense that the Cherokee Nation should follow Arkansas's example. "Your people," Rector continued, "in their institutions, productions, latitude, and natural sympathies, are allied to the common brotherhood of the slave-holding States."[18]

Rector's assessment was accurate. Stretching from just west of Fort Smith to the far northeastern parts of Indian Territory, the Cherokee Nation shared an important socioeconomic connection with western Arkansas and southwest Missouri. Thriving population centers like the Cherokee capital of Tahlequah and wealthy individuals in nearby Park Hill traded with Arkansans at Fort Smith, Van Buren, Fayetteville, and smaller towns in between. By 1861, the nation deemed its relationship with Arkansas one of overwhelming commonality. For Chief Ross, his people and Arkansas shared a mutual adherence to the culture, economy, and political system of the South. In response to Governor Rector's inquiry concerning where Cherokee sympathies lay at the onset of hostilities, he made clear that the nation's "institutions, locality, and natural sympathies" were "unequivocally with the slave-holding States." Moreover, and equally important said Ross, "[the] connection with the daily social and commercial intercourse between our respective citizens, forbids the idea that [Arkansas and the Cherokee Nation] should ever be otherwise than steadfast friends."[19]

Many of these "natural sympathies" grew from the environment. The Cherokee Nation's climate and terrain, and the economic forces based on both, shared a natural connection with southwest Missouri and western Arkansas. The Ozark Plateau gradually disappears into rolling river valleys in the region, carved by four large rivers, the Grand, Verdigris, Illinois, and Arkansas. Indeed, so far as the environment was concerned, all that separated the Cherokee Nation from its western neighbors was a political border.[20]

The Cherokee Nation emerged as a key area of interest for Confederate authorities. "It is well established that the Indian country west of Arkansas is looked to by the incoming administration of Mr. Lincoln as fruitful fields, ripe for the harvest of abolitionism, free-soilers, and Northern mountebanks," claimed Rector in a letter to Ross. "We hope to find in your friends willing to co-operate with the South in defense of her institutions, her honor, and her firesides, and with whom the slave-holding States are willing to share a common future."[21]

Confederate commissioner of Indian affairs David Hubbard was equally forthright in his warning about the Republican administration: "First your slaves they will take from you; that is one object of the war, to enable them to abolish slavery in such a manner and at such a time as they choose." Threat of abolition, no matter how minor slavery was in its society nor how insignificant the institution to its greater economy, should cause the Cherokee Nation to fear Northern "aggression." Federal theft of Cherokee slaves, Hubbard continued, would only be the first step. "They will settle upon your lands as fast as they choose," he insisted, "they will settle among you, and totally destroy the power of your chiefs and nationality, and then trade your people out of the residue of their lands." Winning Cherokee support was paramount to Confederate strategy in the Trans-Mississippi theater. Not only could the Native Americans provide manpower very much needed by the rebels, but they could also provide a seemingly endless supply of beef and other agricultural materials essential to waging war. But Ross hesitated. The Cherokee people, he admonished in a May proclamation, should work to "cultivate harmony among themselves and observe in good faith strict neutrality between the States threatening civil war." Such a neutral ground, the chief warned, was the only way in which to spare their "soil and firesides . . . from the baleful effects of a devastating war." As Ross and his constituents most certainly knew at the time, such rhetoric was merely hopeful if not hollow. The slaveholding Cherokee Nation, connected to the

United States through treaties and alliance, could not hope to remain neutral. Indeed, the very soil and firesides Ross harkened would soon suffer absolute devastation.[22]

While David Hubbard and the Confederacy tried to convince the Cherokees of the Union's devious designs, the Choctaw Nation just to their south also struggled over whom to side with. For the Choctaws, their social and cultural ties to slaveholding and the South pushed them closer to the Confederacy, but they had to balance such ties with the economic realities of aid from the U.S. government. Such support in a time of drought was essential. Yet most promised Federal funding never reached the Choctaws. Persuaded by Confederate representative Albert Pike that the South would provide aid and ensure its security, the Choctaw Nation officially joined the Confederacy in July 1861. In the end, the financial issues and lack of funding in addition to environmental factors led the Choctaws to war against the Union, further complicating the coming conflict on the frontier.[23]

Meanwhile, farther north, the Missouri government began to fracture. Newly elected governor Claiborne Fox Jackson, faced with resolutions from the state house of representatives to remove the state militia from southwest Missouri in March 1861, replied that such action was unthinkable. "The immediate withdrawal of troops," Jackson warned, "would be regarded as the signal invitation, by all the marauding bands in Southern Kansas, to renew their attacks upon our unoffending citizens, with the view of plundering the whole border country." Importantly, by early 1861, this militia force served as more than protection from violence out of Kansas. Due to the intense and violent confrontations in previous years, Jackson, a staunch supporter of secession, understood the importance the border region would play in the impending conflict. He sought unofficially to keep a strong pro-Southern force in the lower Trans-Mississippi. Knowing well the potential for fighting in the region, the governor closed his rebuttal to the legislature by saying, "Without the means of placing them upon a footing of self-reliance and defense, I should regard it as exceedingly hazardous to the safety and security of the people on the border to recall the forces now there."[24] These troops would in March 1861 become a large portion of the pro-Confederate Missouri State Guard, which played an instrumental role in the first campaigns in the Trans-Mississippi theater.

Jackson's tone changed later that spring. In a letter to Arkansas Secession Convention president David Walker, the governor explained, "Missouri and Arkansas have been called upon by an abolition President for troops to whip their southern brethren and friends into the support of a miserable, Black Republican, fanatical administration." Making clear his intentions, Jackson continued, "Whatever have been our prior differences, it seems to me, that the time has come when all true southern men should be united as a band of brothers against the common enemy."[25] By June, Missouri Confederates, enjoying significant support from the state's western border, made their final split from any ties to the U.S. government. But Jackson and the pro-Confederate legislature did not leave the Missouri capital completely of their own accord. Union general Nathaniel Lyon and a force of approximately 2,000 soldiers marched on Jefferson City in June 1861, bent on removing the secessionist state government from power.[26]

Having heard about Lyon and Frank Blair's military actions in Saint Louis, Jackson issued a public proclamation addressed to the "People of Missouri" on June 14. "A series of unprovoked unparalleled outrages have been inflicted upon the peace and dignity of this commonwealth by wicked and unprincipled men," Jackson exclaimed. These supposed agents of the United States government, the embattled governor continued, were promoting "bloody and revolutionary schemes" through which they intentionally sought civil war. Jackson further warned that due to the actions of Lyon, Blair, and their evil-minded cohorts, Missouri would surely be consumed by roving groups of "lawless invaders." Calling for prompt and dramatic action, Jackson pleaded: "Rise, then, and drive out ignominiously the invaders who have dared to desecrate the soil which your labors have made fruitful, and which is consecrated by your homes!"[27]

The governor's proclamation was published in the Missouri Republican for the entire state's edification. Such rhetoric, printed and preached, helped fuel anti-Jackson sentiment within Union ranks and made Lyon's task easier to stomach. Jackson and his supporters within the state government fled to the southwestern part of Missouri. In transit he appointed Sterling Price as the general in charge of the Missouri State Guard. By August, Jackson and all other pro-Confederate congressmen had left Jefferson City, with former state supreme court justice Hamilton R. Gamble appointed provisional governor of Missouri. The Civil War had begun in earnest, and the most immediate and harshest fighting in Missouri would occur along the western border region.[28]

Provisional Governor Gamble, in his inaugural address before the Missouri State Convention on July 31, 1861, spoke prophetically about the future. "We may soon be in that condition of anarchy in which a man when he goes to bed with his family at night, does not know whether he shall ever rise again, or whether his house shall remain intact until morning," he proclaimed. Capturing the urgency of the time and brutal reality of the future, Gamble continued, "That is the kind of danger; not merely a war between different divisions of the State, but a war between neighbors."[29] Try as he may to stop it, the war that Gamble feared had already erupted along the frontier border.

The secession crisis in Arkansas ended far differently. Initially, most Arkansans watched from the sidelines as South Carolina seceded in December 1860. The leading newspaper in the state urged neutrality: "Let no steps be taken against this administration until [the president] has committed an overt act which cannot be remedied." The situation declined further in late January 1861, when Federal proposals to reinforce the U.S. arsenal in Little Rock were announced. Although not fully ready to secede, Governor Rector and the state government refused to allow such reinforcement to occur. Capt. James Totten, charged with maintaining and protecting the Federal post, saw little chance to hold out. "Companies of armed citizens from various sections of this State have already arrived, and it is said there will soon be five thousand here for the express purpose of taking this arsenal," he warned. "Collision seems inevitable if this arsenal is to be held." Following communication with officials in Washington, Totten ordered the evacuation of the post. In exchange for this, Rector agreed to protect the arsenal's stores until the secession convention had made a final decision—especially after the first session voted against secession in March.[30]

Following the surrender of Fort Sumter on April 14 and President Lincoln's subsequent call for troops, Rector recalled the secession convention. In the meantime, over one thousand state militiamen had moved on Fort Smith only to find it evacuated by its garrison; all other U.S. arsenals and forts in the state were seized. On May 6 Arkansas seceded from the Union.

Most citizens were excited by this rapid turn of events, but there remained a sizeable minority in the northwest portion of the state who remained loyal to the Union. During the next four years, these residents, more than any others, would suffer immeasurably from vicious irregular warfare within a society that soon degenerated into anarchy.[31]

Indeed, the dramatic change in the spring of 1861 had been expected by people on the border and not a little foreboding. Although the brutal guerrilla war had yet to fully begin, civilians there knew well that their lives and livelihoods were about to undergo a seismic shift. For Fayetteville resident William Baxter, such sudden and negative change was all too clear. With the onset of hostilities, he noted, the border region underwent a dramatic shift toward war-induced subsistence: "Hardware, school-books, stationary, dry-goods, medicines, implements of agriculture, groceries, carpets, hats, shoes, pins, needles, matches, nay, every thing, one might say, were now foreign articles." For Baxter and his fellow residents on the western edge of the Trans-Mississippi, the first months of the war had initiated an economic shock from which they would not recover until after hostilities ceased.[32]

Except for the threat of violence during Bleeding Kansas, the life people knew along the Trans-Mississippi's western border changed drastically in 1861 as the region tumbled into war and existing political and social disagreements turned deadly. Men who had once argued on front porches and in meeting halls about politics and slavery had stopped squabbling and started shooting. The region's socioeconomic foundation crumbled with each succeeding month of war, halting its shift from a subsistence economy to a growing market economy. What were once supplementary means of securing food, such as hunting and foraging, became necessary to survive.[33]

# 2

## "Civil War Was Fully Inaugurated"

### THE BORDER WAR, 1861

Civil war was fully inaugurated; the popular mind was greatly inflamed; disregard of law universally reigned; there was no military force to enforce law
and preserve order; there was no money in the treasury with which to purchase
arms or subsist soldiers; there was no State credit upon which to raise money;
and, moreover, a very large majority of all public office of the State were in
the hands of persons hostile to the Government of the United States, sym-
pathizing with those engaged in the rebellion, and opposed to your attempt
to restore peace.

—MISSOURI GOVERNOR HAMILTON R. GAMBLE

The Germans oozed beer from every pore as they marched along,"
exclaimed a local Unionist woman as Brig. Gen. Franz Sigel's army
marched by her farm in southwest Missouri. In early July 1861, just
before the Battle of Carthage, Sigel's Yankees, composed largely of German-
speaking immigrants from Missouri, had made a striking impression on
local residents. Like it or not, the woman and her neighbors had become
rapidly entangled in warfare. Although often wearing regular uniforms and
fighting against a recognized foe, soldiers marching through towns or the
countryside early in the war proved an oddity for civilians. But southwest
Missouri Unionists welcomed Sigel's contingent, hoping the troops would
establish Union control to that part of the state and foster a semblance of
stability in a society quickly devolving into mayhem. Happy as Unionists were
to see Sigel's men, the culture and language barrier proved troublesome.

Oozing beer or not, the presence of Federal troops ready for battle, much less those speaking a different language, contributed to the strangeness of it all.[1]

When Sigel's force entered Carthage on July 4, it found the small county seat largely vacated. As a hotbed of Confederate support, most residents had fled or hid upon hearing of the Federals' approach. Local Unionists, however, greeted the army and provided information concerning rebel positions north of town. Although in no way formal participants, these people became part of the war, and their deeds would be remembered by their pro-Confederate neighbors. Few civilians were directly affected by the ensuing battle, though hundreds must have heard and perhaps even watched much of the commotion as Sigel's men soon retreated back through town toward Springfield. Following ex-Missouri governor Claiborne Fox Jackson's battlefield victory, Confederate residents in southwest Missouri came out from hiding to jeer at the retreating Federals. Some troops, led by Capt. Joseph Conrad, had been captured during the battle and were soon paroled. On their journey to rejoin Sigel's forces in Springfield, Conrad and his fellow paroles suffered the wrath of local Confederate supporters who, according to the officer, "threatened to kill us in the streets."[2]

One Carthage resident who fled after the engagement deemed the town a disaster. He reported: "Wagons and hacks passing in every direction gathering up the dead for interment. . . . [T]he stench was sickening." The man witnessed a "whole country . . . laid desolate. Fences torn down, crops tramped into the ground, and houses plundered." On his way to Fort Scott, he encountered groups of fleeing women who had lost everything except what they were carrying. The western Trans-Mississippi border had devolved into chaos, and everyone was affected. Yet some civilians tried to be part of the battle, or at least get very close to the action. "Strange to say that the people of the country," wrote one newspaper editor, "rushed to the scene in large numbers [and] actually crowding up so closely as to incommode the movements of the troops on both sides."[3]

As Sigel retreated, according to one contemporary, the remaining "Union men deemed it safest to fly to the woods and hills for concealment." The Ozark Plateau and the wooded waterways coursing through the rolling foothills served as ideal hiding spots. Starting in the first months of war, Unionists made good use of the same terrain that Confederate irregulars would come to dominate. They left their wives and children behind to take care of their homes and farms, fleeing to the woods where they were "fed clandestinely by their families." According to Wiley Britton, these men had good reason to flee, even this early in the war. "Instead of respecting the rights of property of all classes," Britton explained, "the rebel troops took all serviceable horses they could find belonging to Union citizens." In addition to horses, the "secessionists" sought any other Union property of value. Illustrating the social nature of war, pro-Confederate citizens informed rebel soldiers where Unionists resided. As these troops approached identified residences, Britton continued, "Here and there a wife or mother, in the absence of husband or son, stood at the gate to plead with the armed and hostile men to spare [their] property."[4]

War in all its surreal formality had begun in the region. Soldiers and civilians alike struggled to come to terms with it on a national and local level. Within the very first months of the war on the border, civilians, both Union and Confederate, readily took an active role, if not by fighting on the front lines, then by providing valuable intelligence, openly threatening the enemy, or suffering as victims. As early as 1861, families in the region also had begun a fight for their livelihoods that they would all ultimately lose. Irregular warfare soon spread throughout southwest Missouri and southeast Kansas. Yet although some irregular attacks had already occurred, few in the area could have guessed the drastic route that war would take in the coming months. "Thus was introduced a phase of war of which few, if any, had ever dreamed," lamented Britton.[5]

It did not always require formal battles or irregular skirmishes for civilians to suffer. Just months after hostilities began, two Federal cavalrymen stationed at Fort Scott "accomplished their hellish purpose" on a young woman living nearby. Recorded instances of rape in the region are rare. Such things were seldom mentioned by victims or their families for fear of the social stigma that was sure to follow. In this case, however, the attack had occurred in front of the girl's mother, who had been detained by the rapists. Neighbors, hearing commotion from the house, captured the two soldiers, marched them into town, and turned them over to the military authorities, who then released the men to the local sheriff and the civil courts. Not satisfied with the drawn-out course of events, though, a local mob forced the prisoners from the sheriff and promptly lynched them. "If there ever was an instance in which [lynching] was justifiable," noted a local newspaper editor, "this is the one."[6] Just months after Fort Sumter, civilians had played a direct role in shaping their wartime environment.

About fifty miles west of Fort Scott, the small town of Humboldt represented a hotbed of "abolitionist" and Union activity. Confederate irregulars had long hoped to raid and destroy the Kansas town. With the outbreak of hostilities and Federal activities in Missouri, the time seemed right for an attack. On September 8, hundreds of pro-Confederate soldiers and guerrillas converged on Humboldt. Guerrilla leaders Thomas R. Livingston and John A. Mathews, who had focused much of their early irregular work on the "Neutral Lands" in southeastern Kansas, led their respective bands in the assault. Their men focused mainly on pillage, robbing "stores and houses of whatever they found of value, and what they could carry away with them." The nearest Union soldiers were over a day's ride away at Fort Scott. By the time the alarm had reached the garrison, the raiders had vanished, leaving the town in ruins. A two-hundred-man Union patrol finally picked up their trail on September 20, but the rebels enjoyed a twelve-day head start. Col. James G. Blunt, who would soon be promoted to general, sought specifically the "notorious Mathews . . . the terror of southern Kansas." Hiding out during daylight hours, Blunt's counterguerrilla force traveled only under the cover of darkness. Three days into the pursuit, his troops surprised the guerrilla band and killed Mathews near the Kansas–Cherokee Nation border.[7]

Vengeance had been swift, but only a few of the Humboldt attackers had suffered. Consequently, Blunt ordered the arrest of every fighting-aged man in the region where Mathews had been confronted. Few such persons could be found, however, and those rounded up were largely Unionists, who were immediately released. The troops relieved their frustration on other segments of the civilian population. Cherokees in extreme southern Kansas and northern Indian Territory, for example, suffered destruction, abuse, and in some cases forced removal.[8]

While Blunt's Federals scoured southern Kansas, Unionist John C. Cox headed home in southwest Missouri from a short business trip on a mild September morning. Filled with anxiety by the recent Confederate victory at Wilson's Creek, near Springfield, and continued reports of violence in Kansas, he was concerned about the fate of his family. The hastily coalesced rebel forces had won back-to-back engagements at Carthage and Wilson's Creek in the last two months, effectively squelching Union efforts to gain control of southwest Missouri. Now Confederate irregulars roamed the area. Cox's anxiety itself was nothing new after years of conflict in the region over the fate of Kansas, but it was significantly amplified due to the military situation. His concern turned to terror when he was met by a worried neighbor who notified him that his family had been attacked by a band of guerrillas the previous night.[9]

Before Cox could get the full story, and much to his relief, his wife and two of his sons approached from the direction of their home, ragged and terrified. His wife, Sarah, shaken and tired, explained that a guerrilla band from Indian Territory had approached the house in the evening. Their faces covered by black paint with "streaks around their eyes," the riders demanded to see Cox, intending "to kill the damned old abolitionist." His wife made clear that her husband was away and pleaded with the men to leave her and the children alone. The painted irregulars were angered by the response and hardly convinced. They searched for Cox and any valuables. Unable to corral the livestock in the darkness or to find items of interest, the gang left the residence in frustration. Sarah and two of her young sons soon afterward gathered what livestock they could, determined to save their livelihood for the coming winter, and proceeded south in search of John. She left her oldest daughter behind to look after the younger children until morning. There they huddled together to wait for daylight and the return of their mother and father, never knowing if or when the guerrillas might come back.[10]

In the middle of explaining the situation, Sarah was shocked to see one of her sons approaching from the direction of their house and screaming that the men had returned to pillage. She implored her husband to stay behind and hide as she ran back toward her home, filled with terror at what might had befallen the children she had left behind. Upon arrival, she found two of the guerrillas from the night before, apparently unsatisfied with the situation. In the daylight they ordered the terrified daughter to cook them breakfast and set about once more searching for livestock and anything else of value. Finding only a mule—thanks to Sarah and her sons evacuating the rest—the two men took out their anger on the woman when she returned.

One told Cox that if she did not "produce [the bridles and saddles] then he would set the house on fire." She refused. The man then ordered her and the children to leave so he could burn the house. Clearly fed up with these antics and her terror turning to anger, Cox challenged the man "to set the house on fire if he wished and when it got good to burning [she] would walk out." At hearing this, the guerrilla stormed out, frustrated by her stubbornness and unwilling to set the home ablaze with her and the children inside.[11]

The two men spent the remainder of the morning frantically searching for saddles, bridles, and anything else holding value. Cox and her children, empowered by their successful stance against the guerrillas, remained in the home to wait for the intruders to leave, though the men seemed to be in no special hurry. They continued to enter the house "for water and to talk insulting" to the family. Finally, after what must have seemed an eternity, the guerrillas made preparations to ride off. First, though, they barged in one last time to tell Cox that she "must be gone in two days or [they] would return and burn [them] out." Shaking a rope at the woman and her children, they said it was the same rope they had prepared to hang her husband. Unwilling to let them have the last word, Sarah made clear that they might "burn the house, kill my children, and hang old Cox . . . but I would remain on this hill." Unquestionably shocked by her boldness, the guerrillas listened as Cox insisted that if they burned the house, she would "strike a tent" and remain there, refusing to be "run off by a set of thieves."[12]

This encounter occurred only months after the onset of the war, and it illuminates key contours of the irregular conflict to come. First, and most importantly, this war was not to be one just between soldiers on the front, or only between men, would be fought by people of all ages. It was a political war turned social, in which political and military alliances were only guidelines for fighting and could be easily broken. The event at the Cox farm also illustrates that rivalries could turn deadly, as the guerrillas clearly knew John Cox and his political allegiance. What is remarkable, though, is the timing. Irregulars went to work early in the war. Simultaneous with the initial large battles came smaller ones on the home front. As his assailants exclaimed, "Old Cox" was a "damned old abolitionist."[13]

Finally, Sarah Cox's experience illuminates the nastiness inherent in irregular warfare, an outlaw mentality that infiltrated nearly every move made by guerrillas in the border region. The men who terrorized her family sought revenge and personal profit. They clearly knew that John Cox was a Unionist, but as soon as they found him gone, they turned to theft. In short, guerrillas in this frontier region did not just seek to drive out Unionists potentially harmful to the Confederate cause. As the confrontation at the Cox farm suggests, they mingled terror and theft with their higher goals of military defense. A great many supposed Confederate partisans (as many labeled themselves) were little better than outlaws. They attacked Confederate and Union civilians indiscriminately to search for loot and adventure. The lawlessness of the wartime Trans-Mississippi border, in tandem with a loosely defined Southern "cause" by which they rationalized their destructiveness, served as ideal fuel for most guerrilla bands. For Union captain H. E. Palmer of the Eleventh Kansas Cavalry, "the bushwhackers, who were the demon devils of this border war, personally more for plunder and daredevil notoriety than for patriotic impulses, . . . paid and supported themselves by robbery, by plundering homes and villages, wrecking and robbing trains, attacking weakly protected supply-trains and ambushing soldiers." Although Palmer's postwar description was certainly influenced by a personally intense and zealous hatred, he made an accurate assessment. Even high-toned Confederate officers recognized the chaos that had settled over the region during the war. For Confederate general Joseph Shelby in 1864, the "so-called Confederate forces" along the border were not much more than lawless bands of thieves and murderers.[14]

While Cox's family was being terrorized by pro-Confederate guerrillas, other civilians suffered similar anguish, albeit less directly. As General Price's rebels marched northwest following their success at Wilson's Creek, U.S. senator and Kansas general James H. Lane evacuated the bulk of his men from Fort Scott. Union civilians panicked, and the majority of Fort Scott's residents fled, terrified that Price's Missourians would soon attack the unprotected town. Price never came, but some Union soldiers stayed behind and pillaged the newly created ghost town. One group of soldiers took up residence in a well-adorned house that had been hastily abandoned. They immediately made the place their home, "with four soldiers as servants and a contraband wench for cook." One officer later confided to his wife that they enjoyed all the domestic comforts, including "a good piano which . . .

[a soldier] is now amusing himself with. Preserves and jellies, magazines and book[s], and everything we want are here, so you see we are living high at present."[15]

Civilians slowly returned to Fort Scott after Price redirected his force following a skirmish at Dry Wood Creek near the Missouri border. The local newspaper published a brief article reprimanding local military authorities. "It is with great pain," the editor declared, "that we are compelled to chronicle acts of pillage by our troops, on the houses and property left under their protection." More than that, he continued, "the prospect of immediate destruction of the town seems to have let loose all their evil passions, and we are made to blush for the acts of vandalism" The only courage in the matter had been displayed by "four ladies . . . [who] stood their ground heroically, expressing their determination never to leave until their path was lighted by the flames of their burning homes." It had become quite apparent very early on that few could be trusted in the region, whatever their loyalties.[16]

Pro-Confederate guerrillas did not hold a monopoly on irregular warfare at this time. Civilians had also been plagued by antiguerrilla Union cavalry and militia. Much like their foe, these soldiers and cavalrymen lived off the bounty of civilians. Lane's "Kansas Brigade," also labeled "Jayhawkers," had set their sights on Osceola, Missouri, a town filled with secessionist citizens. Residents of western Missouri (and elsewhere along the Trans-Mississippi frontier) had reason to fear Lane's advance as potentially ruinous. In a Kansas newspaper Lane cautioned Missourians to be loyal to the Union instead of supporting "this wicked rebellion." Those who allied with the Confederacy should beware. "Stern visitations of war will be meted out to the rebels and their allies," Lane warned, "rest assured that the traitor, where caught, shall receive a traitor's doom." The Kansan continued: "The cup of mercy has been exhausted. Treason hereafter will be treated as treason. . . . The two roads are open to you. People of Western Missouri, choose ye between them; the one will lead you to peace and plenty, the other to destruction."[17]

Having heard of the Kansans' advance several hours before their arrival, Osceola males over twelve years old prepared to scatter into the surrounding forest, fearing what might become of them at the hands of the notorious senator turned general.[18] "My husband came in about the middle of the afternoon and told me to pack as much as I could of the best and most necessary things we had," remembered resident Sarah Yeater, "and he would try to get teams to take them away." After packing two large trunks with their clothing, bedding, and silver, Yeater anxiously awaited her husband's return while fearing what might later become of him, her, and their baby. With everyone scurrying to prepare their own departure, Yeater's husband found no available teams to save their valuables. After several hurried, fearful, and frustrating efforts, he had no choice but to flee town and hide in the surrounding bush. Sarah Yeater dragged the trunks into the high grass behind her home in hopes of hiding them during the anticipated Union occupation. As she did so, other residents bustled in much the same way in an atmosphere of terror. Men and teenage boys hurried to prepare their mothers, wives, and sisters for the coming onslaught and hoped the women and children could weather it on their own. For the men and teenagers to stay would mean potential imprisonment or death.[19]

The ensuing raid set a precedent for future attacks across Missouri, Kansas, Arkansas, and Indian Territory. Lane's troops, including some of the nastiest sorts to fight in the border war, entered Osceola late in the evening just after most of the men had evacuated town. They met some resistance on the outskirts from a small rebel force. After dislodging the defenders from their initial stronghold, Lane reported, the enemy "took refuge in the buildings of the town to annoy us [and] we were compelled to shell them out, and in doing so the place was burned to ashes." The Kansan did not divulge the full story, however. Once the majority of his command entered Osceola, one correspondent wrote, "the town had scarcely an inhabitant except women and children." According to another Union observer, "Lane said he meant to make the secessionists of Missouri feel the difference between being loyal and disloyal citizens and he is doing it."[20]

The Kansas troops ravaged the local businesses and moved on to the homes. Built almost entirely of wood, the town was easily burned after soldiers recovered the poorly hidden loot. Some homes were spared for use as living quarters or because women and children pleaded with sympathetic Union officers. Nevertheless, Osceola was largely destroyed. "Here we come to the horrors of war," one Union participant observed, "there are men whose souls are feasted and glutted with delight at the sight of distracted women, weeping children, and burning cities."[21]

Women were indeed shocked by the assault, their economic and social world now ruined. Although they had rarely been violently assaulted, the women suffered continually due to burned-out homes and stolen subsistence. Rushing toward her residence after hiding the previous evening at a family member's house, Yeater found it on fire along with the rest of the town. Her hogs, trapped in a pin attached to the house, were "squealing lustily, having been so near the burning buildings as to suffer from the heat." She promptly broke down the fence to free the overheated swine. Since her husband's "store and warehouse were entirely consumed," in doing so Yeater had saved her family's primary source of meat for the coming winter.[22] The men of the Kansas Brigade somehow overlooked the pigs, which they would have delighted in confiscating.

After turning Osceola into a "heap of smoldering ruins," Lane's troops moved a large herd of beef west toward Kansas. The region northeast of Fort Scott had a sizeable cattle population, and in addition to other forage, Lane sought such valuable food sources to maintain his army, no matter if they belonged to Confederate or Union civilians. He not only stripped beef cattle from the countryside but took milk cows as well. Nearly as prized as pigs by the civilian population, milk cows played a critical role along the Trans-Mississippi border. Infants and young children depended on their milk for nutritional needs in the war-stricken region, where their diet was too often inadequate. Seeing their cattle leaving town with the Union cavalrymen, Osceola's women, the only residents not in hiding, pleaded with the soldiers to spare them the livestock. One bold woman approached officers stationed in her home to ask for the release of her milk cow. Observing these men bow to her request, more ladies followed suit and, at least for the time, reclaimed their milk cows too. They were not as successful in retrieving their beef cattle, though.[23]

The slavery issue was more alive in the Trans-Mississippi than in any other theater early in the Civil War. Continuing their crusade from the days of Bleeding Kansas in the 1850s, pro-Union Missourians, most pointedly Maj. Gen. John C. Frémont, sought the emancipation of slaves. On August 30, 1861, Frémont issued a statewide order of emancipation that incited chaos throughout Missouri and other Border States. The Union military situation in Missouri seemed to be crumbling, and slaves, as much as any other agent, directly aided the secessionist war effort by supporting pro-Confederate families. Yet pro-Union Missourians also owned slaves, as did thousands of Union supporters throughout Kentucky, Maryland, and Delaware. Such brash political action by local commanders served as one of President Lincoln's earliest and most aggravating problems, which led one well-connected Washington socialite to predict that Frémont would be in a "peck of trouble about his proclamation."[24] Indeed he was. Following failed private communication concerning the general's action, Lincoln openly revoked the emancipation order. To allay powerful Upper South slaveholders, he shortly thereafter removed Frémont from his Missouri post and transferred him to western Virginia.[25]

The aftermath of Lane's Osceola raid further illuminated the racial contour of war on the western Trans-Mississippi border. In a characteristically heated letter to Brig. Gen. Samuel D. Sturgis regarding the protection of civilian goods and human chattel, Lane exclaimed that, although his brigade should "not become negro thieves," neither should they be "prostituted into negro catchers." Slaves as well as materials useful for perpetuating guerrilla warfare should be confiscated in order to deny them to Confederate irregulars. They helped rebel wives maintain their way of life in the absence of husbands fighting in the field. "I say that the mass of the personal property in Missouri, including slaves," the Kansan admonished, "is at this moment held by the wives and children, assisted by the Federal army, while the husband and father are actually in arms against the Government." This was unacceptable to Lane and many other Union commanders in the Trans-Mississippi.[26]

From the beginning, officers like Lane took the issue into their own hands, believing that "confiscation of slaves and other property" that could be made useful to the rebels "should follow treason as the thunder peal follows the lightning flash." Frustration abounded in Union ranks, especially when in the field. The very day Lane penned his letter to Sturgis, one of his men was shot in the woods outside of camp, very likely, added the Kansan impertinently, by the same man whose property his superior was "so anxious to protect."[27]

Lane's goal in the raid on Osceola, as in future operations by commanders on both sides, was to terrorize a population he believed supported the enemy. Primary means for achieving such terror were through theft and destruction.

Lane and others learned early that civilians, as much as fighting men, were combatants in the borderlands. From the beginning, a significant amount of this civilian war took place north of Arkansas in small communities like Osceola and throughout the countryside. Whether or not Osceola's men served as Confederate irregulars, Lane struck terror into them during his raid. Following the first attack by the Kansas Brigade, the men cautiously returned to find their town in ruins, their wives and children doing what they could to salvage what was left. At the mere mention of Union troops returning, one townsman declared, "Our men did not wait to meet the enemy, and again the town was left with only women and children to defend it."[28]

The Kansas Brigade moved on from Osceola to terrorize hundreds more throughout western Missouri. A New York reporter who had followed its path "found all through Western Missouri a deadly horror entertained towards Lane," who had "left a track marked with charred ruins and blood." The correspondent, who had interviewed civilians along the way, found brutal stories for his East Coast readers. One elderly man had lost his "horses, mules, grain, his wife's dresses . . . , [and his] log shanty." What was worse, this victim declared to the Yankee reporter, Lane's men had "stole the clothes of my little dead grandson."[29]

The first year of hostilities along the Trans-Mississippi border was a war of exhaustion on par with Maj. Gen. William Tecumseh Sherman's march through Georgia in the fall and winter of 1864. While Sherman's raid lasted only months, actions like those endured by women and children in Osceola occurred throughout the entire conflict. For agents of irregular warfare, including Lane and his guerrilla adversaries, what had transpired at the Missouri town was a necessary step toward victory. To destroy the enemy's livelihood and to leave nothing, quite literally, to which he might return was critical in demoralizing and defeating the other side. This intense social conflict fought daily throughout the immense area of the borderlands, punctuated by events like Osceola, exemplified the nastiest aspects of the Civil War.

Due in part to Lane's campaign through southwest Missouri, Union commanders not connected to the rigors of combat in the field filed a series of general orders to keep a semblance of proper military decorum. One of the earliest efforts, issued in November 1861, reprimanded field commanders for their harsh treatment of civilians. In an attempt to counter these seemingly ruthless policies, Maj. Gen. Henry W. Halleck made clear that "numerous cases" had been brought to his attention of "alleged seizure and destruction of property in this department, showing an outrageous abuse of power and a violation of the laws of war." For Halleck, personal property should be protected by officers unless such material was deemed necessary for the direct benefit of troops or if it proved beneficial for the enemy.[30] The wording left room for a wide range of interpretations, allowing commanders in the field to decide for themselves exactly what constituted necessary forage or potential aid for the enemy. Complaints continued to pour in to Union headquarters throughout the war. While such general orders were reissued, commanders such as Halleck found effective counterinsurgency activities and maintaining amicable relations with the citizenry nearly impossible to balance.

Real and alleged Confederate abuses against private property and civilians certainly did not help Halleck's case for leniency. Before Osceola, with Sterling Price's army maintaining control of southwest Missouri, reports of small-scale Confederate raids into Union-held territory abounded. Parties of regular and irregular troops from both sides roamed southwest Missouri and southeast Kansas in 1861. In one instance as early as September, just east of Fort Scott a party of one hundred rebels drove off a Union wagon train and mule herd "in a hurry." Although a sizeable force pursued the stolen supplies and transport animals, the Federals were unable to recover them. One frustrated soldier lamented, "It is generally believed that the wagon master is a secessionist."[31]

Theft and violence did not stop with the regular or irregular military, for civilians not connected in any *official* capacity with either side brought the war to one another, with women usually at the forefront. As the first cold weather spread south in the fall of 1861, families, still uncertain about the course the war might take, prepared for the encroaching winter. In southwest Missouri, now firmly under Confederate control, neighbor partisanship emerged with vigor. A young lady at the time, Lucy Bryant remembered how one day a man with whom her family was acquainted drove up in a wagon to their house Bryant and her mother looked on in shock as their Confederate neighbor brazenly walked into their house and stole furniture, piece by piece, loading it all on the wagon and taking it away. Such an act of blatant theft would have been unthinkable just a few months earlier. With intense anger, Bryant's mother promptly "hitched up the poorest team of horses . . . to an old wagon, the whole outfit being as unlikely to arouse the cupidity of any bushwhackers she might meet as anything we could get up, and then started . . . all alone." Along the way, she alerted another neighbor about what had occurred—the fellow happening to be the thief's father-in-law—and they proceeded to the transgressor's house. In his yard lay her furniture, a sickly child relaxing on one of the pieces. After a heated exchange, Bryant repatriated her possessions and returned home triumphant.[32]

Particularly brutal fighting also erupted in Indian Territory in late 1861 when bitter sectional rivalries within tribes turned to full-scale warfare. Loyalist Indians refused to adhere to the alliance between Creek chief Motey Canard and the Confederacy. They established an independent, pro-Union organization and appointed influential Creek leader Opothleyahola as their chief. In August Opothleyahola pleaded with President Lincoln for support. Citing an 1832 treaty, he complained, "Now White People are trying to take our people away to fight against us and you." But no immediate aid came. Lincoln's administration and most high-level military commanders were consumed with developments elsewhere, and the Native Americans hoping for government assistance were near the bottom of their long list. Intense political pressure followed as Cherokee chief John Ross and others urged both Opothleyahola's Unionists and Confederate forces in the area to stand down. But this meant little. Just six days after Opothleyahola's pleading letter to Lincoln, Ross finally decided to side with the Confederacy, at least for the time being. He urged the Cherokee Nation to initiate an alliance with the Confederacy, making clear in a carefully worded message that their own "general interest is inseparable from [the South's] and it is not desirable that we should stand alone." Soon after, with Ross no longer to be trusted, Opothleyahola led a column of nearly 8,000 poorly clad and equipped civilians and warriors toward Kansas.[33]

Confederate colonel Douglas H. Cooper and 2,000 cavalrymen pursued the escaping loyalists, meeting heavy resistance. The retreating Creeks had set the tall, dead grass ablaze behind them to slow their pursuers and destroy any possible forage for their horses. According to one discouraged Confederate, the "old fellow" left little in his wake: "We get no feed for our horses scarcely but a little corn & not much grass." The fleeing loyalists had used the environment to their advantage by destroying the fuel for Cooper's horses and making any quick attack impossible. Such use of fire was nothing new among Native Americans, who had used the "Red Buffalo," as some called it, for centuries for both ecological and military purposes.[34]

Then on November 19, Opothleyahola's refugees surprised Cooper at the Battle of Round Mountain, where Union sympathizers led the Confederates into an ambush. Heavy fighting continued into the night "by the light of the prairie burning," until Cooper's forces finally fell back.[35] Still the civilian refugees, aware of the proximity of their Confederate pursuers, had left behind a significant amount of supplies, including livestock and food. Moreover, their civilian status meant that they could not hope to receive further provisions from the Union government. They thus were forced to forage from the countryside.[36]

Disease, cold weather, and combat further hampered the retreat of the refugees. In late November both Confederate soldiers and Union refugees suffered from an outbreak of measles that significantly weakened both sides. Then in early December, Opothleyahola launched another surprise attack against the Confederates at the Battle of Chusto-Talasah, along Bird Creek in the Cherokee Nation. The intense engagement was short lived, but it forced Cooper to retreat to Fort Gibson for resupply. The refugees had no such option and so continued north, only to meet Confederate reinforcements under Col. James M. McIntosh at the Battle of Chustenahlah on December 26. The engagement proved disastrous for the Unionists, who were scattered by the successful Confederate attack. According to McIntosh, the Confederates captured "160 women and children, 20 Negroes, 30 wagons, 70 yoke of oxen, 500 horses, several hundred head of cattle, 100 sheep, and a great quantity of property of much value to the enemy." Beyond contraband and prisoners, the colonel reported that his troops had killed 250 of the Indians. The numbers do not add up, however, unless, as contemporary Wiley Britton noted, the Confederates had killed civilians. Opothleyahola's bloodied column continued north with little food or clothing.[37]

The ensuing journey occurred amid harsh winter weather, and many of the refugees died from exposure. According to one Indian agent, "Quite a number of them froze to death on the route and their bodies, with a shroud of snow, were left where they fell." At least one of their pursuers, a Confederate soldier in Colonel Cooper's command, had also "froze to death" during the campaign. Although the refugees' arrival in Kansas meant some protection from Confederate forces, the weather continued to assault them. Hundreds of Unionist Indians had joined Opothleyahola's exodus along the way, and by December 1861 southeast Kansas had become inundated with thousands of refugees. Union authorities were ill equipped to shelter and feed such numbers, and in the particularly harsh winter, people continued to die from exposure and starvation. Most who survived the trek suffered from malnutrition and frostbite. One of the few doctors available to help the refugees was shocked by the scene and quickly exhausted the modicum of clothes and supplies he had brought for the Indians. At one point a group of children appeared before the physician without "one thread upon their bodies." Utilizing a "triage" approach for dispensing supplies, he focused his efforts first on the "nakedest of the naked." The situation continued to deteriorate throughout the winter. "The destitution, misery, and suffering amongst them is beyond the power of any pen to portray," wrote one witness, "it must be seen to be realized."[38]

The border Trans-Mississippi also faced a socioeconomic disaster as large business operations began to shut down. Near Granby in southwest Missouri, one of the largest and most successful lead mines came under attack by Major General Price's forces in the fall of 1861. Following his victory at Wilson's Creek and consequent control of much of southwest Missouri and northwest Arkansas, Price was the first military commander to commandeer the Granby lead mines. Owned by devout Unionists, including the U.S. minister to Venezuela, Henry P. Blow, the firm claimed to have been nearly completely ruined by the "so called Union Confederacy." In a letter to General Halleck, the company's attorney claimed that Confederate authorities had pressured one of the owners to such an extent "as to compel him to remove his family to his former homestead" far away from their presence. Price's army was not satisfied with confiscating "500 pigs of lead, but also [took possession] of the furnaces and about 200,000 lbs of mineral then on hand, together with teams, stock and everything appertaining thereto."[39] The complex was a complete loss for its owners, and the rebels continued to extract lead for their armies until late 1862. The Confederate quartermaster in charge of its production notified Secretary of War Judah P. Benjamin that he had shipped 32,000 pounds of lead from the Granby mines to Memphis. "Will continue to forward lead," he declared, "and believe that I can furnish all that is wanted for the confederate army."[40]

While Price's Confederates helped supply lead to the Confederacy, civilians along the border faced increased threat from those who took advantage of the lawless atmosphere born by conflict. Most county and municipal political officers, including sheriffs and members of the judiciary, had disbanded shortly after the secession crisis began. Only months into the war, much of the region was void of governmental operations.

One "band of marauders" that took advantage of this void to ravage parts of southwest Missouri in 1861 provides insight into the nature of warfare and society at this early stage. Along their path of theft and destruction, the gang killed George Broome, a well-known and much-liked farmer and businessman. Only partially numbed by the war at this time, residents banded together to find and punish the murderers. The angered locals, seeking justice in a time of near anarchy, captured the suspected killer, gave him a mock trial, and promptly lynched him. It remains unknown whether the man had been involved in Broome's death at all, and it is certain that even if guilty, he was far from the only one. Yet the local citizens, unable to rely on any recognized law in the region, took justice into their own hands.[41]

By the end of 1861, people along the Trans-Mississippi border, both Confederate and Union, were reeling from a newly imposed anarchy. They armed themselves, hid out, sent their families away, and formed vigilante mobs to construct at least a semblance of order. For the residents who, in their minds, vindicated George Broome, this was a fleeting gesture of civility, however uncivil society had already become. By the next year, though, the guerrilla war on the western frontier would become even more intense. People would flee by the thousands, and the once-prosperous region would transform into a natural and social wilderness in which farm fields filled with weeds and the remaining people reverted to a system of severe distrust and survival.

# 3

## "The Depth of Misfortune and Misery"

### REGULAR AND IRREGULAR WAR, 1862

By 1862, political leaders for both the Union and Confederacy worried about how the war had rapidly devolved into a bitter civilian-centered conflict. Confederate president Jefferson Davis complained to Gen. Robert E. Lee that Union authorities were pushing his hand toward an exceedingly severe military strategy, a "savage war in which no quarter is to be given and no sex to be spared." This savage war emerged only intermittently in the eastern theater, where Davis focused his lamentation, but it became real on the frontier Trans-Mississippi—and far from sporadic. For the women and children on the western borderlands, the war had developed as Davis feared it might in Virginia, one in which the rules as "recognised to be lawful by civilized men in modern times" did not apply. Just as the Confederate president protested harsh Federal retribution toward civilians, Missouri's Union governor, Hamilton R. Gamble, reflected on the first year of the conflict. He decried the Confederate war effort in the Trans-Mississippi and the universal "disregard of law" that consumed his state, particularly the western border. In the end, political passions aside, both Davis and Gamble were on to something. "This Wicked Rebellion," as Gamble termed it in 1862, had already developed on the Trans-Mississippi frontier into a complex and dynamic conflict shaped by political, natural, and racial extremes—with civilians always at its center.[1]

The war's second year brought more intense *regular* warfare to the western Trans-Mississippi border than at any other time. By year's end, the Battles of Pea Ridge and Prairie Grove had shifted control of the region in the

Union's favor. They had also exposed those civilians remaining in the area to thousands more Union and Confederate soldiers traversing through farms and towns. Residents were not merely casual observers, however. Instead of reading about the increasingly destructive fighting from afar, people on the western Trans-Mississippi became a part of the war. Women, children, elderly, those usually considered noncombatants, had evolved into a critical part of the conflict. Consequently, their roles as victims intensified. They watched from their front doors as soldiers marched and, at times, fought around them. Wounded men would lie on their kitchen floors and bullets flew through their walls. Large battles like Pea Ridge and Prairie Grove were the exception, though, and not the rule. Although strategically critical for control of Missouri and northern Arkansas, these Federal victories only served to intensify the irregular war in the region. When the armies moved elsewhere, irregulars and their pursuers plagued residents. Union leaders became increasingly frustrated with guerrillas and those civilians suspected of helping them. Even with major battles and large armies, the war on the border in 1862 continued to develop into a civilian-centered conflict. To be sure, 1862 marks an important transition toward a more severe and exacting Federal presence in the region, one that would ultimately help undermine any vestige of civilian support for the Confederacy.

Significant military activity that year began almost immediately. The Pea Ridge Campaign in first three months of 1862 ushered in the largest number of Union and Confederate soldiers during the war. In the winter Brig. Gen. Samuel R. Curtis and his 10,000-man Army of the Southwest had pursued Confederates through southwest Missouri into northwest Arkansas. Maj. Gen. Earl Van Dorn, chosen by President Davis to lead the combined forces of Brig. Gen. Benjamin McCulloch and Maj. Gen. Sterling Price, formed the Army of the West, with approximately 16,000 men. By late winter, both armies prepared to fight near Fayetteville. Their preparations lasted over a month, and the two commands relied on local forage to survive. Civilians, already strained by a year of war and a hard winter, were caught in the middle.[2]

Confederate control of most of the region in early 1862 led to brazen irregular attacks against known Union sympathizers. Thousands of civilians from northwest Arkansas and southwest Missouri had fled to Kansas or points farther north, but some people remained, despite the threat to their lives and property. The same Bryant family in southwest Missouri who had already dealt with attempted theft suffered another scare just weeks later. John A. Bryant, a known Union sympathizer who had been suffering from severe illness for some time, had been unable to evacuate his family from the region. Two rebel guerrillas arrived on the first day he was able to get out of bed. With one man holding a double-barreled shotgun, they barged into the house and ordered Bryant outside. He refused, noting his weakened condition. One of the guerrillas, enraged, exclaimed, "Well if you won't go outside I will kill you anyway right here." He pulled back both hammers and pointed the shotgun squarely at Bryant. "We children set up a scream and my mother sprang in front of my father," recalled his daughter. "I remember yet exactly how the caps on [Joe] Thompson's gun looked as he stood there with the weapon leveled." The tense standoff lasted for what seemed an eternity to Bryant's wife and children. Finally, the other partisan, who had known the family before the war, suggested to his comrade that they move on rather than blasting the man in front of his family.[3]

But the guerrillas were not finished that day. Frustrated by their failure to intimidate the Bryants, they rode less than a mile farther to the house of another known Unionist. They hailed the man, spoke briefly with him, and as he turned to go back to his house while his wife watched, the shotgun-wielding guerrilla unloaded one of the barrels into his back. At such close range the buckshot devastated the victim, hitting him "beneath the shoulder blade and coming out at the breast, killing him instantly." Local Unionists and friends, mostly women, held a secret burial for the man under cover of darkness to avoid detection by other partisans. Some remaining Unionist men, including John Bryant, understood the message and set off for Kansas. The Confederate guerrillas had succeeded. One dead Unionist led to the evacuation of dozens more. The wives and children of these refugees, left behind to fend for themselves, followed two months later.[4]

Residents of southwest Missouri were not the only civilians who sought refuge in Kansas by 1862. Creek chief Opothleyahola's followers, who had fled north from the Arkansas River in December 1861, continued to collect stragglers in the winter and early spring of 1862. Nearly 5,000 Native Americans, most of whom held Unionist sympathies, had flooded into southeast Kansas and the far northeastern reaches of Indian Territory to escape the bitter irregular fighting. The refugees nevertheless continued to suffer from exposure and malnourishment as occasional supply trains brought only enough goods for a portion of them. Yet even had the commissioner of Indian affairs been willing and able to supply those huddled along the Verdigris River, they likely never could have satisfied the dozens more who trickled in daily. Their horses and other animals suffered as well. When the warmer weather in the spring brought with it the increased danger of contamination from the thousands of rotting horse carcasses in and around the river, the refugees had to move once again. This time, hoping that fresher water and milder weather might ensure at least a modicum of survival, they relocated farther north along the Neosho River. The environment had combined with soldiers and guerrillas to bring a different, increasingly harsh, kind of warfare to civilians.[5]

By the time the refugees started to relocate, their numbers approached 8,000 people, and any hope for quick relief was futile. Opotheyahola, among other leaders, sent a storm of protests concerning the deteriorating conditions. One commissioner, who had been ordered to evaluate the situation firsthand, confirmed these reports: "Such covering as I saw were made in the rudest manner, being composed of pieces of cloth, old quilts, handkerchiefs, aprons, etc., stretched upon sticks, and so limited were many of them in size that they were scarcely sufficient to cover the emaciated and dying forms beneath them." The refugees' food was little better. Thousands of Native Americans suffered nearly constant illness due to rotting pork "not fit for a dog to eat." This bacon had been discarded by Union soldiers at Fort Leavenworth, where one men had "pronounced it suitable only for soap grease." Such malnutrition and exposure led to sickening scenes of dying children and gaunt adults. An Indian commissioner on the scene reported "a little Creek boy, about eight years old, with both feet taken off near the ankle." Although spring and summer brought more-bearable weather, the situation for these people scarcely improved.[6]

As reports of a Federal offensive increased, dozens of Confederate families made plans to evacuate the region. Fayetteville civilians watched as the electric atmosphere intensified with increasing reports of the imminent Union approach. Once the first secessionist families started south across the Boston Mountains, according to one resident, there occurred a "general stampede from the town." Hundreds of civilians hurriedly packed their belongings into wagons, collected their slaves, and in a near panic, started across the rugged roads leading to Van Buren and Fort Smith. For Sarah Yeater, the sight was as mesmerizing as it was troubling. "The line of carriages, wagons and horsemen must have been two miles or more long as they crossed the Boston mountains," she later wrote, "and as the road had not been worked for months a wagon would frequently be stalled and the whole procession [had] to stop." This refugee train finally made it to the Arkansas River and dispersed toward either Fort Smith or Little Rock. These civilians had escaped the coming tumult in northwest Arkansas and would not experience the effects of the region's most important battle.[7]

Meanwhile, Benjamin McCulloch, surprised by the immediacy of the Union threat, ordered his army to evacuate Fayetteville. Confederate quartermaster officers, unable to load their supplies in time, opened the balance of their stores to soldiers and civilians. A melee ensued, one resident remembered, and "pillage soon became the order of the day." One regiment after another "poured in to swell the tide of waste and robbery, the [and] the scene became one of riot and unrestrained plunder." Confederates reveled in the free-for-all as, according to one Missourian, almost every soldier "got a ham or a shoulder or a side of bacon, ran his bayonet through them, and carried it to camp." Another officer who witnessed the scene remembered that "stores all along Main Street were thrown open to the Missouri and Arkansas soldiers." Hundreds of frenzied soldiers ran through town, anxiously anticipating the Federals arrival while taking advantage of the lawlessness. "Amid the destruction it could not but be amusing," wrote the officer, "to see great heavy-bearded fellows carrying around fancy little toys—rattlers, made to amuse very small juveniles. Bonnet frames—old French flowers—nearly every man had a looking glass."[8] While burly soldiers pranced down Main Street with their stolen toys and mirrors, residents tried to remain inconspicuous.

The next day, as the townspeople took stock of the situation, a rear guard of Confederate cavalry moved through Fayetteville, with Federal scouts not far behind. Their mission was to destroy anything that the closely trailing Union army might find useful. Most notably, they set fire to the Fayetteville Female Institute, which had served as an ammunition factory and where a large amount of live ammunition, left behind by the retreating rebels, remained. The resulting display made an impression on most of the remaining residents. One young girl later recalled, "The smoke was so dense that it seemed like a black cloud over the town."[9] Several homes had also been burned and much of the town lay in ruins as the Confederate army finally headed south.

The soldiers also realized what they had wrought. "Fayetteville presented indeed a sad spectacle when we passed through," wrote one Confederate officer. "I could not but contrast the beautiful quiet little town of last May when we were so heartily welcomed to the devastation and waste and ruin manifest all around." The soldier was shocked by what he had seen and wondered, as many did, how anyone could maintain any sort of life in such a region. "What Citizens now left in Fayetteville," he observed, "seemed perfectly panic stricken—seemed to be utterly regardless of anything like protection of property." Another Confederate remembered the episode as "one of the most disgraceful scenes" he had ever witnessed.[10]

When Union troops finally arrived, the town and its citizens were in shambles. Brig. Gen. Alexander Asboth issued a proclamation to Fayetteville residents in which he summarily declared the cessation of the "wanton destruction" perpetuated by rebel forces. He reaffirmed his desire for civilians to adhere to U.S. law and rid themselves of any remaining influences imparted upon them by threats and devious persuasion by "bad and designing men." Law and order, Asboth assured residents, would return, even if it meant Union troops must guard them and their property daily. "Deserted fire-sides cannot be guarded," Asboth cautioned, "but every house containing a living soul shall have the protection of power." He then called for everyone present to remain in place and those wayward citizens to return to benefit from Federal protection. For much of the war, Asboth and other Union commanders would work to make good those promises for security. But authorities had not accounted for potential depredations committed by Federal soldiers.[11]

Although Asboth tried to restore a sense of order, his very presence only further complicated matters. The Union army could not stay forever, and for many Fayetteville citizens, Federal soldiers were as unwelcome as Confederates due to their proclivity for theft and destruction, even with the general's promises. Curtis's army had pushed deep into Confederate territory now and was dangerously removed from its supply base at Rolla, Missouri. The Federal force had little choice but to gather forage from locals who had already suffered immeasurably from the Confederate presence. But Curtis's men found little in the rebels' wake. According to Union doctor John T. Buegel, cattle in the area, when they could be found, were emaciated. "It takes two men to hold them up while one knocks them down," he wrote.[12] One Union soldier remonstrated to an Illinois newspaper: "Desolation, horrid to contemplate, marks every section of the country through which the army has passed. Houses are deserted and fast going to ruin; fences are pulled down and burned up [and] orchards are ruined by hitching horses and mules to the trees." A nearly unmanageable mass of Union and Confederate soldiers had pushed an already feeble society past the brink. "An air of sickening devastation is everywhere visible," another soldier aptly concluded.[13]

And that was before battle had even begun. On March 7 and 8 ferocious fighting in the dense woods and rocky terrain known as Pea Ridge, thirty miles to the north of Fayetteville, produced the bloodiest battle west of the Mississippi River. The resounding Federal victory turned the course of the Trans-Mississippi war in the Union's favor and led to the complete demoralization of Van Dorn's army. Curtis's command incurred over 1,300 casualties, but the Confederates had more than 2,000 losses. Southern chances of controlling the region had significantly worsened.[14]

Seven months after Pea Ridge, a Union soldier encamped near the battlefield could not help but comment on the destructive nature of the engagement. "The woods present a scene as if a tornado had passed through it," the Iowa soldier wrote in his diary, "and spent its vengeance in snapping limbs and twisting huge trees from the main trunk." In a region most noted for intense guerrilla warfare and destitute refugees, such a scene was both peculiar and haunting. The dense woods had been mangled. Large trees, now skeletons of their former glory, were adorned with spent cannonballs wedged into them. The ground was still littered with the refuse of battle. Indeed, many of the bullets used in the December engagement at Prairie Grove had been recovered by Union forces who scoured the Pea Ridge battlefield. Such ruination, as historian Megan Kate Nelson has shown, manifested itself in an almost mystical way for soldiers who could hardly comprehend the landscape's sheer physical destruction. Natural forces, like tornadoes, are all they could compare it to. Here was a symbolic display of the terror and destruction wrought by war. For most soldiers in the Trans-Mississippi, however, experiencing combat on battlefields like Pea Ridge was rare and remarkable. Their war occurred daily, and it involved guerrillas and civilians. Unlike the lines of battle resplendent with planned tactical maneuvers, their battle lines were everywhere and their tactics often improvised.[15]

With the Union and Confederate armies needing subsistence after Pea Ridge even more than before, local civilians unwittingly served as quartermasters. The ensuing Confederate retreat south through the Boston Mountains was by all accounts miserable for the defeated rebels, but civilians in their path suffered too. One man reported that the retreating troops took "every fowl of any kind, all the cattle, hogs and sheep, and . . . all the bacon and corn they could find for several miles around." The famished soldiers, another civilian observed, went so far as to "cut out slices of beef and mutton before it was done bleeding and eat it raw." One Confederate described the Boston Mountains, drenched in cold, early spring rain, as "so poor, as some of the men expressed it, that turkey buzzards would not fly over it." Price's Missourians blazed the path of retreat, effectively clearing out what little forage had been available, "even to the last acorn." The retreating Confederates, plodding along, made slow progress over the steep, slick roads, some of the most rugged terrain in the Trans-Mississippi. "Occasionally we passed a small settlement from which the inhabitants had fled," wrote one soldier, "but everything had been carried away by Price's army. In the gardens we occasionally found the remains of some turnips or onions, which were eagerly dug out of the ground . . . and eaten raw."[16]

Residents nearer the battlefield fared little better. Over two weeks after the engagement, Curtis, who had been pleading for supplies, noted that the entire region had been "stripped" and that it required at best "two days' journey north to get anything." Civilians in the area had no more to give, or to have taken. The Union army soon moved north, leaving behind a scene of destruction not only on the battlefield but also all along its path. Certain women and children remained steadfast, but most participated in one of the largest exoduses during the Civil War, leaving behind their homes and belongings for safety farther north. In May a Union cavalryman noted with little surprise that "a large number of union families are leaving." The goods and livestock left behind were quickly requisitioned by local forces, Union and Confederate alike.[17]

While the bulk of regular Confederate soldiers fled south following Pea Ridge, the regionally ubiquitous guerrilla war continued unabated. Late spring brought warmth, forage, and foliage for irregular operations. Small and large bands of "marauders" stepped up their efforts to plunder and kill. A Federal officer traveling alone represented perhaps the most prized quarry for any rebel partisan. One such hapless lieutenant suffered the consequences. Having taken a brief Sunday leave from his company to court a southwest Missouri belle, the smitten officer was spotted by two men, one of whom was noted guerrilla Hugh McBride. McBride and his alleged accomplice, Smith Crim, watched as the lieutenant hitched his horse to a post outside the girl's home. Once he was inside, the two men quickly and quietly approached. As they crept up to the door, McBride, holding his double-barrel shotgun, smashed through the door and immediately "cocked both barrels." The Federal could do nothing and was taken prisoner. The group traveled into the nearby woods, had dinner, and moved on for another half mile. Finally, deciding that the officer "must die," McBride ordered his comrade to shoot him. When Crim refused, McBride angrily walked up and unloaded one of his barrels into the lieutenant. Occasionally, guerrillas kept their captives alive, but nearly always such mercy served a direct purpose. If no prisoner exchanges or other advantageous outcomes were available, the most common policy was murder.[18]

Civilians were not exempt from such violence. Not long after the fight at Pea Ridge, local physician Jaquillian Stemmons invited more than twenty other local Unionists to his home for a meeting. Guerrillas got word of the meeting and promptly descended on the dwelling. Opportunities like this were rare, and the irregulars were determined to take full advantage of having these men in the same place. As the rebels surrounded the house, taking care to hide behind brush and trees, Stemmons and his guests soon caught on to their predicament and prepared for battle. Shots rang out. Not willing to linger in a prolonged fight, the guerrillas tried to smoke the Unionists out by setting fire to the building. At this the doctor stepped out to try and reason with the attackers, some of whom he knew well from having treated them before the war. According to one witness, he made clear that "if they must kill [the men], that was one matter, but the firing of the house was another thing." With his former patients and neighbors surprised by his boldness, Stemmons went on to explain that "he was ready to die if he must, but [they] ought not to burn down the shelter for his wife and kids who would be left when he was gone." The assailants, having listened to the doctor's appeal, promptly shot him to death. Stemmons's wife and children (not to mention his friends inside the house) heard him groaning outside while the guerrillas once again prepared to set the structure ablaze.[19]

In order to burn the building without getting shot by its remaining occupants, the rebels fired a wagon full of hay and pushed it against an outside wall. They "soon had the house blazing." Most of those inside escaped into the surrounding woods. Stemmons's son remembered seeing his mother running out of the burning house while carrying his one-year-old sibling. The boy, with the help of an older man, was one of the last to leave. His companion recognized one of the guerrillas as a longtime neighbor who, according to the younger Stemmons, took mercy on the man and told him to run, all the while continuing to shoot at the other fleeing Unionists.[20]

Three years later, after struggling to take care of her children and keep what little property remained, Susan Stemmons filed a lawsuit against eleven of the known attackers. In an exceedingly rare occurrence, she asked for and received $10,000 in damages for the murder of her husband and the loss of the house and its contents. But at the time of the attack, the guerrillas had achieved their aims: killing a Unionist, destroying his property, and terrorizing the people of the surrounding region.[21]

Another victim of the attack on Stemmons's home was Miles Overton. In his separate postwar testimony, he emphatically claimed that his neighbor and friend had been "a respectable man and actively loyal towards the government of the United States." The attacking guerrillas, he stated, "did not have the fear of God before their eyes but [were] instigated by the devil." As Overton had attempted to make his escape from the burning house, the assailants opened fire on both him and his colleagues. Though saving himself, he lost to the guerrillas a mare and saddle worth $1,500.[22] As if this first violent experience was not enough, Overton was attacked again later the same year. Overtaken by a completely different group of irregulars, he lost his horse, saddle, bridle, boots off his feet, Navy Colt revolver, and $5.50, the last of his cash. In addition, he was shot in both an arm and a thigh as he tried to escape. The wounded and beleaguered Unionist managed to evade the guerrillas but lost the use of his leg for life. The theft of his belongings, in addition to the loss of his leg, Overton estimated, was valued at $5,000.[23]

In an attempt to thwart the violence endured by Stemmons, Overton, and others, more Union troops entered the border region by the spring of 1862. Their job had become as much to hunt guerrillas as it was to fight the regular Confederate forces. The latter would become less of a problem by the end of the year, but guerrilla activity would more than take the regulars' place. Many of the Federals who entered the western borderlands took great pains to write about the wilderness that surrounded them. Jacob Haas, a German immigrant and Yankee soldier, entered Fort Scott in March. He and his comrades were not impressed with the frontier fort. "People may think that it is strongly fortified because of the name but such is not the case," Haas wrote, "one sees nothing but dilapidated buildings and fallen over walls." By May, his Wisconsin regiment had moved into southwest Missouri to hunt guerrillas, entering Carthage and finding it abandoned. "It is a fine town and must have been a lively place commercially," Haas observed, "but at present it looks deserted and in ruins." The Federals found plenty of food there, though. They chased down chickens and raided cellars full of "mutton, veal, lard, apples, butter, [and] ham," all stockpiled by hiding civilians.[24]

In June 1862 approximately 6,000 Federal troops composing seven regiments—including two Indian regiments—prepared to invade Indian Territory. The "Indian Expedition" was the first significant Union operation into Indian Territory during the Civil War. Federal commanders intended to secure the Cherokee Nation from regular and irregular Confederate forces and also hoped to return to their homes the longsuffering civilian refugees who had been camped near Baxter Springs since Opothleyahola's exodus. The ill-fated expedition reflects not only Union strategy and troubled leadership in the region but also serves to illuminate the racial and ethnic diversity on the Trans-Mississippi frontier. In addition, the campaign serves to highlight the central role the environment played in shaping and, in this case, derailing an entire operation.[25]

Some Union commanders found the "skulking" abilities of their Native American soldiers ideally suited for the nature of warfare in the region.

Maj. E. C. Ellithorpe put such able scouts to good use in the Indian Territory's rough terrain. Ellithorpe's Native American soldiers repeatedly proved themselves during the campaign. In one case, his men located a small force of Confederate irregulars in a "thickly timbered bottom" near the Verdigris River in the Cherokee Nation. "The brush was so thick that I dared not undertake to penetrate without first learning the strength of the enemy," the major wrote, "and to do this was a difficult task not having any cannon to shell the woods." Ellithorpe instead sent in his Indian scouts. They crept silently through the brush to gauge the enemy's strength, and thanks to their valuable intelligence, the major ordered a successful attack the following morning. "Here I saw the value of the Indian as a daring scout," he later wrote.[26]

For most Union soldiers, though, experiences in the brush were far different. Even on horseback, cavalryman Chester L. White suffered directly from the difficult terrain. Soon after an engagement with Col. Stand Watie's Confederates in northeastern Indian Territory, White got lost in the brush. "I got entangled in the d—dst place I ever got into nothing but Grapevines—rattlesnakes and wood-ticks," the cavalryman lamented. "[A]fter trying for about an hour to get out I finally succeeded in doing so by jumping my horse down a perpendicular bank 15 feet into a swampy creek where I was not much better off than before." Thickets and tangles notwithstanding, the motley and increasingly frustrated Union army moved farther south into Indian Territory.[27]

Along the way, the soldiers suffered from an inconsistent and unpredictable water supply. Early in the summer expedition, one Kansas soldier complained about the lack of fresh water when the troops moved away from the Grand River. According to the artillerist, "We had, on occasion, to depend for our water supply upon stagnant pools in the partially dry creeks, where roaming herds of cattle were in the habit of standing to protect their legs from the attacks of the green-head flies." Struggling through difficult terrain and hunting an elusive enemy, the thirsty Federals had little choice but to make the best out of water seasoned by mud and cattle. It was so bad at times that it "assumed the consistency of soup, but by boiling and skimming, and then spiking it with coffee until it was black, we managed to exist." Although such Yankee ingenuity in the war-induced wilderness made the expedition slightly more manageable, the environment proved to be just as troublesome as the enemy they pursued. By July, the thirsty troops had reached a breaking point. A prolonged drought had dried much of the water in northeastern Indian Territory, and what little did exist became increasingly unpalatable. The situation was desperate, according to one Ohio cavalryman, who remarked that the beleaguered men had nearly broken into mutiny when they passed a rare spring and were not allowed to stop and fill their canteens. On top of this, the trooper noted, "there has been no rain of any consequence for about two months."[28]

As thirsty and increasingly angry Federal troops continued their expedition into Indian Territory, Union authorities hoped to move the Native American refugees back to their homes in the Cherokee Nation. In July, just as men were filtering cattle feces from their drinking water, Brig. Gen. James Blunt told Col. William Weer to survey the land through northeastern Indian Territory. "As it is desirable to return the refugee Indians now in Kansas to their homes as soon as practicable," Blunt ordered, "you will therefore take measures to ascertain if the corn crop in the Indian Territory of the present season will be sufficient to subsist them." The general also instructed him to pressure Chief John Ross to reconsider his position with the Confederacy. Part of Ross's concerns reflected those of Native American civilians throughout the area. According to a Union officer who conducted talks directly with the embattled Cherokee chief, Ross was "very much concerned about the people of his nation, and anxious that the United States Government should send sufficient force . . . to protect them from lawless bands that are daily threatening them, committing robberies and murders." He also showed considerable fear for "his own personal safety and the safety of his family." In the end, though, with the Union army's strong show of force in the territory, Blunt would gain Ross's careful cooperation and that of over 1,500 Cherokee civilians.[29]

But regaining Ross's tepid loyalty was the expedition's only success. As Weer's motley army of Native Americans, German immigrants, and Midwestern farmboys moved south, they met stubborn resistance from both regular and irregular Confederates. Guerrilla bands from southwest Missouri, most notably the group led by Thomas R. Livingston, teamed with Colonel Watie's regular forces to frustrate Federal progress. Trudging through thick brush and across numerous creeks and rivers while being constantly harassed by partisans and Confederate pickets, the Union expedition slowed considerably. Moreover, by the time Weer's Yankees had reached the outskirts of Fort Gibson in mid-July, they found the place desolated. Anticipating the Union assault, Brig. Gen. Albert Pike had ordered his troops to set fire to a four-mile radius of prairie and brush surrounding the fort. The extreme heat and drought (one soldier reported a likely exaggerated 125 degrees) only added to the misery.[30]

The Confederates, meanwhile, took full advantage of the adverse environmental conditions. In a letter to Confederate secretary of war George W. Randolph, General Pike made clear the harassing actions taken against Weer's expedition and carefully noted what in the end would prove decisive in thwarting any further Union advance. "The excessive drought, the utter destruction of corn and grass, the intense heat, and the scarcity of water may prove our best allies," Pike reported. Indeed, he continued, thanks to the environment, "no large force of the enemy can march now any distance into this country."[31]

Colonel Weer's proclivity for whiskey, his habit of staying where none but "putrid, stinking water" was available to his men, and the subsequent discontent among his troops led his second in command, Col. Frederick Salomon, to take action. Salomon, a German immigrant, had seen enough. "I have stood by with arms folded and seen my men fade and fall away from me like the leaves in autumn because I thought myself powerless to save them," he explained. "I will look upon this scene no longer." The colonel removed his superior officer, took command of the expedition, and promptly ordered an evacuation from the Cherokee Nation.[32]

The embarrassed and broken Union army turned around and started back north toward Fort Scott. Their return journey was little better. "The ground was as loose as an ash pile," exhausted Ohio cavalryman Isaac Gause wrote, "the clouds of dust would rise up from under the feet of the thousands of animals so that the air was often stifling and blinding." The demoralized Yankees moved back through what they deemed a wasteland. Along one stretch of the return route, they marched over a burned-out section of prairie and brush, with blackened grass and dust under each step. To make matters worse, many Federals were barefoot. "The ashes of the burned grass, mixed with alkali," Gause remembered, "caused our feet to swell and crack open until they bled profusely." The horseless cavalryman, with blackened, cracked, and bleeding feet, reflected most of his miserable comrades. With keen and brutally cogent observation, Gause defined not just the failed expedition but also much of the war on the frontier: "When we arrived at the water, Indians, Mexicans, negroes, whites, with mules and horses, plunged into it, stirring the green scum which was two or three inches thick on top of what little water there was. . . . They quaffed the mud down as if it was good."[33]

Nearly 3,000 additional Native American refugees followed Salomon's retreating army back north, where they joined those who had fled to Kansas with Opothleyahola's band the previous winter. "They had been robbed of all their means of subsistence," Indian leaders noted in a letter to Ross, so following the Union troops into southeast Kansas was their only option. Although large armies were mostly absent from the Cherokee Nation by late 1862, the area was once again "overrun by guerrilla bands; committing every conceivable depredation." Most of the able-bodied Indian men among the refugees were mustered into Union regiments, while their wives and children remained along the wooded creek near Fort Scott. The families subsisted on what little food and shelter the Federal post could provide. Their condition remained both pitiable and deadly, especially as winter set in, during which they suffered immeasurably due to poor shelter and bad weather. Although Blunt took temporary charge of supplying the growing number of refugees camped near the fort, he was unable to secure appropriate shelter. "When the fall rains came on and the winter frosts," lamented Cherokee leadership, "these women and children were thus exposed and were most miserably clad." Hundreds died. The fields surrounding the refugee camp became a vast unmarked graveyard filled with men, women, and children. Intense guerrilla war had again kept them from rebuilding their homes in the Cherokee Nation, while harsh environmental conditions killed them in Kansas.[34]

In late November 1862 the Fort Scott Bulletin published an editorial titled "Lo! The Poor Indians," in which the editor remarked, "These women and children, squatted down in the timber, in our vicinity, have selected this locality as a place of safety, and security, against the marauders of their own nationality in the rebel army." The Indians were still not safe, though better off than if these "suffering creatures [had remained] in their own country." The situation was bleak. "Unless something is done for them very soon," the editor worried, "these poor people will before the winter is over, make one move more, to the country where they will be troubled no longer by the wicked, and where the weary rest forever." They needed better shelter and new clothes to survive the winter, but such materials had to come from civilian donors who were themselves starving and freezing. And more refugees continued to trickle in throughout the winter of 1862–63, sometimes in groups as large as six hundred people.[35]

While environmental factors played no small role in thwarting Federal efforts to corral guerrillas, there also existed a growing discontent among civilians in regard to Union conduct. In the late summer of 1862, Governor Gamble had assured Missouri and its neighbors to the west that the state militia would be more rigidly codified and organized into a regular force. Thus far, at least for scores of anxious Kansas residents, the militia had been woefully ineffective. "Too many of [them] are cowardly, treason-sympathizing scoundrels," one newspaper editor declared, "or bushwhacking would have long been put down." Brig. Gen. John M. Schofield was chosen to clear up the mess as the new, if short-tenured, commander of the Department of Missouri. Missouri and Kansas residents were confident that, as an ebullient editorial put it, Schofield would "shoot guerrillas wherever found." Such rhetoric had won him temporary respect and relative trust in an atmosphere otherwise dominated by fear and confusion. The general, the editorial continued, "has shown himself to be a man well fitted for the position he occupies, and . . . we think that the guerrillas will be effectively stopped in their plundering, murderous work."[36]

Although Schofield proved nearly as unyielding toward guerrillas as the newspapers said he would, political squabbles over manpower shortages, pro-Confederate civilian support, and the guerrillas' skilled use of the environment as an ally together meant that he could only occasionally control the partisan problem, but he could never fully resolve it. With Samuel Curtis pushing regular Confederate forces farther south into Arkansas, Schofield felt abandoned. Short on supplies and support, he found it nearly impossible to make much headway with the growing and pernicious guerrilla problem on the border. For the harried commander engaged in an almost impossible counterinsurgency campaign, such irregular warfare was unparalleled in "extent and intensity." By September, Schofield had been reappointed to command the Army of the Frontier, but guerrillas continued to be among his chief problems.[37]

If both random and calculated murders happened often along the western Trans-Mississippi border, theft and property destruction was an everyday occurrence, becoming so widespread as to affect local economies. Abandoned or stolen goods and livestock served not only to supplement regular military supplies but also to supply the civilian market. Federal soldiers may have stripped farms for sustenance, but it is also clear that they sought to profit from the confiscated goods. When captured cattle from Missouri were driven to Fort Scott that summer, for example, an advertisement in the Fort Scott Bulletin announced: "A large lot of captured stock to be sold. . . . This will afford our farmers a fine opportunity to procure cattle cheap, and of any kind they choose."[38]

Guerrillas and local collaborators in southwest Missouri focused their own efforts to plunder and steal against residents, further redirecting the conflict into one centered on civilians. Elizabeth James, a widow with two young children, had been attacked by a guerrilla band that stole more than two hundred dollars' worth of goods, including clothing and food. According to James, the same local partisans later returned to torch her house, effectively making the destitute family refugees. Countless thousands of women became widows during the Civil War, but those like James, who had watched their homes and livelihood consumed around them, surely felt the horror of war more immediately than wives who were notified of a husband's death hundreds of miles away. These women were victims of both revenge and terror. Governor Gamble, in his typical grasp of the importance of events, remarked early on, "People of most loyal States know nothing of the species of war through which we have passed." For him, and for most people who had unwittingly become victims and combatants along the border, the war was quite literally in their backyards. Their homes became miniature battlegrounds, encompassing small-scale but immediate losers and winners, victims and aggressors. Gamble, eloquently expressing the sentiment of civilians throughout the border region, continued: "They send their sons to distant battle fields, they bear the interruption of their ordinary pursuits and the burdens of taxation, but they know nothing of the horrors of war in which families each night fear that before morning they may be aroused by bands of armed men coming to plunder their dwellings and probably murder their protectors."³⁹

Such frustration led to further drastic counterinsurgency policies. Special and general orders poured out of district headquarters in Springfield, echoing and sometimes intensifying the language used in Halleck's spate of general orders in late 1861 and early 1862. These commands called for swift punishment for guerrillas and their supporters. In one such missive, Brig. Gen. E. B. Brown, clearly exasperated by the situation, declared, "the country is infested with bands of murderers, robbers, and other outlaws . . . who by their deeds, boasts, and threats [have] placed themselves beyond the pale of law." He admonished that such characters "must be dealt with accordingly." Just a year into the conflict, Union authorities on the border had reached a level of frustration often regulated in the last year of the war elsewhere. So far as Brown and his colleagues were concerned, guerrillas were little better than outlaws, and "reasoning with outlaws is of no avail." Seething with equal parts impatience and anger, Brown further stated that such "agents of anarchy . . . must be subjected to their own code, and punished without mercy upon the spot when found enacting . . . their foul deeds."⁴⁰

Brown's remedy was clear and forceful: should any individual or band be caught and suspected of guerrilla activity, they were to be "shot down." Moreover, to better address the foundation of the problem, the general ordered that any civilian suspected of harboring or otherwise encouraging guerrillas "in their nefarious deeds" was to be immediately placed under arrest and tried by military commission. The war, hardly a year old, already had devolved into something very close to what Brown called anarchy. If they had not already, civilians—a critical ingredient in any sustained guerrilla campaign—now became directly implicated as suspects in aiding such activity. The war on the border became one of uncertainty, terror, and nearly constant frustration. And at the heart of it were regular people struggling to adapt and survive. Many did not, and those who did survive often were forced to flee.⁴¹

After General Brown's announcement, an editorial in the *Leavenworth Daily Times* cautioned its readers about the declining conditions on the southern Kansas border with Missouri and Indian Territory. The residents there, the editorial declared, "are not unjustly alarmed at the prospect of difficulties by invasion from Missouri." Such fear and uncertainty had led to an exodus from the area. "The border counties are rapidly becoming depopulated and will be entirely abandoned," the writer noted. He closed with a gloomy yet entirely accurate prediction: such fear and uncertainty "will be extremely disastrous upon the future of Southern Kansas, and must be lamented by every lover of our State."[42]

Early that fall in the Cherokee Nation, Unionist Hannah Hicks lamented the state of things. Her husband had been killed during the summer, and her children were sick and hungry. To make matters worse, Hicks's house had been torched at the end of July, and Confederates at Fort Gibson were holding her brother captive "with a herd of wretches, guarded like a criminal, with no comfort at all." Her neighbors suffered similarly. One woman had lost contact with her husband, William Spears, early that fall. She searched for him for weeks in the area where he had last been seen, eventually finding only his bones and tattered clothes. The community later heard that Spears had been captured and summarily executed. "It is said they told him to pray," Hicks reported, "and [he] was kneeling in prayer . . . when he was shot." Amid her deep personal turmoil and that of the people around her, Hicks assessed the general state of things in the region. "Alas, alas, for this miserable people, destroying each other as fast as they can," she wrote in her diary that September. "My heart cries 'Oh Lord how long?'" With five sick children, no house, and few prospects for reprieve, Hicks's tormented uncertainty would persist.[43]

In the meantime, many towns and villages on the Trans-Mississippi frontier had been abandoned. Carthage, Missouri, was but one example. For Robert Todd McMahan, the town represented the region as a whole. "Most of the buildings that had escaped the usual destruction by fire were desolate and going to wreck," he explained, "as is the case in most little villages in South W Mo." The cloudy, windy evening in late October during which his Union cavalry force occupied Carthage created an altogether eerie feeling. Stationed in the courthouse on the town square, McMahan envisaged the worst. "During the night," he reported, "almost every old door & Window-shutter in the town was at the mercy of the winds, break! break! Slam Slam slam! Bringing to mind all the old hobgoblin and ghost stories I had ever heard." Such sharp noises punctuated by howling wolves in the nearby forest resulted in a sleepless night.[44]

During his stay at Carthage, McMahan heard stories about the brutality that had inundated the region. He learned how Unionists "had been taken out but a short distance into the bushes and brutally murdered." To make it worse, "their bodies [were] left to bleach without burial and many left dangling from the limbs to which they had been suspended by blood thirsty traitors." McMahan's fellow soldiers returned the insulting treatment to dead secessionist citizens, whose bodies had been left "to be torn to pieces by hogs and dogs and birds of prey." Their fleshless bones lying around provided macabre amusement for some Federals. "Early in the evening," McMahan reported, "I saw one of the boys carelessly placing the heel of his boot in the under jawbone of some poor victim." Such hate-fueled warfare permeated the Trans-Mississippi borderlands. The relative absence of "regular" warfare between organized armies wore on soldiers and civilians from both sides, leading to countless uneasy nights like the one endured by McMahan.[45]

To be sure, conditions in southwest Missouri were largely indicative of the border as a whole. According to Iowan Benjamin McIntyre, the ubiquity of desolation and depopulation in the region had become almost expected. "The country through which we have passed presents the same desolate appearance," the soldier recorded in his diary, "houses burned, fences destroyed, farms laid waste." Even in larger communities, Union troops found a crumbling society. As McIntyre toured Cassville, Missouri, he found the town nearly void of any male inhabitants. The presence of both Union and Confederate units in the region, as well as dozens of guerrilla bands, McIntyre reasoned, had encouraged men of all "proclivities to skedaddle, both parties leaving their families who seem to have enjoyed the protection that they could wish." Yankee sarcasm aside, if it was not already clear, few could overlook the devastating results of the war by the fall of 1862. Rural homesteads had been destroyed and small towns were populated mostly by women and children. The entire border had become a massive battlefield, and everyone left in it, willing or not, were active players.[46]

This war-torn atmosphere had been perpetuated by what McIntyre admitted was Union "jayhawking." Whether members of large Union armies or small cavalry patrols, Federal troops relied heavily on the land and its people for food and supplies. "Whenever or wherever we found what was needed, it was taken," noted McIntyre. Most of what had been taken came from homesteads void of men. As his Iowa unit crossed through southwest Missouri and northwest Arkansas in anticipation of a nascent Confederate attack, the men laid bare the farms and homes in their path. Yet McIntyre makes clear, "the utmost propriety was shown to the families" from whom they secured food, supplies, and fence posts. And all of this in October, just as a hard winter approached.[47]

The Federals were hungry, frustrated, and spoiling for a fight, and disloyal or ambivalent locals would serve well as unwilling suppliers. Maj. William G. Thompson unapologetically articulated the unofficial Union policy toward the residents of the region. The people, he wrote, only seemed to show Union sympathies when Federal troops were present. Their support, Thompson said, was only "skin deep," and he continued, "I would not trust many of them further than I could throw a fly." Consequently, like McIntyre, Thompson and his men considered the residents' food and supplies free for the taking. "Hogs, sheep, Orchards, Horses, cornfields, hen roosts, in fact everything is drawn on at will," the major boasted, very little would remain "for anyone after our forces have once foraged through the country."[48]

The fall of 1862 saw a resumption of conventional warfare on the border of the Trans-Mississippi. Thousands of Union and Confederate soldiers traversed southwest Missouri and northwest Arkansas as their commanders poised for another fight. Soldiers also took the time to comment on what they saw. Most were awed by the natural beauty and ruggedness of the terrain, where the Ozarks melted into the wooded lowlands of Indian Territory. So too were they disconcerted by what society had become in the region. Yet they played no small role in exacerbating the war's brutality.

In late October a large Union force moved through northwest Arkansas in search of Maj. Gen. Thomas C. Hindman's Army of the Trans-Mississippi. As most armies had done, the Federals stopped in Fayetteville to rest and resupply themselves from the civilian population. Minister and former college professor William Baxter, although a Unionist, remembered, "My yard was soon stripped of poultry, my house was filled with soldiers." The troops had "appropriated everything they could lay their hands on." Reflecting on the incident, Baxter made clear that "there was neither time nor inclination for discussing the rights of property; they had learned, too, that every man who had anything to lose, almost invariably became a Union man on their approach."[49] Baxter and his neighbors were not casual observers of the war but part of the action. Their yards and houses were quite literally a key part of the larger frontier battlefield.

Even with the theft and destruction, Baxter and his neighbors fared better than residents north of Fayetteville. The thriving town of Bentonville at one point had boasted a population of over 1,500 residents. By the late fall of 1862, that number had dwindled to approximately 300 mostly women and children. One Federal officer was shocked by the depressing scene. "The dissolution is almost complete," he confided to his diary, "very few men are here and those mostly old and decrepid." Bentonville had been torched earlier that year by troops who had suspected it harbored guerrillas and their supporters, even though the town had been a center of pro-Union support.[50]

But Union soldiers could hardly tour the war-torn region in peace. As Hindman's army prepared for battle, irregular activity intensified throughout northwest Arkansas. Federal troops had to remain vigilant in the face of continual harassment. Remarking on the plentiful resources at hand, one officer complained, "[the] bushwhackers are also plenty, and our men are fired upon several times daily." Unexpected, though generally inaccurate, shots from underbrush and trees terrorized the men. "The country is covered with thick brush," wrote one ducking Yankee, "and admirably adapted to this cowardly mode of warfare." The environment had again proven an ideal ally for guerrillas. Indeed, it was essential for their survival and success. Yet the antiguerrilla patrols, often chasing these "ghosts" through the brush and forests, sometimes caught their quarry. When they did, punishment could be swift. "We killed one and took one prisoner," a Federal boasted of one encounter near Bentonville, "he probably will be shot."[51]

In the absence of large enemy units to fight, Union cavalry was forced to focus on counterguerrilla operations. If not patrolling for the express purpose of chasing partisans, the horse soldiers regularly escorted supply trains. Many such operations occurred in the rugged country between Fort Scott and northwest Arkansas. For Albert Greene of the Ninth Kansas Cavalry, these patrols were often arduous and perilous tasks. Although the cavalry rarely participated directly in full-scale battles, Greene made clear, it constantly suffered from "hard work and long hours of service, and the chances of being picked off in detail without warning by an unseen foe." Guerrillas utilized the natural landscape against long, slumbering wagon trains, for there was nowhere better to both harass Union troops and secure much-needed supplies than from slow-moving caravans passing through the rugged terrain. These trains often consisted of over a hundred wagons loaded down with food and supplies—ideal bounty for any partisan. Using a typical route from Fort Scott into Arkansas as an example, Greene noted the futility and terror involved in transporting such cumbersome and coveted loads in the region. Although wagon trains could move ten miles per day on open ground, the rugged landscape of the border made for a slow and exceedingly dangerous journey. "In a wooded country, cut up with streams and featured by canyons and passes and rocky defiles," Greene made clear, moving and protecting wagons "was a far different proposition." Federal escorts not only had to deal with the inhospitable terrain but also, and especially, the guerrillas who might be infesting it. "Every foot of that road must be scouted and inspected and combed over for a lurking enemy," Greene lamented, "bridges must be examined and repaired, often under the fire of snipers . . . and flankers must be stationed all along the route before the first wagon could be allowed to pass." In the end, he admitted the reality of the war on the border: "It is a hard service and there's precious little of the pomp and circumstance of war about it, but it's the only way to get food and supplies to an army with a base several hundred miles in the rear."[52]

The topography hindered supply wagons and counterguerrilla patrols alike. In late October the First Kansas Colored Infantry set out from Kansas to hunt guerrillas in western Missouri. They had received a number of reports from local civilians that a large irregular force was operating in the region. The patrol of over 200 men not only found over 100 guerrillas but also a small regular Confederate force moving through the area. The intense fight that followed at Island Mound, Missouri, on October 29 exemplified both the African Americans' determination and ability in action and the nature of race relations along the Trans-Mississippi border.

Much of this small battle took place in the bush and included especially hard fighting at very close proximity. In what had become typical for antiguerrilla patrols, the first day proved to be, as one Federal officer quipped, full of "desultory skirmishes." The Confederate irregulars had employed their chief strategy of hiding in the brush just out of range or sight of Union arms. By the next morning, the frustrated First Kansas Colored took the offensive. A brutal chase ensued as guerrillas yelled above the ruckus of combat "come on, you damned niggers." The irony of the moment was lost on neither Union soldiers nor their officers, for as guerrillas issued such challenges, they were riding horseback to escape from the marching African American troops. By afternoon, the deadly cat-and-mouse game had covered four miles through thick brush, but the chase finally stagnated as many of the irregulars escaped. As the Union troops returned to camp, however, the guerrillas launched a counterattack; more intense fighting ensued. Union commanders quickly sought to control a nearby hill and sent a twenty-five-man African American force to hold the height while the fighting raged around camp. Upon seeing the high ground compromised, the bulk of the mounted guerrillas quickly turned their attention toward the occupying small band of Union troops and charged. "Nothing dismayed, the little band turned upon their foes," a Union officer reported, "and as their guns cracked many a riderless [horse] swung off to one side." The guerrillas soon demanded the small band of black soldiers to surrender, though to do so invariably meant certain death. According to a Union officer who witnessed the ordeal: "I never saw a braver sight than that handful of brave men fighting 117 men who were all around and in amongst them. Not one surrendered or gave up a weapon."[53]

Nearly as soon as the nasty little fight had begun, more Union troops charged the hill to relieve their besieged comrades. At this, the now-outnumbered guerrilla force abandoned their attack and set fire to the dry brush to thwart the counterattack. As they retreated, the partisans tried to finish off any wounded Union soldiers within reach. One lieutenant who had been hit in the leg by buckshot lay in their path. Soon, according to a witness, "one of the cowardly demons dismounted, and making the remark that he would finish the damned son of a bitch, placed his revolver to his head and fired." Fortunately for the badly wounded Federal, the bullet glanced off his head, though ripping open a cavity between his skull and scalp before exiting from behind. But unfortunately for the patrol, as was nearly always the case, the vast majority of guerrillas made good their escape.[54]

The brutal skirmish at Island Mound illustrates the tactical and environmental nature of combat between the Union army and Confederate irregulars. The fight represents what historian Mark Lause calls the racially charged radicalism that permeated much of the Union army on the border. Within a little over a year after Fort Sumter, white officers and black soldiers were fighting side by side against Confederate guerrillas in a heated contest in which surrender was not an option. In a broken nation that had yet to see formal emancipation even within those states in rebellion, such a fight was radical indeed. In his official report concerning the skirmish, white Union captain R. G. Ward exclaimed that those wounded and killed African American troops "deserve the lasting gratitude of all the friends of the cause and race."[55]

When not hunting guerrillas, Federal soldiers hunted forage for their animals and food for themselves. "The supply of wheat and corn is quite abundant," wrote one officer, "to the loyal we pay to the Rebels confiscate." To process their bounty, Union soldiers commandeered three abandoned and broken gristmills, rebuilt them, and put them to use. Cornmeal and flour proved an excellent supplement to confiscated chickens, hogs, and cattle, but their foraged feast lacked an important ingredient, salt, "an article we stand in need of much." The region was desperately short of the essential mineral. "The inhabitants here have been without salt for months," wrote Colonel Ellithorpe, "and are suffering extremely for the want of it."[56]

The Union army had needed salt for some time. As early as June, one officer complained that his men were suffering due to an "utter destitution of salt." Just weeks later that same command had been forced to halt all military activities and "go to manufacturing salt" at Grand Saline, near the Grand River in Indian Territory. Again in October, General Blunt assigned much of his command to acquire salt in the Cherokee Nation. Finally, in November, as the Hindman's Confederates moved closer to Federal positions in northwest Arkansas, a "strong force of mounted men and howitzers" was ordered again to the Grand Saline for the express purpose of acquiring the mineral.[57]

Meanwhile, Federal patrols continued to deal with the upsurge in guerrilla activity, which by November increased with each passing day. Scouting parties rode on the outskirts of the main camps, hoping to dissuade or catch guerrillas. On one such foray, a scout captured over four hundred cattle that had belonged to Stand Watie's First Cherokee Cavalry (C.S.). As the troops pushed their prize back toward northwest Arkansas, guerrillas checked their enthusiasm by killing three of the Federal wranglers. Enraged, the Union patrol wheeled on the partisans and succeeded in capturing one of their number. The man pretended to be an innocent bystander who fervently supported the Union cause, but his concealed weapons and "swetty horse with his back wet and hot from the saddle" spoiled that story. The scouts made quick work of the situation. "In 10 minutes he swung a lifeless corpse from a tree and left hanging there as a warning to piratical bush murderers," reported Ellithorpe. Furthermore, the scouting party "desolated the houses in the vicinity as a warning to such acts in the future." Angered by what had occurred and fed up with the irregular war in general, the colonel vented, "They may bushwhack but I will follow them with the torch and the halter until they cease this mode of warfare."[58]

Union troops were clearly fed up with the guerrillas plaguing their every move, but they had also become increasingly miffed with the local civilians who seemed primarily responsible for aiding these partisan bands. That November in southwest Missouri, Livingston's guerrillas surprised the Ninth Kansas Cavalry as they slowed their horses to cross Spring River. The characteristically rapid attack ended within minutes, leaving the frazzled and angry cavalrymen looking for someone to blame. The assailants, one trooper guessed, "had been fed and harbored" by local pro-Confederate civilians. These "well-to-do farmers [who] had so far escaped the ravages of war," he continued, "lived in a fine house and owned a number of slaves." The men of the Ninth Kansas decided to "make an example of them" and promptly torched their house, stole their livestock, and confiscated their slaves, numbering almost one hundred animals and over ten slaves. The following evening, the newly freed slaves "laughed spasmodically . . . over the discomfiture of their former owner who would have to start all over again with a pile of ashes." This action represented the war on the border in microcosm. Confederate guerrillas succeeded in a rapid hit-and-run attack against a wary and frustrated Federal cavalry unit. Union forces, in turn, sought retribution against alleged civilian supporters. After burning the suspects' house and confiscating their livestock, the troops also freed their slaves—the very symbolic core of the conflict.[59]

While troops chased guerrillas and punished civilians, some Union combatants adopted irregular tactics themselves as their primary method of fighting. Thomas Wilhite, who would later serve in the First Arkansas Cavalry (U.S.), had organized a band of Unionists in the Boston Mountains to plague Hindman's Confederates as they marched north. In the late summer and early fall of 1862, with plenty of foliage and rocks to conceal themselves, Wilhite's group challenged any Confederate force to enter the region. Their challenge was effective. In September Hindman offered a seven-thousand-dollar reward for Wilhite's body. The Union guerrilla band had dealt the frustrations of irregular warfare to those who had relied on it most. One Union officer, commenting on this success, made clear that Wilhite's inherently risky style of warfare depended upon familiarity with the terrain and "consciousness of the fact that the environment would permit only a few men to operate against him at a time." For Federal soldiers and civilians, Wilhite's band served a gratifying purpose by "annoying the enemy and taking vengeance upon those who had so cruelly robbed and maltreated Union men."[60]

Some regular Union regiments had also become particularly effective guerrilla hunters. The First Arkansas Cavalry—comprised mostly of local northwest Arkansas Unionists—was the most notable. The men of the regiment that Wilhite would later join knew the terrain and many of the people in the region and had been able to keep a nearly constant pressure on irregulars. For Union observers from farther north, these Arkansas Yankees were particularly impressive. By late 1862, according to one Iowa officer, the First Arkansas had wreaked havoc on the local guerrillas and "avenged" the longsuffering Unionists. "Secesh property melts whenever it comes near them," he wrote, and "they kill a rebel easier than they can kill a chicken." No matter how effective the Arkansas guerrilla hunters were, they could never quite fully control the guerrilla problem. Indeed, with their harsh tactics and retribution, they further exacerbated the intensity and severity of the region's irregular war.[61]

A month later Union soldier Edmund G. Ross, serving with the Eleventh Kansas Infantry, wrote home to his wife from Cane Hill, near Fayetteville: "There are some very beautiful features of this country . . . but nearly every fireside is desolated by the ravages of war. Families are robbed of everything they have and oftentimes fathers and sons murdered or sent to imprisonment." Ross, destined for fame as the U.S. senator who cast the vote that acquitted Pres. Andrew Johnson during his 1868 impeachment trial, presented an eloquent account of war in the region. "This whole country is in the depth of misfortune and misery and must always be so, so long as the war continues," he observed. "Families are stripped . . . of all their bedding, cooking utensils and provisions and left to starvation." In the end, he wrote, "I feel very grateful that my family is far from all this."[62]

What Ross described to his wife devolved even further just a week later. Thomas Hindman's Army of the Trans-Mississippi had been organized to gain control of northwest Arkansas, an important region that had been in Union hands since March. Hindman raised approximately twelve thousand men, but most of his troops lacked sufficient training and supplies. On December 7, 1862, Brig. Gen. Francis J. Herron, commanding three thousand men as a part of James Blunt's Army of the Frontier, met Hindman's "ragtag" army on a ridge near Prairie Grove Church, thirteen miles southwest of Fayetteville. Herron's men had been in southwest Missouri when Blunt, at Cane Hill, called for immediate reinforcements. Swiftly marching a hard 120 miles, they ran directly into Hindman's Confederates, who cut them off from a direct route to Blunt. Intense fighting occurred through the morning as Herron, hoping to stall long enough for the Federals at Cane Hill to arrive, ordered two frontal assaults into the rebels' right flank. The fighting was severe as the Confederates countercharged and were repulsed by strong Federal artillery. By the afternoon, Blunt's five thousand men had finally arrived to spoil Hindman's hopes of crushing Herron's beleaguered force. The cool, sunny day ended with a stalemate, neither side gaining a clear tactical advantage.[63]

The Union troops awoke on December 8 expecting to charge the hill again, but they found it empty, save for the dead and mortally wounded. The Army of the Trans-Mississippi had expended what little ammunition and supplies it had and retreated south during the night. Hindman had hoped to catch the Army of the Frontier divided, which he did initially, so that he might crush Herron, then turn and attack Blunt. His plan nearly worked, but a full day of hard fighting had exhausted any hopes for a prolonged campaign, much less a second day of battle.

Union soldiers turned to the grisly chore of collecting and burying the dead, some of whom were frozen and half-eaten by feral hogs. One Federal remembered the condition of a wounded soldier. "A shell had torn away part of his abdomen," he said, "and his bowels were protruding. At these wild hogs were chewing." He scattered the animals and watched helplessly as stretcher bearers carted the man away. The mortally wounded soldier "had been overlooked and had lain in this condition not less than eighteen hours," claimed the cavalryman, "although the hogs had evidently just found him."[64]

Dozens of women, children, and elderly residents endured the battle as well. After having been warned that a large fight was eminent, women ran from house to house to check on their neighbors and implore them to take cover. According to one witness, "Each mother, in a frantic haste, took her children to Mr. Morton's cellar where they remained all day in dread horror listening to the cannon's roar, with hardly a cessation of smaller guns." At least twenty people crowded into this small root cellar and listened as the battle raged above them. "They fought through and around the house, the shots flying like hail in every direction," recalled one woman. These civilians witnessed regular warfare in all its violence.[65]

When they tried to push open the door after the fighting had died down, they found it unusually difficult. "There was a dead man across the cellar door," remembered nine-year-old Caledonia Borden. The scene outside made a lasting impression on the young girl. There were "wounded and dying men all around. I can still hear them calling 'help-help-help.' . . . One soldier's leg was just hanging by the skin and the doctor cut if off and threw it outside." As the women and children spread out over the battlefield, they were disgusted by the carnage. "It was scary and pitiful," Borden recalled, "some of us got sick."[66]

Thousands of wounded Union soldiers poured into Fayetteville over the next few days. One resident watched as hundreds of casualties were crowded into the Fayetteville Female Seminary: "The entire floor was so thickly covered with mangled and bleeding men that it was difficult to thread my way among them." People from all over town watched and helped. It was quite impossible to avoid the scene, for such makeshift hospitals were constructed "in about twenty other buildings, including the churches, all of which were thronged with the sad wrecks of humanity." Men, women, and children once again faced war at their doorsteps. This time there was no shooting or burning, but there was plenty of dying. "Some were mortally wounded, the life fast escaping through a ghastly hole in the breast," reported on witness, while "the limbs of others were shattered and useless, the faces of others so disfigured as to seem scarcely human; the bloody bandages, hair clotted, and garments stained in blood."[67]

The Union army took control of local gristmills and used them to supply their bloodied but successful troops. One of the most prominent mills in the region, owned by William H. Rhea northeast of the battlefield, had been controlled by both Confederate and Union forces. During the battle, Stand Watie had guarded Rhea's Mill until it fell into Federal hands. Pro-Confederate Rhea claimed after the war that the Union army's occupation had cost him over one thousand dollars; dead Federal horses, putrefying in the mill race and surrounding area, accounted for half that sum. In turn, he calculated, the army's use of his mill resulted in the production of over six tons of flour.[68]

In addition to enduring the brunt of the battles, locals also had to contend with the irregular warfare that followed in the weeks after the Union victory. In one of the few surviving houses near the battlefield—the same homestead that had provided a cellar for protection—a band of irregulars rode up to talk with Nancy Morton's father. Initially, the men acted as if they only intended a friendly visit. They seemed unconcerned by Morton's avowed Confederate sympathies, and the girl and her mother went as far as to offer them apples, a delicacy in the region at the time. Then as her father retired, one of the visitors approached him and exclaimed: "Old man, it's not your politics I care for, it's your money, and we're going to have it." Four of the men restrained her father. They "heated two shovels," as Nancy recalled, "for the night was cold and we had a big fire, and they began burning the bottoms of his feet." The intruders meant to torture him until he told them where his money was hidden, but Nancy threw water on the shovels, even as one of the men pointed a pistol at her face and struck her back and arms until she was "black and blue." Still undeterred, the girl doused the fire with water.[69]

Now incensed at how the situation had unfolded, one of the guerrillas stormed over to the fireplace, picked up a shovel full of simmering coals, and dumped them over Mr. Morton. His "heavy all-wool underwear" saved him from serious burns, but the situation continued to deteriorate. "They then took him out to hang him," Nancy remembered, "[and] they choked my mother for screaming and abused us for looking out the window." Finally, Nancy's father talked, and the guerrillas pushed him back inside—on his blistered feet—to ransack the house and carry off what paper money they found. In a rare bit of luck amid this horrific night, the intruders soon left, apparently satisfied with their loot and the terror they had inflicted.[70]

While a cruel mixture of full-scale battles and localized guerrilla activity raged in northwest Arkansas, a band of more than thirty irregulars attacked fifty-two-year-old farmer James McFarland in southwest Missouri. They stole a wagon and work animals along with many clothes, blankets, and other personal items worth almost two thousand dollars. Worst, the guerrillas took McFarland captive for a day. As they had done to many before him, the assailants planned to hang the man after getting his valuables. When satisfied that he would talk no more, they strung a rope around their victim's neck and unceremoniously hoisted him until he dangled in the air. Just as McFarland was facing strangulation, his attackers cut him down. Gasping for breath, the old farmer realized that he had known one of the men—an old acquaintance or neighbor—who had mercifully allowed him to live.[71]

McFarland's case illustrates an important theme of guerrilla warfare on the border. The men who attacked McFarland did so because he was a known Unionist in the county. Yet similarly, his salvation was in having known one of his assailants. A great number of combatants—civilians, guerrillas, and soldiers—knew their enemies or had at least heard of them. The war was a personal, indeed a social, affair. Much of the time this personal acquaintanceship fostered a desire for revenge, as it did in McFarland's case, but the same thing that nearly got him killed was also what saved him.

McFarland could count himself lucky, however, compared to his neighbor William Hood. David Rusk's band of guerrillas had taken Hood captive. Soon after, within his wife's clear view, one of the men "willfully" and "maliciously" shot Hood. According to his widow, who gave gruesome details of the event after the war, the bullet had entered into her husband's torso at an angle and penetrated "twelve inches deep." Hood was targeted because he was a Unionist, even though he posed little threat to the large, well-armed guerrilla band that had called him out of his house.[72]

Danger did not always originate from guerrillas or Union militia. Indeed, the environment continued to create perilous situations. A self-described

Confederate "partisan ranger," having escaped capture by Union authorities near Fayetteville, ran south of town into the heavily wooded Ozark forest. It was dark by the time he entered the bush. Reveling in his successful retreat from what would have surely been a death sentence, the rebel remembered, "I thanked God and laid down in the very dry grass and leaves to sleep." Later in the night he was "aroused by a heavy, sliding tread in the dry leaves . . . ; a 'bear' flashed across my mind. . . . I sprang to my feet and felt for my bowie knife, when I remembered it had been taken by the Federals." The guerrilla, normally feeling secure deep in the brush, had met his match. Before him he saw the silhouette of a black bear standing on its hind feet and "uttering a hissing, guttural sound." But the animal, not interested in the man, moved on. Relieved and exhausted, he "thanked God again and returned to [his] bed of leaves," unaware that he had chosen as his be a trail used by the bear to move to and from a cornfield where it fed at night. The man was rouse once again in the morning to the sound of the bear tramping toward him. This time, with clarity of sunlight and not being so exhausted, he "gave one bound into the air," and with "long and rapid strides" soon reached a tall sapling. "With the agility of a cat," he reported, "I sprang up this tree and secured myself in its branches." The bear stood once again to examine the frightened man, then continued up its trail.[73]

While Confederate guerrillas evaded Union patrols and black bears, in late December 1862 General Blunt moved south in pursuit of Hindman's retreating army. The Federal route over the Boston Mountains toward Van Buren was trying, especially when the army followed the meandering Cove Creek down the southern slope of the mountains. One cavalryman complained: "We crossed [Cove Creek] thirty-seven times to-day. The winter rains have swelled it until it is a river about forty yards in width, and at no ford less in depth than up to the bellies of the horses." In crossing and recrossing the swollen, icy stream in late December, those on horses could not help but feel for their infantry comrades who "had to hold their guns at arm's length above their heads . . . , the water being up to their armpits."[74]

The hardest part of the march came to an end as the front of the columns emerged into flatter terrain and encountered more civilians as well as signs of Hindman's Confederates. As the Union army spread through the opening valleys just north of Van Buren, women, children, and old men peered from their homes in shock. "The citizens came out of their houses as we passed by," remembered one soldier, "some to cheer, some to curse, and the women to cry." As the Federals encountered Confederate pickets, a nasty running fight ensued, with the rebels retreating toward Van Buren and the Arkansas River. According to another Federal, the pickets "did not attempt to stop us— in fact—[they] skedadled like wild turkies." Blunt's men, reaching a hill overlooking Van Buren and the river below, shelled a Confederate battery on the south side of the Arkansas. Federal cavalry then spread through the town. The Southern troops continued to skedaddle across the river toward Fort Smith as three supporting steamboats full of supplies moved downriver in a feeble attempt to avoid capture. The vessels did not make it, and Blunt's troops had the town and three boatloads of Confederate provisions to themselves.[75]

The Union occupiers received a mixed welcome from the locals, most of whom were Confederate sympathizers. Area slaves, though hiding their excitement, did what they could to welcome the Federals. One older woman had noticed a couple of cavalrymen walking by and slyly waved them over to her. To the soldiers' astonishment, she wanted to prepare a special meal for them and would wave from the window of her slave quarters when it was ready. The two hungry men did their utmost to appear blasé in front of their comrades as they paced in front of the window, not wanting to attract any attention to their nascent feast. Finally, after keeping "a sharp watch of that window," they noticed the slight movement that indicating their dinner was ready. The elderly slave "slipped out a frying pan of spare ribs, candied yams, corn pone, butter, milk and some knives and forks," all from the larder of her Confederate owner.[76]

Most white Van Buren residents jeered as the Federal band played the "Star-Spangled Banner," although "when they struck up 'Dixie' they shouted themselves hoarse." The one concession they made was that the Yankee invaders made a better appearance than their own troops. "We could hear their comments, which were usually quite complimentary," recalled one solder, "and the remark, 'They look like sure soldiers,' was quite common." After filling up on Confederate food, some of which had been provided by generous but still cautious slaves, the Army of the Frontier celebrated the end of its successful campaign. The captured steamboats also provided enormous amounts of liquor to help enliven the festivities. By one soldier's count, they enjoyed "corn whisky, rye whisky, moonshine whisky, white whisky, apple brandy, peach brandy, grape brandy, prune brandy, blackberry brandy, and so on to the end."[77]

Though the Prairie Grove Campaign was over, all was not well. Those same people who watched Federals stumble around in inebriated celebration would suffer immeasurably through the next two years of war. And those soldiers too had only begun what would now turn into an ever-more-vicious guerrilla war. Hindman's army had failed. With few exceptions, no further major Confederate forces would threaten western Arkansas, and the region would increasingly transform into a middle ground where society, the environment, and the military intersected to create a full-scale social war.

Even with prewar political violence and the nearly immediate economic, political, and social breakdown along the border at the onset of the war, conditions in the region only worsened through 1862 and 1863. Certainly there had been areas that held out longer than others: Fayetteville, for example, maintained at least occasional periods of "normality" throughout the war. But citizens there and elsewhere could little predict when the next army (Confederate or Union) might march through, when the next battle might erupt nearby (or in the town itself), or when Confederate guerrillas or Union forces chasing them might ride through.

Even with such uncertainty, Fayetteville fared far better than its sister towns along the Trans-Mississippi border. Carthage had witnessed one of the first battles of the conflict in July 1861, then transformed into a central hotbed for irregular warfare, its hardy remaining citizens literally burned out by 1864. Fort Smith, though not witnessing any major battles, was central to both Confederate and Union strategy in the region. Held tenuously by Confederate forces until late 1862, it represented the key to western Arkansas and a large part of eastern Indian Territory. As Union forces increasingly threatened the area, guerrilla activity increased, and local civilians were caught in the middle. Citizens residing outside the fort's walls and those across the Arkansas River in Van Buren lived in the very heart of the conflict. They fared only somewhat better than those thousands who lived scattered in the countryside.

People living outside such towns had already begun to leave by the end of 1862. Their isolated homes and farms were center points of what had rapidly turned into a vast and brutal battlefield. Unlike any other year of the war, 1862 witnessed an especially destructive combination of regular and irregular warfare. For soldiers, guerrillas, and civilians in the region, that year's fighting verified not only that Missouri would remain firmly, if only politically, in the Union but also that the Trans-Mississippi war was anything but over following two compelling Union victories. Nasty, civilian-centered guerrilla warfare, inaugurated a year before, quickly expanded to take the place of large armies and grand campaigns. Union control of the region occurred only where Federal troops were literally positioned—and even then it was tenuous.

Maj. Gen. James Blunt.
*Wilson's Creek National Battlefield*

Col. Charles Jennison.
*Wilson's Creek National Battlefield*

Brig. Gen. John McNeil.
*Wilson's Creek National Battlefield*

Brig. Gen. James Lane.
*Wilson's Creek National Battlefield*

Third Wisconsin Cavalry troopers at Fort Scott.
*Kansas Historical Society, Kansas Memory, Item 484*

Lt. Col. Albert C. Ellithorpe.
Kansas Historical Society, Kansas Memory, Item 304833

# 4

## "The Arch Fiend Could Desire Nothing More"

### THE DEVOLUTION OF WAR, 1863

On a bitterly cold January night in 1863, Confederate irregulars pushed the war on the western Trans-Mississippi frontier to new levels when one "marauding band of robbers" stole clothing and food from a smallpox hospital in Newtonia, Missouri. The intruders, storming up and down the aisles of sickbeds, took every stitch of clothing they could find and nearly all of the "eatables." Deadly and highly contagious smallpox apparently did not discourage them. After traumatizing the already suffering patients, they rode off into the night, laden with their spoils: infected clothes and food.[1]

In addition to the relative lack of sustenance in the region, these irregulars may have been so desperate because of the extreme cold and heavy snow that greeted civilians, guerrillas, and soldiers alike in January 1863. And they found scant relief when the frozen, snow-blanketed ground gave way to thick mud two weeks into the new year. This maddening winter downpour reflected the mood of combatants along the border. The cold rain melted the snow and made mud the "King of terrors." "We poor devils awoke this morning with about 4 inches of water in our tents," wrote one disgruntled Yankee, "ditching and draining is the order." Soldiers were attacked as much by the environment as by their human enemies. "We get news from bushwhackers daily. Kill some—take some and some come in and surrender." Beyond that there was snow, rain, and mud.[2]

For both Federals and Confederates, this frustration would exemplify the year to come. Along the Trans-Mississippi border, the elements proved more as annoying for the Federals and their supporters in a conflict that had severely shaken their resolve. Important Union victories in the eastern and western theaters would change the course of the war in 1863, but these successes would mean little to most Federal troops and civilians in the Trans-Mississippi. The struggle there would drag on, with little visible progress for either side, as the region devolved ever deeper into a civilian-centered guerrilla conflict. And as the war increasingly tore apart the built environment, the natural environment became both adversary and ally to soldiers and civilians alike.

Federal cavalry and infantry units patrolled the steep terrain, riverine thickets, and burned-out towns in an ever-maddening attempt to track down and summarily punish guerrillas. They also visited war upon civilians who might or might not have aided their enemies. Much like their elusive foe, Union troops not only interrogated civilians but also relied upon their meager subsistence. Hogs and corn became contraband of war, and residents suffered dearly. Save for a handful of regular Confederate maneuvers in the region in 1863, the war had devolved into a game of cat and mouse, with those women and children who dared remain caught dangerously in the middle. A seemingly perpetual stream of ruthless vignettes now had emerged, together illuminating an almost daily occurrence of homes being destroyed, men murdered, and people left destitute. Taken together, these stories reflect hundreds of microbattles fought for food and supplies—or in some cases due to a mere lust for violence.

In addition to the environment's growing key role in the conflict, 1863 ushered in a dramatic shift in Union strategy regarding guerrillas and civilians. Federal commanders shared a growing and intense animosity toward irregulars, whose prominence on the border grew as regular Confederate forces became less common. Frustration became the rule of the day, and the official orders that came from such aggravation reflected the Union's loathing of those they termed "bushwhackers." From Brig. Gen. Thomas Ewing's Order No. 11, which forcefully cleared all civilians from several counties in western Missouri, to Brig. Gen. John McNeil's very real threats to torch civilian homes in western Arkansas, Federal authorities' harsh, if ultimately futile, attempts to crack down on guerrillas and residents thought to be supporting them initiated a dramatic elevation in the war's severity. With the onset of 1863, any modicum of support for guerrillas or the Confederate war effort on the whole was quickly and decisively negated by increasingly aggressive Union policies. Here, if not before, began the dissolution of any direct civilian support for the rebellion on the border.

In northwest Arkansas an old Union man known only as Hyatt had attempted to remove himself from the conflict and live as peaceful a life as possible near Fayetteville. On a brief trip to visit a neighbor, Hyatt was ambushed by a band of guerrillas hiding in a thicket. "A half-dozen balls pierced the body," according to a Union chaplain, and the old man's corpse was "dragged into the woods, & there left to be devoured by the swine." The bushwhackers took their victim's horse and other belongings and left. Hyatt's family and friends found his body before the hogs did, and they vowed to get vengeance for his murder. Catching word of this vow, the guerrillas responsible visited Hyatt's widow and demanded to see her son, who they now considered a threat. When she told them that he was gone, "they seized her by the throat, pointed deadly weapons at her breast, & swore they would kill her if she failed to disclose the hiding place of the young man." The woman refused, and the enraged men forcefully dragged her out of the house and threatened to torch the place if she did not talk. She said nothing. Although the guerrillas refrained from killing or burning, they nevertheless "despoiled her house of numerous articles of food, clothing & other valuables." They would continue to hunt for her son.[3]

The assailants never found young Hyatt, but their leader was soon caught and summarily dealt with by two Union soldiers who recognized him as a local guerrilla "captain" who had directed the murder of Hyatt. After some questioning, the two Federals shot guerrilla leader Haywood S. Thompson at least six times. According to one witness, "a yell of agony" rang out after the shots. The dying irregular leader had been "pierced in the breast, neck, & head. . . . Blood was flowing profusely, as if a carotid artery had been severed." Such "bloody revenge," as the onlooker called it, defined the nature of the conflict by 1863. The Trans-Mississippi frontier had turned into a lawless and unpredictable environment rife with unmitigated violence. Moreover, guerrillas like those who shot Hyatt and terrorized his widow represented only half the threat.[4]

★   ★   ★

By 1863, antiguerrilla policies became increasingly focused on the civilian dimension of irregular war. Realizing that simply sending cavalry detachments into the brush to track down and destroy irregular bands had little effect, Federal forces brought the war to the few hardy civilians who had refused to move into towns or completely out of the area. Indeed, Union soldiers, having been sniped at and frustrated by guerrillas for over two years, had lost any patience they might have had in 1861. In turn, both Confederate and Unionist families throughout the western border region were affected by these harsh policies. Proof of aiding or abetting an irregular, or being suspected of helping one, was grounds for severe penalties, including imprisonment, loss of property, and sometimes death.[5] In southwest Missouri civilian Thomas G. Walton received such summary justice. Accused of supplying guerrillas with information about Federal positions, Walton was visited by Union militia members. Calling him to the door of his residence and asking no questions, the men abruptly shot him down and rode away.[6]

The same militia company responsible for killing Walton, headed by Capt. Thomas Sutherland, was known for its harsh measures against other families suspected of helping guerrillas—that is, everyone living along the border in 1863. One resident remembered that Sutherland's men were "a bad outfit. . . . [T]hey burned a lot of houses [and] it seemed to be their belief that everyone in the country was actively aiding the bushwhackers." Many pro-Union families had been forced to move to Carthage and give an oath proving their loyalty. A sense of urgency and fear filled their conversations, not just concerning guerrillas, who were bad enough, but also about the Union militia. Word had spread through the region that the militiamen were "going to raise the black flag . . . and shoot every man and burn every house in [the] neighborhood and would not believe that there was anyone out there that was loyal to the north."[7]

Although rarely so frustrated that they inflicted violence on women and children, Federal troops had come to see all civilians as sources of food and plunder. Just outside of Fayetteville, a group of "harassing and plundering" Yankees focused their efforts on a residence inhabited only by women. After cleaning the house and smokehouse of almost everything of material or culinary value, one man grabbed the last of the women's coffee. At this, one of the younger ladies exclaimed, "I have stood by and watched you take all the rest without objecting, but the coffee my old mother needs above everything else, and I ask you to leave it." The soldiers, bemused by her request, took the coffee anyway. As one was leaving the house, the young lady, clearly incensed, "rushed for an iron poker and dealt him such a blow that he fell limp to the floor." His shocked comrades left the coffee and quickly rode away.[8]

Union soldiers betrayed their frustration and antipathy by attacking even the staunchest Unionists. William Baxter, having survived both the Pea Ridge and Prairie Grove Campaigns, had long considered the prospects of fleeing northwest Arkansas for Union-occupied Missouri. Federal maltreatment in the wake of Prairie Grove pushed him to act in early 1863. At one point he confronted a group of soldiers tearing down his fence posts to tell them his property was protected by Union authorities. As Baxter walked back to his house, with his wife and children watching from the windows, a lieutenant caught up with him and demanded to know if he had told the soldiers to stop tearing down the fence. On hearing his affirmation, the young officer grabbed Baxter's beard, shoved a pistol in his face, and swore that "he would blow the top of [his] head off." After further cursing and violent threats with the pistol butt, the lieutenant released him.[9]

Baxter's assurances that he had connections with the young officer's superiors, and his calm demeanor in such a heated situation, probably saved his life. He walked into his house, "trembled in every limb," and rejoined his wife and children. Soon after Baxter and his family prepared to leave, for staying any longer, he believed, would be "tempting Providence." To be pillaged by Confederates was one thing, theft and violence at the hands of Unions soldiers quite another. In February Baxter took at least a modicum of control of the situation by joining a Union wagon train bound for Springfield.[10]

Fayetteville, the town that Baxter left behind, reflected in many ways the plight of the civilians who had struggled to survive there. By 1863, the once-thriving town had been largely abandoned. Large regular armies had passed through numerous time during the previous two years, and there existed a nearly constant guerrilla war outside its boundaries. According to Rev. Francis Springer, a Unionist who carefully assessed the town's condition early that year, "fences are torn away, houses broken down or consumed by flames, gardens, fruit-trees, shrubbery & grass plots are marred, mutilated & laid waste." More than just Fayetteville's fences and greenery had been affected. "Numerous piles of unsightly ruins mark the sites where hotels, shops & storehouses once invited the concourse of customers," Springer continued. Most troubling for the Yankee chaplain was the human suffering of its residents. "The people likewise are wrecked & wasted in spirit," he wrote, and the only ones who remained were so rattled by the conflict that "they live in constant dread of all armed men whether loyal or rebel." While Springer's general reflections on the state of Fayetteville provide even more evidence for the increasing destruction on the Trans-Mississippi frontier, his final appraisal of the situation gets straight at the heart of the civilian-centered guerrilla war that ravaged the region. Much as William Baxter had experienced, no matter one's loyalty, Confederate and Union combatants alike, regular or irregular, were direct and deadly threats to civilians. Springer summed it up clearly: "Forcible appropriation, pilfering, rudeness, & obscenity are the slimy traits of character which the demon of war begets."[11]

People like the Baxters were desperate by the first half of 1863. Civilians had fled the region by the thousands, adding to the troubles of Union and Confederate authorities who now had to deal with the massive numbers of refugees. Yet some were unwilling to run away. Instead of giving up their homes, these people begged military authorities for relief. One southwest Missouri resident sought Federal help to rid the region of guerrillas. In a letter to Brig. Gen. John Schofield, Nathan Bray explained the need for Union forces near Carthage and Lamar, a hotbed of irregular activity. With just a few companies, Bray assured him, "We could clean out the whole of the Spring River valley and its tributaries of bushwhackers." These densely vegetated areas, he continued, had served the guerrillas as ideal cover since the commencement of this "unholy war." If Schofield would only comply, the units might rout the irregulars and foster a renaissance in the region, which in turn would encourage the repopulation of that "very productive part of the state." Bray cited the region's destruction, the total loss of court records, and the absence of any law and order as justification for action. If the Federal army could only provide "permanent relief . . . and have these desperadoes driven from the country or planted in the sod," southwest Missouri could serve as a beacon for what might be done elsewhere.[12]

For Union soldiers, fighting an irregular war was at once exhilarating and frustrating. Conventional fighting methods did not apply. Indeed, as one soldier proclaimed, "Whackers must be dealt with after their own style." The odds were almost always against the Union pursuers, however. Beyond knowing the best hideouts or escape routes, local guerrillas were able to blend in to the populace. "Call at their house and if they are at home they are all good union men," one artilleryman lamented, "and perhaps before you are a mile distant from the house they will waylay and shoot at you from the bush, cowardly devils. Hanging is too good for them."[13] Increasing Federal frustration on the border was palpable, and the tension would only worsen as the war continued.

As spring approached, some pleas for a greater Union presence had been answered, but irregular actions intensified. Skirmishes between soldiers and guerrillas occurred on a regular basis. A typical fight on February 19 and 20 in southwest Missouri pitted Thomas R. Livingston's guerrilla band against a section of Enrolled Missouri Militia. The Unionists had "overtaken Livingston, with about 60 men . . . [and] had fought him a little, and came charging back through Carthage, swearing because they did not catch him." Hearing about this missed opportunity, Maj. Edward B. Eno proceeded to fight fire with fire. After dividing his command into several smaller bands, Eno sent his men in different directions to hunt for the guerrillas.[14]

As his own section approached the small town of Fidelity, Eno's men "charged into the place [and] came upon a small party of the rascals, wounded 1 [and] captured 3." To the major's disappointment, however, the guerrilla band largely escaped thanks to exhausted Union horses. "Many of the best friends of this guerrilla chief," Eno later reported, "solemnly own to me that they see and fully appreciate the injury he is doing the country, and they talk seriously of presenting a petition to him to leave."[15] It is unknown whether Livingston's "friends" ever asked him to leave. What is certain, though, is that the guerrilla leader remained in the area.

A month later, near the town of Sherwood in southwestern Missouri, Capt. David Mefford of the Sixth Kansas Cavalry found Livingston's trail. Like Major Eno, Mefford had with him a small segment of the whole regiment, commanding only three companies. But smaller numbers meant more mobility and speed, both advantages critical in any encounter with irregulars. Union antiguerrilla patrols that had once been encumbered with an unwieldy amount of men and supplies had evolved into light, fast, and elusive cavalry force. On March 9 Mefford's search-and-destroy column took up the chase. Shocked guerrilla pickets engaged the Union vanguard and, by blasting one sergeant in the face, bought just enough time for Livingston's men to escape into the dense brush. Mefford's force rode into the guerrilla camp, only to find that the enemy had fled "in great haste," with cut halters and ropes scattered on the ground. Mefford explained his failure to eradicate this guerrilla band. "The bush being so thick," he contended, "it was impossible for us to follow them." Once again, the guerrillas had lived up to their moniker, bushwhackers, and frustrated Union attempts to bring them to bay.[16]

But this deadly game of chase had not ended. Fuming, Mefford directed his men to follow an intervening creek in search of Livingston's band. After nearly two miles of hard riding, the Federals made contact and gave chase for over a mile. Suddenly, Livingston's force turned on them and obliged the pursuers to await the arrival of their full force. Having rallied his horsemen from the initial surprise, Mefford hastily ordered them to dismount and prepare for a prolonged engagement. But the ensuing fight, fierce as it was, lasted a matter of mere minutes. The guerrillas came uncharacteristically close to the dismounted Federals, firing at them, according to Mefford, from about one hundred yards. Soon after stalling their pursuers, Livingston and his men once again effected their escape into the timber. Mefford ordered his troopers to remount and pursue the guerrillas, but increasing darkness had made the task untenable and dangerous. The next morning the captain made one last effort to catch Livingston. But after a pursuit of nearly thirty-five miles, depleted supplies and exhausted horses brought an end to the chase.[17]

Mefford's experience was common. Although he successfully surprised the guerrillas in their hideout, the captain still had to deal with environmental, logistical, and command problems. Dense vegetation, as much as anything, proved the undoing of the operation. Additionally, although they had increasingly turned to foraging and theft to supply themselves, Mefford's cavalrymen had received most of their necessities from their base of operations (in this case Neosho, in Newton County). Local guerrillas, by contrast, not only knew where to find ample food, forage, and fresh horses but also were often far more familiar with the terrain than were their pursuers, offering them no limits on how far they could run from a sticky situation. During Mefford's pursuit, for example, Livingston and his men had ventured deep into Indian Territory. The Union troopers, on the other hand, could not chase them for hundreds of miles into hostile country without reinforcements or supplies, nor could they stray far beyond their area of command.[18]

As counterguerrilla forces chased elusive irregular bands throughout the region, the women and children who had remained struggled to survive. The spring season, in all its emotional and natural hope, could be exceedingly difficult for people in 1863. "Of the hundreds of farms all over this region, very few can be cultivated this season, for the fences around most of them have been destroyed, burned as fuel by the armies," Wiley Britton noted. Even worse, Britton and his fellow Federals noticed that there had been "nobody left to cultivate [the farms] except women and children, cripples and old men," and even these civilians were fleeting. In a reflective moment Britton rationalized that "mothers and daughters who, before the war, never dreamed of having to work in the fields" would have to raise their own crops now, having already seen some local women plowing their fields. These women and their children would need all the food they could grow.[19]

But Britton's Union colleagues made it exceedingly difficult for these people to scratch out any kind of subsistence, especially when they were suspected of aiding guerrillas. To be sure, civilians on the border, no matter their true allegiance—or any allegiance at all—lived in constant danger from all combatants. In early May a large Federal foraging party, consisting of nearly three hundred men, moved into southwest Missouri with the express purpose of confiscating any food or supplies they could find among the population who had been suspected of aiding guerrillas. The foragers found their first batch of civilians and food near present-day Joplin. According to one cavalryman, they placed all the residents under guard and arrested "a woman and boy with a load of wheat, which was being made into flour for the bush-whackers." The Federals then commandeered twenty horses and mules. Shortly after, two women rode up on horseback and, when questioned, "very defiantly" told the Yankees they were counting the size of the Union force "so as to inform Major Livingston." The officer in charge, Maj. R. G. Ward, no doubt bemused but also a little troubled by the scene, ordered that the women's saddles be taken and their horses confiscated. He allowed them to leave and deliver their reconnaissance report on foot if they were so inclined. The women protested and let loose "curses . . . loud and deep." When they demanded their horses and saddles back, Ward told them they must walk to Baxter Springs to retrieve them after the completion of his foraging mission. The Union patrol moved on, filling their wagons with as much corn, bacon, and other supplies they could find in the rapidly diminishing rural community.[20]

At Fort Scott Col. James M. Williams, commanding the First Kansas Colored Regiment, sought to keep pressure on the irregulars in the area, especially Livingston. "I am here . . . to put a stop to the Guerrilla or Bushwhacking war which is now being carried out," Williams informed Livingston. "I therefore propose that you collect all the enemies of the United States in your vicinity and come . . . attack me, or give me notice where I can find your force and I will fight you on your own ground." The colonel knew well that neither Livingston nor any other guerrilla would accept such a challenge, for it contradicted their strategy. He therefore declared that if Livingston and his followers did not fight as regular soldiers, he would treat them as "thieves and robbers who lurk[ed] in secret places fighting only defenseless people." In closing the colonel warned, "I shall take any means within my power to rid the Country of your murderous Gang."[21] Just after sending this letter, Williams set out to resupply his post for the irregular conflict to come. The supply wagons, manned primarily by African American troops, headed into southwest Missouri and stopped at the Rader farm, near the little town of Sherwood.

The subsequent fight at the Rader farm, and the events it spawned, illustrate the complex nature of irregular warfare along the western Trans-Mississippi border, serving as a microcosm of the fighting in the region: unrestricted killing, intense racial hatred, sneak attacks, Federal anger, the devastation of entire towns, and the consequential evacuation of hundreds of women and children. All of this occurred at Sherwood in a matter of days. The guerrilla attack against Williams's supply column did little to hurt the larger Federal war effort, and the Union counterattack did equally little to suppress guerrilla operations. But the Union retribution dealt to Sherwood and the larger area devastated the population. Civilians—almost entirely women, children, and the elderly—thus suffered the most. Out of frustration against the guerrillas and their perceived supporters, Williams torched the area. Nevertheless, Union cavalry and Confederate guerrillas would continue to play a macabre game of chase despite the dwindling civilian presence.

Major Ward led twenty-three soldiers from the First Kansas Colored Regiment, supported by twenty men from the Second Kansas Artillery, on the foraging mission. Such expeditions were nothing out of the ordinary—Union and Confederate soldiers and irregulars had supplied themselves from the land (and from area residents) since the war had begun. But to see African American soldiers at this point of the war was memorable. One resident recalled watching "six wagons with six armed Negroes standing in each" ride past her house en route toward the Rader farm and any other place that might provide significant sustenance. When just inside Jasper County, Missouri, about fifteen miles northeast of their post at Baxter Springs, Kansas, the soldiers reached their first stop, a large two-story house that had been used by the Rader family and their friends to store corn. Mrs. Rader and two other women were promptly forced out of the building, whose top floor had been packed with corn, a real boon for any foraging party. Excited by their discovery and disregarding any need for caution, the troops left their muskets against the fence and busily tossed their bounty out of the upstairs windows into the wagons below.[22]

Hugh Thompson, a trooper from the Third Wisconsin Cavalry, watched as the soldiers emptied the house of corn. He suddenly heard "shooting from the rear, and almost instantly all around." Livingston and a band of sixty-seven mounted men had rapidly approached from a wooded ravine behind the house and surrounded the surprised Federals. Leaving a small force behind to hold the soldiers in the house, the remaining guerrillas chased the balance of Union troops for more than eight miles, losing them in the dense brush around the Spring River. Meanwhile, their comrades closed in on the Rader house. Well aware of what would befall them should they be captured, the soldiers of the biracial foraging party were unwilling to surrender, and those few with weapons tried to "fight [their] way out."[23]

As the desperate scene evolved, Livingston and his men returned to the house and began killing the unarmed black troops who had been trying to flee. Thompson, trying to remain unnoticed until he found an escape route, watched as a "bushwhacker [pointed] a double-barreled shotgun . . . at the head of a Negro soldier who had been shot in the face and was not armed." The wounded soldier exclaimed, "Massa, don't shoot, I'll give up." Knowing well what the guerrilla's answer would be, Thompson shot him through the chest as he was about to pull the trigger. Though having saved this black soldier's life, confusion and bloodshed continued all around. In the noise and terror Thompson tried to fire at the guerrillas on horseback, but his carbine repeatedly jammed. At one point he thought he had a dead bead on Livingston himself, but the gun misfired yet again. As the frustrated cavalryman tried in vain to operate his weapon, another guerrilla rode up and promptly kicked him in the head. "Using a vile epithet," Thompson remembered, the guerrilla told him to "look up." The beleaguered Yankee complied, and the rebel kicked him in the face. "It was with great difficulty that I could speak," Thompson noted, "but I did so . . . and asked him not to kick me any more as I was dying." The Yankee trooper was not mortally injured, but in the blood, smoke, and confusion, the guerrilla believed him and rode on. Thompson was finally able to flee through the underbrush and eventually make his way back to Baxter Springs, but he "carried the mark of [the guerrilla's] boot heel on my right check for three months."[24]

The Wisconsin trooper was one of the lucky ones. According to Union estimates, Livingston and his men killed sixteen Federal troops, most of them unarmed African Americans who had been shot down when they tried to escape or surrender. Bragging to Maj. Gen. Sterling Price (to whom he occasionally pretended to answer), Livingston stated that he had defeated the black troops, filled with "the hellish passions of their race," stationed at Baxter Springs. His men, the guerrilla reported, also captured a large amount of supplies from the routed artillerymen and the fallen infantrymen, including "30 mules and 5 wagons, a box containing 1,400 cartridges and caps; [and] a good many guns, pistols, & c."[25]

Arriving at the scene as part of a Union detachment the following morning, one soldier reported that he and his comrades "proceeded to gather up all our dead, 11 that we found, and piled them in the house, a hard pine one two stories high." Colonel Williams, Livingston's nemesis, accompanied Federal forces to the site and was shocked. "I visited the scene of this engagement the morning after its occurrence," Williams wrote, "and for the first time beheld the horrible evidences of the demonic spirit of these rebel fiends in their treatment of our dead and wounded." After taking account of the situation, he further explained, "Men were found with their brains beaten out with clubs, and the bloody weapons left by their sides, and their bodies most horribly mutilated."[26] Not allowing the grisly scene to spoil their appetite, the recovery party dined on the food that had been left behind. Afterward, they piled the dead soldiers in the house. As soldiers worked to clean the mess, cavalrymen on the outskirts of the farm discovered a guerrilla suspected of having been a participant. The man, who donned a new pair of Union boots and a bloody shirt, was "marched into the house and shot, his body placed upon the pile, and the house burned."[27]

After cremating their comrades and the unlucky guerrilla, Union soldiers torched the area around the Rader farm. "We burned some dozen houses," one told his wife, "those that had families in them [we] gave . . . a few minutes to move out." In a reflective moment, and perhaps to justify his actions, the soldier remarked, "it is pretty hard, but war is a serious business." Indeed it was. Suspecting the local populace of having aided Livingston's men, even of having taken part in some of the killing after the initial fight, Williams ordered every structure within a five-mile radius of the site burned, including the small town of Sherwood. Destruction had become the fruit of Federal anger.[28]

The next day Livingston asked the colonel for a prisoner exchange and took the opportunity to protest Federal retaliation. The guerrilla leader offered to trade three white soldiers for the same number of any Confederate soldiers or irregulars in custody. His men had also captured two members of the First Kansas Colored, but he "could not recognize them as soldiers and in consequence [had] to hold them as contrabands of war." Livingston then complained about the execution of the captured guerrilla. "If that is your mode of warfare to arrest civil citizens who are living at home and trying to raise a crop for their families," he warned, "let me know and I will play to your hand." Even though word had reached him that the man had been killed and "burnt up" in the house, Livingston concluded in his letter to Williams, "I am satisfied that you are too high toned a gentleman to stoop or condescend to such brutal deeds of barbarity."[29]

In a quick reply Williams cautioned the guerrilla chief that the black soldiers in his custody should receive the privileges of prisoners of war. Should any ill befall them, there would be trouble. "You can safely trust that I shall visit a retributive justice upon them for any injury done them," the colonel warned, "and if twenty days are allowed to pass without hearing of their exchange I shall conclude that they have been murdered by your soldiers."

But murder was hardly the only punishment Williams feared might be visited upon his black soldiers. Indeed, dreaded even more was the prospect that they might be forced back "in chains to the slave pens of the South." If this happened, he closed his letter to Livingston. "they will be presumed dead."[30] As the colonel feared, the guerrillas soon killed one of their prisoners. Williams demanded that Livingston turn over the "assassin" within two days, but the rebel claimed that the killer was no part of his band and had escaped. Nevertheless, Union commander fulfilled his promise of retributive justice by shooting a Confederate prisoner.[31]

As for the suspected guerrilla who had been killed in the Rader house, Williams assured Livingston that he had been rightfully "shot and shared the fate of other soldiers for whom spades could not be found to dig their graves." After all, he reasoned, the guerrilla had not suffered as much as many of his own men. If Livingston considered the act "brutal barbarity," Williams noted, he should "compare it to the fiendish treatment . . . visited upon one of my men and of the bodies of club bruised, and brain spattered corpses . . . left on the prairie by your men and leave it to a candid word who profits by the comparison."[32]

Union commanders responded bitterly to Livingston's exploits and did everything possible to stop him. As much as these officers despised the guerrilla leader, they admitted his importance in perpetuating the irregular war in the region. One cavalry officer, frustrated by the skill of the guerrillas in evading attack, suggested that "a quick succession of vigorous assaults" could "destroy and disperse them." Indeed, he contended: "Kill Livingston, and there is no one else to mass and congregate these bands. He is a man of much influence."[33]

Yet Livingston and other guerrillas were by no means without problems. Federal counterguerrilla patrols had taken a toll on their bands. Constantly pursued by Union cavalry and hated by much of the population, the guerrillas were spread thin. Immediately after his attack on the Rader farm, Livingston complained to General Price that his forces were inadequate and exhausted. He later showed his desperation by pleading with Price to send Confederate troops into southwest Missouri. "Can you, and will you, use your influences in sending a sufficient force to relieve the sufferings of the people," Livingston asked, "who are being subjected to outrages unparalleled in this, and unprecedented in any other war?" At the time he penned this letter in late May 1863, Confederate troops were in short supply and had barely managed to oppose Union forces in southern Arkansas, much less Missouri. Livingston's request went unanswered.[34]

Less than two months later, Livingston was killed in central Missouri, although his death did not bring the peace expected by Federal commanders. Other irregular bands roamed through the region to create havoc. Some of Livingston's men afterward joined these groups, including William Clarke Quantrill's outfit, but most returned to southwest Missouri to fight under their fallen leader's "lieutenant," David Rusk.[35] Union cavalry commanders continued to chase guerrillas, and although the pressure made it increasingly difficult for irregulars to survive, they maintained an almost perpetual presence on the western border.

A significant part of counterguerrilla policy was to destroy irregular supply bases. While Livingston's men harassed the Union foragers near Sherwood, other Federal troops set out to destroy a noted guerrilla haunt over sixty miles to the north. On the morning of May 26, soldiers went from house to house in Nevada to order its residents to evacuate. According to one witness, the men were polite but blunt. "We are going to burn this house," they said, "get your things out in twenty minutes; if you want any help, we will help you, but the house must be burned." The only people remaining in town were women, children, and the elderly, any fighting-aged men having joined the Confederate or Union army.[36]

As the houses were ignited, according to one witness, "volumes of black, thick smoke rolled up into the blue May day sky." Women and children huddled near their belongings piled in the streets, undoubtedly wondering what they should do next. "The door yards and vacant lots were piled with household articles," remembered one onlooker, "around which wailed and mourned, or scolded and stormed, the dispossessed women as they kept the flying brands from their goods, or quarreled with the torch bearers." Months before General Ewing's infamous Order No. 11, which forced civilians in the middle Missouri border counties to abandon their residences, Union soldiers had taken it on themselves to evict civilians from their houses and destroy their property. Although women and children had not suffered direct violence, they now lost their homes and most of their belongings. The region had not been carpet bombed or gassed, and women and children had not been tortured or shot, but they all suffered indirect, and potentially deadly, destruction.[37]

Meanwhile, pro-Union Native American refugees began to trickle back into their former farmsteads near Fort Gibson and Tahlequah. Having suffered in Kansas for over a year due to the elements and lack of supplies, they hoped for a fresh start, but such optimism soon ended. As the refugees trudged into Fort Gibson and the surrounding area, their troubles became acute. "Where are the supplies to come from for the people?" a doctor bitterly complained. "Farms are ruined—corn and meat eaten up." At first overjoyed to have returned to the Cherokee Nation, these thousands who had originally joined Opothleyahola found the region reverting to wilderness. Weeds had overtaken farms, wooden fences had been torn down, and houses burned. "You have no conception of the desolation the different armies have caused," the doctor confided to his friend, "you may well believe nothing is spared." The refugees moved in anyway, even though their lot looked bleak. Hunger, disease, and violence continued to haunt them throughout the year.[38]

The capital at Tahlequah and the neighboring community of Park Hill suffered similarly. These towns had been at the center of Cherokee culture and commerce before the war, and they had played a significant role in the economic growth of both the Cherokee Nation and the Trans-Mississippi border generally. By 1863, most people in the area supported the Union or, at the very least, wished to be left alone. But nobody, no matter their loyalty, could be untouched by the war. This became all too clear for the hundreds of civilians living in the two towns and in the nearby countryside.

During the first half of June 1863, Confederate colonel Stand Watie led eight hundred Cherokee soldiers in a raid on Tahlequah and nearby Park Hill. He achieved surprise by snaking his regiment through the rugged and dense Cookson Hills and approaching the two towns from the south. In the ensuing attack the Confederate Indians "robbed the women and children of everything they could find, and took off horses, cattle, wagon, [and] farming utensils . . . and laid open their farms to be entered and eaten up by stock." Satisfied with their successful strike, the unmolested rebels left the area. Unionist survivors once again abandoned the ruined region. "Some fled into the mountains," a congressional report later noted, "and these remained for months in the winter season, exposed, in their destitute condition, to all the

inclemencies of the season, and many died of exposure." On top of their
renewed refugees status and suffering, the loyal Union Indians endured a
smallpox outbreak that killed hundreds. The attempted reintroduction of
Indian refugees in 1863 thus failed, and the situation in the Cherokee Nation
and throughout the border region would only continue to erode until the end
of the war.[39]

Due in part to Watie's ongoing pressure in the region, the Federal army
prepared for a full-scale assault in Indian Territory. Maj. Gen. James Blunt
hoped to secure Fort Gibson and rout the Confederates from the northeastern
section of the territory. Their first engagement occurred at Cabin Creek on
July 2–3. After an intense fight, the rebels fell back. Although Blunt captured
Fort Gibson, he had not fully defeated the army under Brig. Gen. Douglas H.
Cooper. But on July 17 the Federals surprised and defeated Cooper at Honey
Springs, about thirty miles southwest of Fort Gibson. By August, Brig. Gen.
William Cabell again challenged Union control of the region, but his cam-
paign, beset by supply problems and desertion, crumbled. Blunt continued
to drive the Confederates toward the Arkansas line.[40]

As regular Confederate forces in Indian Territory and western Arkansas
fell apart, the rebel irregulars in the region intensified their efforts. Guerrillas
filled the thickets and river bottoms. One such man happened upon a small
section of the Union army in eastern Indian Territory and mistook them for
Confederate reinforcements. This Native American guerrilla, according to
one Federal, "boasted how true he was to the Southern cause, and how many
Feds . . . he had killed, that he had shot one yesterday & one today, & one
of them a dead shot in the head, & how he had ripped open the flesh of the
other with his sharp knife." The old and unsuspecting irregular reveled in his
success, never knowing that one of the men whom he had shot in the head
had been a friend and scout of the Yankees to whom he was bragging. "It is,
perhaps, needless to say that the sneaking bushwhacker was not long permitted to remain among us," the Federal reported. Just after sharing his stories,
the Indian, who was "half Spanish & Choctaw," was summarily executed.[41]

The Confederates abandoned Fort Smith on August 31 as Blunt forced
Cabell toward Arkansas. The Federals marched in uncontested. Unionist
and Confederate refugees soon trudged into the new Union stronghold on
the Arkansas River. Pro-Confederate Creek soldiers and civilians fled en

masse. Most attempted to go back to the Creek Nation, while others more practically judged it safer to desert to Fort Smith. "Numbers are coming into our lines," Blunt reported with some satisfaction, "some to volunteer in the United States service, others pledging their allegiance and asking protection." Reverend Springer was shocked by the refugees' appearance. "The frightened & deluded creatures, toiling along the dusty road with their crazy wagons & lazy oxen," he wrote in his journal, "presented a pitiable spectacle of human degradation." White locals also tried to take advantage of the power shift. While hundreds of Confederate citizens abandoned their farms and fled south with their slaves as the Federals approached, still more civilians remained. Many had supported the Southern cause but, like their Creek neighbors, judged it safer and more practical to take a neutral stance and live in or near the garrison. Civilians from nearly one hundred miles away moved to Fort Smith to ride out the conflict. Not all of them treated the occupiers well, however. According to one Union officer, the women and children there "looked upon Federal officers and soldiers as rough, ignorant, uncouth barbarians, without any regard for truth, integrity, or virtue." Whether or not this was a universal view, one thing is certain: the civilians were wary of the newcomers. "It was pitiable to see and hear of their distress," the officer continued, "they were afraid to venture out of their houses and afraid to stay at home without a guard."[42]

Although initially gratifying for Blunt and the Union army, refugees would continue to trickle into their lines, causing ever-more problems. From September 1863 until the end of the war, Fort Smith served dual roles as a garrison for equipping and protecting Union soldiers and, increasingly, as a relative safe haven for civilians and Confederate deserters who understood the deadly risks associated with living beyond immediate armed protection. Such practical thinking resulted in an ever-more desolate landscape, allowing the war-induced wilderness to thrive. Union soldiers knew well their desperate situation even in light of their recent victories. At Fort Smith, one officer noted in his journal with not a little trepidation, "here we are, only a small band of Federals, cut off from communication with all the great world around." The garrison was surrounded by guerrillas and the remnants of the Confederate army, who by the officer's estimation, were as "thick as hops on our west [and] plenty as blackberries south of us." Flowing toward Little Rock to the east was the unpredictable and often-unreliable Arkansas River, its banks plagued by irregulars waiting in ambush. In the end Union forces on the Trans-Mississippi frontier had been stretched thin and were tasked with somehow maintaining "northwestern Arkansas, southwestern Missouri, southeastern Kansas, & all Indian Territory with all its shades of humanity." Ultimately, the increasingly frustrated Federals could only keep control of the very places they stood, though even then there was little guarantee of success.[43]

Relative isolation and a preponderance of guerrillas notwithstanding, General Blunt did not halt his entire force at Fort Smith. On September 9 he sent Col. William F. Cloud and two hundred members of the Second Kansas Cavalry east along the Arkansas River to follow and harass the retreating Confederates. Cloud soon made good on his orders, killing or capturing nearly forty rebels while seizing two hundred cattle and a large supply of wheat and processed flour. Moreover, the colonel's force grew significantly when nearly three hundred men joined his cavalry, "with Stars and Stripes flying, and cheers for the Union." Civilians along the river—the majority of whom had favored the Confederacy—quickly adapted to the new situation. Although some certainly continued (or began) to harass Union patrols through guerrilla tactics, the majority simply hoped to survive. Refuge in Fort Smith helped as did feigned enthusiasm for the Union cause.[44]

On September 10, just days after Blunt had entered Fort Smith, Union general Frederick Steele captured Little Rock. With Steele's success, the regular war along the Arkansas River from Fort Gibson in Indian Territory to Little Rock had largely ended, the region now nominally under Union control. Indeed, by late September nearly all territory north of the Arkansas River had been secured by the Federals. Sterling Price would cross the Arkansas River the next year on a raid into Missouri, but Federal control of the Trans-Mississippi border was otherwise complete, if only in terms of conventional army actions. That summer Gen. Robert E. Lee's Army of Northern Virginia had been defeated at Gettysburg and Maj. Gen. Ulysses S. Grant had taken Vicksburg. For the Union, regular military success had come in every theater of the war. But as one southeast Kansas resident wrote in July, while the "great and glorious victories for the Union" were well received by all, people living along the western Trans-Mississippi border still faced one brutal fact: "There are yet Bushwhackers."[45]

But bushwhackers, who used the environment to their advantage most of the year, faced increased challenges with the onset of fall and winter. In late October 1863 one Arkansas resident noted the unsettling nature of the conflict in the region, especially in regard to the ongoing fight between Federal patrols and guerrillas. Along with reporting what had become almost typical at this point in the war—"both armies are in the country eating up the little bread and forage a few old men and women have been able to make"—the man noted with lucidity how the style of fighting shifted with the changing seasons. "The Federals say that they will be able to hold Fayetteville now," he wrote, "as the leaves are falling from the trees and the bushwhackers will not be able to annoy them." While the lack of effective cover in the form of foliage had induced many guerrilla bands to seek refuge farther south in Texas or southern Indian Territory, some nevertheless remained. Indeed, instead of defeating the guerrillas, frequent Union patrols and the increased general Federal presence in the region had also amplified the intensity of fighting. By the fall of 1863, it was clear that "bushwhackers . . . have grown in importance" and would remain year round. As a consequence, residents caught in the middle would rarely catch a break. Regular armies, guerrillas, counterguerrilla patrols, and a host of other military-centered manifestations would continue to plague Union and Confederate civilians alike.[46]

For civilians—especially women and children—Union strategic success in Missouri and northern Indian Territory and Arkansas meant very little. To be sure, for them the conflict only intensified as Union patrols focused almost solely on counterguerrilla operations in which civilians, who were often accused of aiding them, were closely connected. In northwest Arkansas women had dealt with full-scale battles and nearly constant irregular warfare since 1861. An elderly Fayetteville resident believed that local women had borne "hardship with patience and fortitude." Impressed with such resolve, he declared, "[they] will live in story, aye will they, till their grandchildren have reached their dotage." Some women formed groups bent on the "protection of themselves and property." Instead of leaving the area like hundreds had done previously, they agreed to face all threats and danger. Indeed, the elderly chronicler admired "their dexterity in the use of the broomstick, poker, and wash basin on Federal noggins."[47]

Yet Confederate guerrillas and Union soldiers rarely used violence against women. Although women had certainly become an integral part of the war, they simply had not been the targeted for physical brutality. According to one historian, "truly total war would have meant the erasure of all lines between civilian and soldier and the treatment of men and women." Yet while soldiers and irregulars generally stopped short of killing or abusing them outright, women on the border often suffered, and sometimes died, as a direct consequence of the style of warfare directed toward them.[48]

One northwest Arkansas woman managed to face down an entire squad of soldiers. Having penned her hog to fatten it for the coming winter, the "old lady" heard Federal troops approach her house and open fire on the animal. Incensed, she grabbed a club and started for the yard. Forcing herself between the men and the dead hog, which they were about to drag away, she exclaimed, "You have killed my hog . . . but you cannot carry it away." Unwilling to face hunger or starvation in the coming winter, she had determined to test how far the soldiers might go to secure their prize, and she meant to use the club if they persisted. The men, shocked by her blatant physical threat, "cursed and threatened her," but she stood fast. Frustrated, one of them entered her house and "commenced tossing her bedding about and kicking her sheet of wool rolls over the floor." She did not budge. The enraged soldier returned "as near as it was safe for him, turned his ugly end towards her, pulled down his pants and emptied his bowels of [a] stinking load in her presence." The woman coolly reproached the young man: "You have made a dog of yourself. I am old and not thus to be abashed." The squad left without the hog. In an act of bravado, anger, and desperation, the woman had saved what would be a major part of her winter sustenance.[49]

While profane soldiers attempted to secure food from women and children in northwest Arkansas, Native American refugees continued to suffer in southeastern Kansas. The remnants of Opothleyahola's band, in tandem with thousands more refugees who had joined them through 1862 and early 1863, had found no relief there from hunger and the elements. A letter to the superintendent of Indian affairs from refugees acknowledged that the agency faced many problems. "But, sir, is all this to be counted with the lives of the Cherokee women and children?" the letter chided. "We all know our great and magnanimous government makes no account of cost, that they may be just and fulfill a promise." Conditions had gradually improved, but most of that progress was due to the men in the Indian Brigade, who had sent provisions home, rather than to the Indian commission. On the whole, however, the hardships of these refugees continued.[50]

One of the largest and most vicious irregular engagements on the border occurred just before noon on October 6, 1863. General Blunt and a small contingent traveling south to Fort Smith felt secure as they approached the small and nominally armed Federal garrison at Baxter Springs in southeast Kansas. The post there, Fort Blair, was only four hundred yards away yet still out of sight of the party just beyond the next hill. But Blunt, his staff (including Maj. Gen. Samuel Curtis's son Maj. H. Z. Curtis), a fourteen-musician band, and a small group of the Third Wisconsin Cavalry noticed a large body of mounted men atop another nearby hill. The general rode forward to meet this approaching force of horsemen apparently dressed in Union blue. As he came within two hundred yards of the strange-acting "Yankees," Blunt realized that he had been tricked when they opened fire on him.[51]

Guerrilla chieftain William Quantrill's 250-man force, riding southwest from the Missouri River to spend the winter in Texas, had attacked the Union garrison at Baxter Springs earlier that day. They spotted the hapless Union escort by chance and decided to make the most of the situation. Immediately upon recognizing the enemy, Blunt ordered his men into line of battle. The skittish Union troopers, many of whom had little combat experience, trained their carbines on the screaming guerrillas as they galloped to within sixty yards. Quantrill later reported, "They gave us a volley too high to hurt anyone, and then fled in the wildest confusion on the prairie." Blunt, ashamed of his escort's "disorderly and disgraceful retreat," followed in a vain attempt to rally the panic-stricken men. Wielding revolvers and shotguns and riding superior horses, Quantrill's men were ideally suited for close combat. Easily chasing down the bulk of the Federals over a four-mile stretch, the guerrillas made "fearful havoc on every side." Indeed, one Wisconsin cavalryman recalled, "it immediately became close fighting . . . principally pistol work . . . and when the pistol was empty the butt was used."[52]

Dressed in civilian clothes and mounted on an inconspicuous mule, Blunt managed to escape the carnage, but most of his men did not survive. The general's fourteen-member brigade band, loaded on a small wagon, had few weapons. Scrambling from the guerrilla onslaught, their teamster diverged from the rest of the fleeing Federals in hopes of getting away unnoticed. His evasive action might have worked but for a faulty front wheel that worked loose during the attempted escape, leaving the wagon on a hill in clear view of Quantrill's men. A guerrilla contingent converged on the wagon and, one of their number having been shot by a band member, opened fire on the musicians as they begged to surrender. Upon shooting each man multiple times, the guerrillas piled their bodies onto the useless wagon and set it ablaze.[53]

Somewhat safe behind Union lines, Maj. B. S. Henning, sickened by his inability to offer assistance, despaired as he witnessed the band's drummer boy "shot and thrown under the wagon." "When the fire reached his clothes," Henning reported, "it must have brought returned consciousness, as he had crawled a distance of 30 yards, marking the course by bits of burning clothes and scorched grass." The twelve-year-old boy's gallant effort to escape had failed, and he was "found dead with all his clothes burned off except the portion between his back and the ground as he lay upon his back." Those bodies not consumed by the fire were "brutally mutilated and indecently treated."[54]

Most of Blunt's remaining men were chased down and shot. According to survivors, the guerrillas demanded that they give up their arms in return for their lives. Once the Federals complied, however, the guerrillas opened fire. One soldier, feigning death after receiving multiple gunshot wounds, recalled that his attacker requested that he "tell old God that the last man you saw on earth was Quantrill." Another soldier, playing dead while lying face down, reported that the man who shot him "jumped upon his back and essayed to dance, uttering the most vile imprecations." By most accounts, the guerrillas shot each trooper multiple times in the torso and head, even though they had tried to surrender.[55]

While the butchery continued outside Baxter Springs, Quantrill sent another large contingent to attack Fort Blair, manned only by a company of the Second Kansas Colored Regiment and two companies of the Third Wisconsin Cavalry. Fortunately, the garrison had recently acquired a small mountain howitzer, which Lt. James B. Pond employed with great effect against the guerrilla onslaught. Pond, loading and firing the cannon as fast as he could, did not ready the fuses on every projectile, consequently firing mostly nonexplosive rounds at the guerrillas. But the boom of the gun alone helped turn the tide of battle for the Federals, and it had some effect on guerrilla morale when one of the rebels, Dave Woods, was decapitated by an artillery round.[56]

Pond did not repulse the onslaught alone. In his postbattle report he makes clear that the company of Second Kansas Colored "fought like devils" and inflicted severe casualties by firing solid lead bullets topped with buckshot, affectionately known by soldiers as "buck and ball," into the guerrilla ranks. Their outdated smoothbore muskets worked exceedingly well at such close ranges. Although all Union troops risked death if they surrendered, these African American soldiers knew that they stood no chance if the guerrillas succeeded in taking the fort. Less than five months before, irregulars had butchered black troops at the Rader farm in Missouri, not far from Fort Blair.[57]

Quantrill's actions this day exhibit several important features of irregular warfare on the border. The opportunistic nature of guerrilla fighting was most prominent. Quantrill's men attacked an inferior contingent of unaware Federal troops. Their attack only intensified when Blunt's cavalrymen fled, leading to all-out slaughter. "Had the escort stood their ground, as they should have done, instead of becoming panic stricken," the general later claimed, "all would have been well, and the horrible massacre would not have occurred." This self-serving statement notwithstanding, the soldiers might have increased their chances for survival had they not immediately fled.[58]

It is also important to note the guerrillas' recalcitrance in attacking Fort Blair. A very small Union force with a mountain howitzer held them off because the risk of dying was simply too high for the rebels; it was far easier for guerrillas to run down and shoot panicked cavalrymen and largely unarmed bandsmen. Indeed, one trooper from the Third Wisconsin Cavalry admonished, "Their game is not to fight an equal number even with the advantage of the thick bush to hide themselves in, but they find a person alone or a small squad of men to rob and kill."[59] Another theme repeated in the Baxter Springs massacre is the bloodlust so common in guerrilla warfare. Not only did Quantrill's band take no prisoners but also shot dead and dying Union troopers several times, often in the face and head. Some danced on and kicked the dead and wounded while shouting obscenities as their victims drew their final breaths.

Although Quantrill's men succeeded in spreading fear amongst both Federal soldiers and Unionist civilians, the guerrillas failed to kill Blunt. Their action, as brutally victorious as it was, would do little to change the shape of the general war along the Trans-Mississippi border. Blunt's victories in Indian Territory and at Fort Smith remained intact, and Quantrill's efforts served merely to perpetuate the quagmire of nastiness that had submerged the region since the first months of the war. Indeed, Unionist citizens in Fort Smith, still reeling from their liberation from Confederate control, discounted the Baxter Springs affair. "Maj. Gen. James G. Blunt and staff returned to us again yesterday, after an absence of nine weeks," the local newspaper reported; "the rebels among us, who would have it by all means that he had been killed in the attack made by Quantrile upon him and escort last month will take notice and find to their chagrin that they were sadly mistaken."[60] Quantrill's band would winter in Texas, safe from Union patrols, and revel in their macabre victory against a much smaller force.

Farther south, Fort Smith was quickly filling up with civilian refugees running from what Thomas Alexander and others had already endured. Writing about this flood of humanity, the local newspaper made clear that "many families . . . had their houses burnt, after having been robbed of everything, and have come to town in the most pitiable circumstances." If they had yet to fully understand the destructive nature of the conflict, most people had quickly realized its severity by the fall of 1863. Refugees and Union soldiers agreed that the "only remedy is to clean out the bush-whackers, and give them no mercy wherever and whenever found; and then, and not till then, may we look for revival of prosperity." For Unionists, guerrillas represented an illness that continued to cripple the socioeconomic health of the region— precisely what many irregulars had sought to do. By late 1863, most significant regular Confederate military threats had largely dissipated. All that had kept locals from farming and rebuilding had been the constant guerrilla activity amplified by increasingly frustrated Federal patrols targeting both irregulars and civilians. Such redoubled efforts to eradicate "bushwhackers" led to a larger Northern military presence and increasingly harsh countermeasures against the guerrillas and those suspected of supporting them.[61]

Not all civilian refugees sided with the Federals, though. To be sure, a large portion of the population had been committed Confederates who now bitterly resented the Union presence in Fort Smith. The ever-inquisitive and perceptive Rev. Francis Springer speculated in his journal about the nature of Confederate women under Union occupation. "I wondered how it could be that these individuals of the 'gentler sex' to whom was universally accorded the title of *ladies*," Springer wrote, "should exhibit so much devilish fury." Those in Fort Smith had abandoned all sense of civility when the Federals took the western Arkansas town, Springer said, and had fallen into "protracted & violent fits of weeping & exclamatory utterances." The reverend placed much of the blame on the misperceptions spread early in the war regarding the brutalities sure to be wrought by "*Lincoln's low-bred Dutch & hireling Yankees*" upon the Southern population. From interviews with these women and children, he deduced that they fully anticipated "robberies, arsons, murders, flaying alive; the massacre of children, old men, & helpless women." This perception persisted unabated no matter how Springer and other Federals tried to show them otherwise. While mass murder and "flaying alive" certainly did not happen, at least not on women and children, the guerrilla war on the Trans-Mississippi frontier had come to fit some of these residents' fears. Theft, destruction, and murder did happen, and the countryside was quickly becoming void of any semblance of civilization. This state of war had as much to do with Confederate guerrillas, though, as it did with the Federals chasing them. With persistent and troublesome irregular action came equally dogged and destructive Union reprisal. But for Reverend Springer, the Confederate women in western Arkansas were simply "the most vainglorious & fool-hardy set of people I have ever met with."[62]

In mid-November 1863, with the trees rapidly dropping their leaves, another local guerrilla group played havoc with Union communications in the western Ozarks. Federal telegraph lines between Fort Smith and Fayetteville, crossing through the Boston Mountains, had been cut by irregulars through much of the fall. Union general John McNeil by now had had enough. With conventional Confederate forces at least temporarily absent from the region, McNeil reasoned, the wire-cutting culprits could only have been that "common foe of mankind—the Guerrilla and Bushwhacker [who] have no claim to be treated as soldiers, and are entitled to none of the rights accorded by the laws of war to honorable belligerents." Furthermore, the general exclaimed in a published order, "it is hereby ordered that hereafter, in every instance, the cutting of telegraph wire shall be considered the deed of bush-whackers." He went further. Every time a telegraph communication faltered due to tampering, "some bush-whacking prisoner shall . . . be hung at the post where the wire is out; and so many bushwhackers shall be so hung as there are places where the wire is cut." By this point in the war, harsh as this order sounds, residents were not terribly shocked by the wording. But McNeil's closing sentence certainly caught everyone's attention, especially those living near the telegraph lines: "The nearest house to the place where the wire is cut, if the property of a disloyal man, and within ten miles, shall be burned." According to a Kansas soldier, McNeil had even kept alive captured "bushwhackers" in order "to have them ready to hang to telegraph poles when ever the wires may be cut."[63]

Warfare had become intense, unqualified, and exacting, and readers of the local newspaper that published McNeil's order knew it. Just after its publication, some "infernal scoundrels" attempted to shoot the general while he was visiting with his assistant adjutant general, Joshua T. Tatum, who had sent the order to the press. Neither officer was hit. Turning to see where the shots had originated, McNeil watched as the "cowardly assailants . . . fled precipitately."[64] Whether the attempted assassination was due to his draconian order is unknown, but the shooters certainly knew their target. What is more, even in the vicinity of a major Federal post, garrisoned by hundreds of well-armed soldiers, officers (or civilians) were not safe.

Moving long, slow, and vulnerable supply trains between garrisons was more dangerous still. In early November Union colonel Samuel J. Crawford led had been tasked with moving much-needed supplies over two hundred miles from Fort Scott to Fort Smith. "When strung out on the march," Crawford explained, the supply train "covered a space of six miles, over a rough road." His own escorting forces stretched thin to protect such a vulnerable prize from guerrilla bands, the colonel's men kept busy fighting off several small attacks. At one point Union forces were "fighting on both sides of the road at the same time [against] bands of bushwhackers prowling about the woods on both flanks, watching for an opportunity to capture or burn the wagons." Within two weeks, the Union escorts were able to get their wagon train to Fort Smith with remarkably little damage.[65]

Irregular war in the region was underscored by the need for regular foraging, and Union soldiers knew well the potential benefits that the countryside offered. As the winter cold moved in, troops from the Twelfth Kansas, marching through southwest Missouri from Fort Scott to Fort Smith, encountered an area nearly devoid of human life but brimming with food. Pigs easily adapted to the desolate environment, and perennial crops, especially apples, needed little human labor to produce. In fall and early winter, orchards provided an ideal food source, and discovering such natural bounties made for diary-worthy news. "Come across a fine lot of hogs which we more than went for," recorded Union private Henry A. Strong. Two days later Strong and his fellow soldiers "got two wagon loads of apples at a Rebel's. . . . All in gay spirits." Again, three days later, they ventured "into the country after some eatables. Got plenty of apples and fresh pork."[66]

The Kansans ate heartily on their journey down the length of the Trans-Mississippi border, but other natural factors made the trip both miserable and dangerous. Heavy rain drenched the Union caravan on Christmas Day, then turned to snow on New Year's Eve; the year was ending as it had begun. As they marched through the Boston Mountains, heavily laden with apples and soaking-wet supplies, the soldiers experienced the environment at its harshest. At one point the patrol had to wade across the same bloated Ozark creek thirteen times. The next day, after marching a difficult twelve miles, the men were forced to camp "on the side of a mountain as the teams could not get over it. It was so wet and slippery." They finally crossed the flooded Arkansas River on wagons into Fort Smith, their once plentiful rations by then exhausted. Overjoyed that the trip was over, Strong noted, "Fort Smith is a very pretty place, or was before the war. . . . I am glad that we are at our journey's end for the present, as I am pretty well tired out."[67]

Civilians suffered a worse holiday season than did these Kansans. "There are bands of robbers passing through the country in the night," reported one Arkansan, "blacking themselves, who carry off bed clothing, wearing apparel, etc. A few nights ago they were at most of the houses in the neighborhood of our farm, robbing." There was rarely a respite from war.[68] By winter, most of the foliage that provided cover for irregulars had disappeared. And although Quantrill's band had moved south to Texas, many more stayed that winter despite their increased risk of being caught. Union soldiers, however, were still regularly frustrated by guerrilla attacks and their subsequent inability to track down the assailants, even with the leaves off the trees. Flora in northwest Arkansas and through much of the Ozark region includes a mixture of deciduous and evergreen forests. The natural topography is littered with scattered rocks and caves. Hiding places remained in winter, though they were fewer.

In December the Union garrison at Fayetteville attempted a new anti-guerrilla policy that called for burning the forests. Not only would such conflagrations kill the dead underbrush that screened the bushwhackers, but it also would potentially ignite the pockets of evergreen trees that proved good hiding places year round. Such fires often got out of hand. According to one Fayetteville resident, "The Federals, in burning the woods for bushwhackers, have burned up much fencing." And while one woman had been out "saving her property from the fire, a band of Federals were at the house shooting and carrying away her chickens."[69]

The success of such preventative measures was dubious at best. While soldiers were burning the brush around Fayetteville, guerrillas responded by igniting Van Winkle Mill to the north, which the Federals had been using to cut lumber "to rebuild Fayetteville." Useful or not, these counterguerrilla fires not only reflected a growing frustration in the unending irregular war but also offered an innovative, if ultimately unsuccessful, strategy for striking back. Such strategic defoliation certainly would not be the last attempt by an American army to defeat guerrillas who used the environment to their advantage.[70]

Elsewhere, Union refugees continued to crowd into Federal strongholds. At Springfield, nearly four thousand civilians put intense pressure on Union quartermasters to supply and shelter them. Charged with caring for the overwhelming number of refugees, hospital chaplain Fred H. Hines sought order in the perpetual and ever-growing chaos. In December he asked Brig. Gen. John Sanborn for permission to organize some form of employment for the refugees. The problem, according to Hines, was that those from northwest Arkansas and southwest Missouri could "do nothing well, except to manufacture homespun cloth." "Even if they could work," he continued, "their number is so great, that they cannot find employment sufficient for their support, and they become a burden to the Government."[71]

Hines seemed not to appreciate that these "burdens" had fled or been forced from their farms, or that farmers simply had little experience in trades that might help them better meld within the growing refugee society. While he sought to have them "clothe the rebel prisoners," they had to do something. To continue to give them food and other supplies "without requiring of them any labor in return" would only encourage "their natural indolence and . . . increase and prolong their poverty." So the refugees spun wool and cotton into cloth while stuffed into an overcrowded town, although they were, at least, free of attacks by guerrillas or Union militias.[72]

For those willing to remain on their farms by late 1863, a new bounty increasingly became available—wild game. According to Wiley Britton, "the game in this region, such as deer and wild turkeys, have increased in great numbers in the past two years." Indeed, by desolating much of the prewar human civilization, the brutal conflict along the border had fostered a tremendous growth in wildlife populations. "Many hogs have become wild in the river bottoms," the Union soldier continued, "and flee from the sight of man like deer. When the houses have burned and the fences around the farms destroyed, as we find here and there, animals like hogs . . . soon run wild." Other witnesses reported that "game of all sort had increased tremendously during the last years of the war and . . . wolves were so tame that they could be shot from the wagon seat of those . . . who drove along the seldom used roads."[73]

Federal victories at the local and national level had changed the war's dimensions by the end of 1863, but both Union and Confederate civilians living along the western Trans-Mississippi border were still very much mired in a guerrilla war. Confederate sympathizers rebuked "Lincoln's galling tyrannical yoke" over the region and observed that the few people left had "no means for resistance," their "forage, bread, stock, beds and bed clothing taken" by the enemy. Unionist civilians fared no better. Their food and supplies were subject to use by Federal soldiers and theft by guerrillas. Still, Unionists yearned for progress in the war-torn region, especially in light of the recent turn of events. In Fort Smith, for example, they had created a small newspaper named after what they hoped was materializing, the *New Era*. "Rome wasn't built in a day," the newspaper's editors cautioned, "and we expect, some of these days, to see the *New Era* as big as a small sized barn door."[74] That the paper could begin to write openly about significant progress, while located in the harshest region in the South, had been something to editorialize about indeed.

# 5

## "Deplorable Condition of the Country"

### CIVILIZATION EXTIRPATED, 1864–1865

Harsh winter weather announced 1864 on the Trans-Mississippi border. "Never, in the memory of the oldest inhabitant, was so severe a spell of cold experienced in this latitude," exclaimed a Fort Smith editor. The temperature had plummeted to twelve degrees below zero at one point and hovered near zero for weeks. In a rare occurrence, the newspaper reported, "The Arkansas river is completely frozen over and crossed by heavily loaded wagons at Van Buren." "Very cold weather, I think, for the 'sunny South,'" one Federal soldier noted. "Rather a rough introduction to this 'Sunny Land.'" Fort Smith residents informed occupying troops that the winter had been the coldest in two decades, and a Union officer at Fort Scott, Kansas, complained that soldiers exposed to the weather "returned with fingers, toes, and ears froze, and some profanity and groaning was indulged in as soon as they came to the fire."[1]

In northwest Arkansas there had been "much suffering amongst the soldiers, as also amongst both Union and Rebel women and children." According to one Fayetteville resident, "I saw one Fed with his ears and fingers frost-bitten [and] one boy driving a wagon for a Federal forage train was so badly frosted that he will, it is thought, die." Civilians suffered the worst. "There are doubtless hundreds who will die from the cold," another resident worried. "Many families, both Union and Rebel, are without houses and sufficient clothing for even a moderate winter."[2] The frigid blast also affected the food supply for everyone. Fort Smith lost its primary supply route when the river froze. The commander of the post, Brig. Gen. John McNeil, sent an urgent message on January 4 stating that the fort was running out of sustenance. "Steam-boats loaded with supplies should be at the mouth of the river ready to ascend," he declared, for soldiers and civilians were on "half rations of bread, and in a week shall be destitute of bread supplies."[3]

Such a welcome was appropriate for 1864. Unusually severe winter weather in tandem with depleted food supplies plagued not just the war effort but also civilians' chances for survival. By 1864, any trace of civilian support for either side had nearly disappeared. Yet, importantly, residents on the border had begun to take control of their own security and livelihoods in a more cooperative effort than ever before. While vast swaths of countryside between Federal strongholds remained abandoned and deadly, civilians—Indian and white—attempted to gradually resettle very specific and guarded areas. Under the watchful, if often corrupt and dangerous, eye of Federal authorities, people in northwest Arkansas created farm colonies in a communal effort at protection. Survivors of the Indian exodus to Kansas trickled back down to Union strongholds in eastern Indian Territory in an effort to return to their way of life. Although the vast majority of civilians on the western Trans-Mississippi frontier had died or remained in exile in the last months of the war, hundreds of brave residents returned. They found a wilderness of war. Even high-toned Confederate officers recognized the guerrilla-fueled chaos by 1864. For Brig. Gen. Joseph Shelby, the "so-called Confederate forces" along the border had devolved into lawless bands of thieves and murderers.[4]

Although most regular military campaigns had ceased in the western Trans-Mississippi theater, irregular warfare had intensified. Reporting the condition of much of the region in February, Brig. Gen. John Sanborn noted that the abandoned countryside, thanks to the relative absence of residents, had a remarkable amount of forage for the winter, while the regions to which refugees had fled were stripped of resources. In an ironic twist, the severity and brutality of the border conflict had allowed the natural landscape—both flora and fauna—to thrive. By early 1864, it had heralded the return of the wilderness, however briefly. "The people . . . will not return to their farms in the border counties," Sanborn lamented, making clear that such a wilderness would persist there until Union protection could be established.[5]

Unpredictable weather, isolation, and constant danger bred "immoral behavior" and sloth among many in the region. Refugees who sought protection in towns and forts did not always have jobs, and according to Union authorities charged with maintaining these districts, bands of unemployed men incessantly lurked around these posts. Seeking to impose a strict sense of order at Fort Smith, General McNeil made clear that "vagrancy and idleness" were "a bane to any community where they exist[ed]." In his characteristically straightforward approach, McNeil continued: "Hereafter, every able bodied man in this District will be compelled to enter the service of the United States, either in the ranks of the army, or in the trains or workshops, or they must seek other lawful avocations." He sought not only to rid the streets of vagrants but also, if possible, to increase enlistments. In closing his special published order, and providing insight into refugee-laden military posts on the Trans-Mississippi border, the general cautioned, "Gambling, pimping, prostitution, and other grossly immoral pursuits, will not be tolerated."[6]

The efficacy of McNeil's order was short lived. Union soldiers hit the town just a few weeks later. "I had the pleasure of attending an Arkansas dance," one jubilant Yankee reported. "A regular HO DOWN. Had a young 'lady' to ask me for a 'chaw of tobacco.'" Soldiers manufactured their own fun too. "Ball playing is got to be a chief amusement," one reported. "Well, anything to drive away the Blues when a fellow is short on rations."[7] Baseball and dancing, although often done on an empty stomach, proved useful emotional and physical reprieves for Federal soldiers who had dealt with war for nearly three years.

Yet food-shortage-induced blues typically overshadowed the temporary relief brought by dancing and baseball. Food and equipment was nearly wholly dependent on the navigability of the Arkansas River connecting Fort Smith to Little Rock, over 150 miles to the east. A drought in early 1864 resulted in very little riverboat activity and, consequently, empty stomachs. According to Iowa soldier John A. Mitchell, who had been assigned garrison duty at Fort Smith, "times is hard as usual [we] mostly live on half rations here and not much likely to be any better without the River gets up." In addition to the unpredictable waterway, a growing number of refugees brought increased pressure on the already precarious food supply. "There are so many refugees here," Mitchell lamented, "most all of the rations" were allotted to them. Adding insult to hunger, "the bigger portion of them are negroes," the frustrated Iowan continued. "[A] neger is much better thought of down here than a white soldier among the shoulder straps." Such persistent hunger only compounded the relentless drudgery of garrison duty amid a region defined by terror. That officers allotted valuable rations to African American refugees only further frustrated their soldiers. But even "shoulder straps" struggled with rations. According to one Kansas lieutenant, "the river don't raise and we can barely get enough for [soldiers] to live on."[8]

Disease also plagued civilians and Union soldiers on the border. In Fort Smith sickness had taken a toll, with most afflicted during the winter months. In January 1864 there were over sixty patients suffering from pneumonia and over thirty with smallpox. The most pernicious and widespread ailment, however, continued to be syphilis. "This unfortunate and detestable disease," according to the Federal surgeon for the garrison, had "spread among soldiers and citizens to the extent of five and six hundred cases." Medical officials in concordance with military leaders determined to stem the growing outbreak. Although syphilis had clear-enough causes, it was the most difficult to combat due to the very nature of such causes. But other, nonsexually transmitted diseases could be more easily prevented. Daily sanitary inspections of all military encampments in and around Fort Smith became the order of the day. "The camp shall be each day carefully policed," read the order, "and all tents and clothing well aired and kept clean."[9]

Yet additional refugees—white and black—increased the likelihood of disease and tasked Federal leaders with more responsibilities and fewer supplies. Soldiers regularly complained that white refugees, who they believed to have mostly been Confederate sympathizers, were too busy "feeding at the local crib," as one soldier in Missouri viewed it, when they should be gainfully employed in order to earn their food and protection. But the long lines of increasingly downtrodden women and children (and progressively fewer able-bodied men) gradually softened the hateful resolve of most. Soldiers and civilians alike worked to supplement their meager rations throughout the war, always depending directly upon the environment for their survival.[10]

Unwilling and unable to wait for the steamboats, Union troops regularly traversed the countryside searching for any signs of food or supplies. The surreal landscape they found was devoid of human activity and offered only abandoned farms and plantations, many vacated for months. At the first sign of Federal troops the previous summer, these pro-Confederate farmers had fled south with their slaves, leaving their unharvested crops to wither and die. Soldiers noted that feral hogs flourished in the abandoned areas and roamed largely unmolested—unless spotted by a foraging party. "There is . . . an abundance of fat hogs running loose that we more than 'go for,'" commented one soldier; "made the hogs suffer that crossed our path." Union patrols stripped the residences of everything useful. This new war-induced wilderness of feral hogs, overgrown crops, and weeds where thriving plantations and farms had once been would only expand until the war's end.[11]

Unionist newspaper editors in Fort Smith complained about the same overgrown plantations witnessed by the hog-hunting troops. "Many of the finest farms belonging to rebels have been abandoned by their owners," one noted, "and instead of being allowed to be taken possession of immediately by Union men, of whom there was a great number here . . . , they were allowed to go to ruin and waste, and the fences to be burnt." Even if Unionists were allowed to cultivate the vacated farms, their lives might be severely shortened. As the same editors clarified, "The main reason, why farmers do not follow their usual occupation, is the great dread they have of bushwhackers, and bands of lawless persons infesting the country and this fear is only too well founded." He continued, "It cannot be denied that there is scarcely a farm within a large circuit of this place, that has not been robbed more or less." When the majority of soldiers left Fort Smith the previous summer, Unionist civilians feared that irregular activity would intensify, that "bushwhackers—those fiends in human shape, [would] become more daring than ever."[12]

Food also became the primary concern for civilians in the region. The bitterly cold winter had drained resources from even the best-supplied families. People did all they could to find food and supplies, but even when they could, it was threatened by guerrillas and Union soldiers. Theft or confiscation in such lean times was tantamount to a violent attack. Sickness and death due to poor diet was a brutally real threat for everyone living in the region. The futility and danger of large-scale agriculture provided yet another dimension of food scarcity. To attempt to farm outside of town had often meant courting a death sentence. Either Union patrols would suspect farmers of helping guerrillas or irregulars might suspect them of aiding the Federals.

It was a difficult situation either way, further fueling an exodus from the countryside.

Civilians crowding into towns sought various ways to accumulate food, sometimes succeeding, but their efforts were often foiled by regular visits from hungry soldiers. One Fayetteville slave, for example, spent a great deal of time on the outskirts of town "building his traps and catching prairie chickens and partridges." Wild game was a welcome supplement to the typical diet of salted pork and bread, though any full meal was a delicacy. "We still have little to eat ourselves and have to divide that little with those who are worse off than we are," complained Robert Mecklin. His family also had to divide their food with Union soldiers occupying the town, many of whom visited at dinnertime. If not openly confiscated, cows, pigs, and horses simply went missing. "Mrs. Mecklin is still cow hunting," he wrote with a hint of sarcasm. "I have very little hope of her finding them, for I think they have gone the way of our horses, hogs and some of our cattle heretofore went. But I encourage her in looking for them because it will improve her health."[13]

Indeed, food—and who it sustained—became a central point of conflict between civilians, guerrillas, and Union forces. While Mrs. Mecklin was hunting for her stolen cattle in northwest Arkansas, a mother and her daughters in southwest Missouri suffered a fate altogether too familiar in the region. Frustrated Union troopers had just skirmished with a guerrilla band nearby when the women saw the partisans ride by their house at a full gallop. The cavalrymen were close on their heels, but some nevertheless stopped the pursuit to interrogate the women, approximately thirty Federals slowing as they approached the small house. Instead of continuing the chase, they pulled up in the front yard, and the officer in charge barged into the house. Noting that a meal had recently been served, he shouted to his men, "These people had fed them and the dishes are still on the table." "We denied the accusation vigorously," claimed the daughter, "explaining that we ourselves had just finished dinner and that the bushwhackers had not even come in." The women's pleas made no impression on the soldiers, who prepared to burn the house. "We began to carry out what little household goods we had left," asserted the daughter, "and the [soldiers] stood by watching until the roof of the house was ablaze." Once the building was well afire, the Federals slowly rode off "in the same direction the bushwhackers had taken." Whether or not the women had assisted the guerrillas in any way is impossible to know, but the absolute frustration at the never-ending pursuit of the guerrillas had fueled the cavalrymen to take their anger out on these residents. Clearly, anyone even slightly suspected of aiding the enemy suffered. Clearer still, the border region had become almost entirely inhospitable outside garrisoned towns.[14]

But even getting to those Federal strongholds proved risky. That February, Union officer Ozias Ruark and his Eighth Missouri State Militia were tasked with escorting civilians—mostly women, children, and the elderly—from the border region into Springfield, Missouri. While always wary of the potential for guerrilla attacks, the soldiers and refugees suffered most dearly from the harsh environmental conditions. Pushing hard through the Ozarks, Ruark noted, the group "traveled late at night [and] it grew very dark [so] we could not see our hands before us in heavy pine forest." Worse still was the frigid winter weather. "The snow fell thick and heavy," the officer lamented. "Men and Angels pity thy poor suffering women and children." After finally delivering the refugees to the camps in Springfield, the regiment returned to the border and found a desolate countryside. Residents, Ruark remarked, guarded their dwindling stores of food. Most no longer cared (if they ever really had) about large campaigns, battles, or strategies. For Unionist and Confederate civilians like those encountered by Ruark, the war had become squarely about simple survival.[15]

Amid such chaos and seeming anarchy, Union general Samuel Curtis set out on a tour of his District of the Frontier, a sprawling landmass that included Nebraska, Colorado, Kansas, and Indian Territory. Focusing the bulk of his time on Kansas and Indian Territory, he was shocked by what he found. "The people everywhere are in a great state of anxious fear," he reported to Secretary of War Edwin Stanton. The lower Trans-Mississippi border resembled more a wilderness than civilization. Moreover, Curtis found that irregulars had blended into society "disguised as citizens." They had become adept at not only hiding in the hills, hollows, and thickets of the region but also among the civilian population. Concerning the significance of the guerrilla threat throughout the region, the general concluded, "The public apprehension of danger is well founded."[16]

Curtis pleaded with Stanton to send more help to the area. The state of things in his district was "sickening and painful," he wrote, "the people [of

Kansas] are devoted, innocent, patient lovers of our institutions, but they have been denounced, distrusted, and . . . cruelly neglected." Even worse, Curtis observed, the "villains who have perpetuated the horrid crimes against all civilized and savage warfare" had been neither stopped nor punished. Something needed to be done. With only a force of "dismounted, decimated, half-starved, and undisciplined Indians" south of Fort Scott, he noted, there was little chance to wage an effective war against Confederate and guerrilla forces.[17]

No matter how vigorously Curtis sought reinforcements, he was denied them at the highest levels. The war elsewhere had drained manpower and resources from the Trans-Mississippi border. Campaigns the previous summer and fall at Helena, Vicksburg, and Little Rock had pulled thousands of guerrilla-fighting Federals from the western regions. By the spring of 1864, provost marshal reports stated that the Department of Kansas had over fifteen thousand troops. In reality, Curtis had less than ten thousand men, and most of them were busy patrolling northern portions of the borderlands around Lawrence and Kansas City. The area between Forts Scott, Gibson, and Smith remained largely unguarded.[18]

Commanders in Washington, however, believed the provost marshal general's inflated report concerning troop levels in the department. In reality, Curtis's counterguerrilla force had dwindled to less than seven thousand men by April 1864. Word reached General in Chief Ulysses S. Grant that Curtis wanted more troops to thwart guerrilla actions. Knowing only the inflated figures, Grant balked at his request and told Chief of Staff Henry W. Halleck, "I am satisfied you would hear the same call if they were stationed in Maine." Halleck, for his part, assumed that any increase in troop numbers for Curtis would give him twenty thousand men in his command, far more than necessary, he reported to Grant, to "oppose 2,000 guerrillas." Such misinformation only exacerbated the irregular warfare along the Trans-Mississippi border.[19]

By March, Union officials sought a clearer picture of the border region than that provided by Curtis. The War Department ordered Inspector General Randolph B. Marcy to tour parts of the western Trans-Mississippi and to suggest more-effective policies for waging war there. Marcy reported that Union forces in general *perpetuated* irregular warfare in the region through their harsh treatment of guerrilla prisoners and the civilians suspected of aiding them. "It has been the custom in many parts of the department for officers and soldiers, when operating against guerrillas," he reported, "to immediately put to death all who fall into their hands, even after they have thrown down their arms and asked for mercy." Officers to the rank of colonel had regularly given orders to "bring in no prisoners." Such strategy, though emanating from the inherent and ever-growing frustration experienced by Federal forces, had "induced many [Confederate sympathizers] to continue their guerrilla warfare, and to make them fight to desperation, as they dare not return to their homes or give themselves up to the military authorities for fear of being instantly put to death."[20]

Viewing clearly an increasingly complicated situation, Marcy also suggested that soldiers stationed near their homes be relocated. The proximity of local men recruited to use deadly force, and who had often sought revenge for wrongs committed against their families or property, was unhealthy for controlled warfare. Such soldiers, Marcy warned, were "very prone to use the power which their military positions give them to accomplish unwise purposes." "The evils of this are seen on every hand along the beautiful country bordering Kansas," he continued, "where nearly all the houses, barns, and fences have been burned to the ground, [and] it is unsafe for a man, either Union or rebel, to live away from the immediate vicinity of the military stations." The inspector general's perceptions were partially correct. Union soldiers and militiamen often exacted harsh retribution against irregulars who operated in their communities, but Wisconsin and Indiana soldiers visited destruction on the region as well. In the end, relocation of locally recruited soldiers rarely occurred, and "murder, highway robbery, pillage, and other kindred crimes" continued unabated until the end of the war.[21]

The Confederate perspective was little better. The confused and broken state of things on the border disturbed J. O. Shelby. No stranger to the destructive nature of warfare in the region, General Shelby was nevertheless shaken by what he observed. "The condition of this country is and has been pitiable in the extreme," the Missourian wrote in late May 1864. But the Federals were not entirely to blame. Indeed, the war had devolved into a state of anarchy for which, even Shelby admitted, pro-Confederate combatants held some responsibility. "Confederate soldiers in nothing save the name, robbers, and jayhawkers have vied with the Federals in plundering, devouring, and wasting the substance of loyal Southerners," lamented the general, with typical flair. Loosely organized Confederate forces and guerrillas had made unlikely acquaintances with what Shelby called "predatory bands of Federals, unmolested and unfought, [who] roamed about like devouring wolves and swept whole neighborhoods at a breath." Such irregulars, albeit disowned by Shelby, had joined the Yankees in running "rough-shod over defenseless families." The country and its people were in ruins. Regular and honorable Confederate forces moving into the region would "find an enemy worse than armed men—starvation." Loyal residents, Shelby lamented, had been compelled by the actions of Confederate and Union forces alike to take refuge in Federal posts. Everyone in the region—rebels, Yankees, and civilians—agreed at least on one thing: the war had become desperate and unyielding.[22]

Within such a complex and frustrating situation, Union commanders continued to deal with an increasing flood of refugees. In March 1864, over 220 African Americans left Fort Smith for Kansas. They were soon replaced by several Unionist families from the surrounding area. A thirty-five-man Federal scouting party set off to escort local civilians to the fort, soon rounding up "20 teams, a large number of cattle and sheep . . . , [and] scores of women and children." The motley wagon train quickly moved back toward Fort Smith with bounty and burden. On the column's last night before reaching town, at around 10:00 P.M., guerrillas attacked. According to one soldier, upon hearing the shots, "our boys sprang to their posts, carbine and revolver in hand, ready to receive the bandits." But as soon as the firing had started, all was quiet. The assailants melted back into the darkness, leaving the terrorized civilians huddled in or behind their bullet-riddled wagons.[23]

Union commanders issued orders to get the upper hand in the increasingly maddening struggle. In a detailed and well-planned "Circular of Instruction," Col. Thomas Moonlight of the Eleventh Kansas laid out strategy for control, if not victory, over the guerrillas. Union counterguerrilla patrols would be organized in southeast Kansas to cover the countryside on a daily basis, never allowing the irregulars a break. The soldiers' duty was not "to simply go from station to station, but . . . to scour the country searching for armed men in rebellion." Nor should these patrols fall into a predictable routine. They must leave and return at different hours and from different directions, less the enemy memorize their schedule "with murderous intent" and lay in ambush. Rigorous adherence to such a policy would not only ensure the safety of Union patrols but also convince the guerrilla that "*there is no safety for him on Kansas Soil.*"[24]

Beyond such counterinsurgency missions, Moonlight instructed the patrols to befriend loyal residents and to win their trust. "Every farmer will become a sentinel," the colonel pledged, "and every homestead a dwelling place of loyalty and happiness." The only factor that might bring such a policy to a crashing halt were the actions of the troops themselves. Here, Moonlight provided a stern warning by guaranteeing "punishment meted out as deserved" to any soldier or officer who violated "the rights and privileges guaranteed to every loyal citizen of the United States." This circular represented yet another attempt not only to achieve an upper hand against irregulars but also, and just as importantly, to rein in federal troops. Nonetheless, little notable change occurred, and frustrations on the western border simmered.[25]

Commanders' tours, unanswered recommendations, and new strategies notwithstanding, warmer days with the onset of spring led to increased guerrilla activity. Here again, the environment shaped the course and conduct of the Civil War on the border. With a more hospitable countryside, less extreme weather (except for occasional severe storms), and ample food for animals and soldiers alike, the brutality redoubled in the spring and summer of 1864. Guerrillas now had not only increased access to food and forage but also more places to hide. Central to their general attempt to frustrate the Union forces and terrorize Unionist civilians remained their ability to melt into the landscape as quickly as they emerged from it to attack.

In early April just outside of Fayetteville, a small group of Union cavalrymen took their horses out to graze in fresh grass. A group of over twenty guerrillas soon approached and hid in a nearby thicket undetected. A few of them had on Union uniforms and rode into the Yankee camp. Their ruse was so successful that the troopers invited them to dinner. The guerrillas-in-disguise then lured eight of the men into the nearby woods, where they were shot down. An editorial in the Fort Smith *New Era* later reproved the irregulars' proclivity for such deception. "It was shown to be a common practice of this class of the secesh pro-slavery chivalry," the writer said, "to put on the Federal uniform for the purpose of rendering their schemes of assassination and thieving more effective."[26]

After the killings, the balance of the guerrillas made their escape, though four were soon captured, given a speedy trial, and sentenced to death by firing squad. Union troops moved these young rebels to Fort Smith, where they were put in chains and forced into small holding cells. In the unusually lengthy time between their capture and execution, they had the opportunity to write letters to their loved ones. Each showed elements of defiance and remorse. Guerrilla John Norwood admitted to his family that he had "been a verry wicked [man] in time but I hope that God will forgive me. . . . My short life is done." His colleague William Carey wrote that he thought he would "die in a just cause if not I hope God wil forgive me." The guerrillas seemed to bend under the hardships of confinement. "As hopes of escape grew dimmer and vanished away," wrote Rev. Francis Springer, who accompanied the condemned partisans, "the wretched men became indifferent about the cause for which they had enlisted as soldiers and marauders." On the day of execution, each young rebel was released from his small cell, loaded onto a wagon, and taken nearly a mile to a clearing where over sixty men from the Thirteenth Kansas Infantry awaited. Forty-eight of the Yankee soldiers would carry out the simultaneous executions, with the remainder in reserve in case the first volley did not fully do the job. Each guerrilla knelt beside his coffin, and an officer read aloud the charges against them. They were soon blindfolded, with their hands tied behind their backs. Some could be heard praying aloud, and one of the guerrillas started singing "We'll all meet in heaven to part no more." The soldiers in attendance remained silent. For one witness, "it was the awful and significant silence that immediately proceeded the provost's signal, the ominous click of forty-eight guns pointed directly at the kneeling [convicts]." A moment later the four guerrillas lay "prostrate and bleeding by their coffins." Such was only one of hundreds of executions in the region, yet it reflects anxiety and anarchy punctuated by small bits of harsh retributive justice; to be sure, it went both ways. Reverend Springer made sense out of this generally senseless situation: "The most painful reflection awakened by the sad ceremonial was that selfish, faithless, and traitorous citizens should have stirred a strife that precipitates into the vortex of crime, ignominy, and ruin of so many of the young men of our once peaceful, prosperous, and happy country."[27]

Amid this new season of war, newspapers issued warnings of nascent violence and terror to their readership. "We desire to forewarn our citizens of any movements made by the guerrillas," one editor cautioned in May, "so they may be prepared for any emergency." Civilians along the border doubtlessly read such words with foreboding. "It is certain that the former successes have whetted the appetite for plunder and blood of these outlaws," the editorial continued, "and should an opportunity offer, we may be certain there will be further robbery and murder . . . in the coming season"—dire predictions, indeed. The few newspapers in regular publication spent a remarkable amount of space not simply reporting the war but also cautioning readers to beware of imminent attack. "Let our citizens, especially on the border be on alert," one paper instructed, "it is impossible to exercise too much vigilance. . . . Every man that has a gun or a horse in the country, should have them ready for service." According to another article that May, "the country . . . seems to be infested by daring outlaws, many of them having gone to the 'brush' since the opening of spring." Such an atmosphere of fear and terror defined the very nature of the border war, as did the regular inclusion of civilians either actively defending themselves with guns and saving themselves with horses.[28]

Hundreds more civilians simply fled the region altogether that spring. "During the past week about 100 wagons belonging to refugees have crossed the river . . . on their way to Kansas," a Fort Smith editor noted, "in search of peace and quietude, which they are not permitted to enjoy . . . on account of the ravages of bushwhackers." Like the thousands who had preceded them, a seemingly endless line of refugees continued to pour through Fort Smith for Kansas or other points north. In addition to the very real and ubiquitous threat of violence, they feared the harsh environment that they could no longer control. They fled north with what little they could carry, an observer wrote, in order "to avoid utter destruction for want of food next winter, as there will be but little raised outside of the influence of the different Forts we occupy."[29]

The flood of refugees put considerable strain on Federal commanders. In late May Brig. Gen. John Thayer complained to Maj. Gen. Frederick Steele about dwindling supplies and urged him to "send up all the boats that can be spared from the Rock, as the river is in good boating condition." The soldiers' livelihood, not to mention that of the civilians, was at the mercy of the Arkansas River's fluctuating water levels, which Thayer recognized: "it is of vital importance to get all the supplies here which it is possible to do while the river lasts." The continuing influx of people from the countryside only compounded the supply problem and lent extra urgency to taking advantage of the navigable river. "There are over 1,000 refugees, completely destitute, whom we have to feed," Thayer lamented to his superior. Having little ability to feed them all for long, he immediately ordered hundreds to Kansas under military escort and warned Steele that he would "have to send a lot [of civilians] down the river by boats in order to get them to some pointe where supplies are more plenty, for I cannot feed them here, and they must starve if I do not." Caring for hungry and destitute noncombatants was a big enough job to keep all the Union troops busy, yet they still needed to maintain pressure on guerrillas and stay vigilant for any regular Confederate movements in the region. Although it always had been complex and brutal, the war on the border had evolved into something much more by 1864. Environmental hardships and guerrilla warfare underscored a situation wrought with anxiety and terror.[30]

Farther north, Charles Fletcher "Fletch" Taylor's partisan band, having returned from a winter respite in Texas, raided Lamar in southwest Missouri. Receiving belated word of the irregulars' presence in that part of the state, the Third Wisconsin Cavalry gave chase from Fort Scott. The regiment arrived in Lamar too late. Local Unionists, including approximately twenty-five enrolled militia and as many civilians, had taken the matter into their own hands. According to one Federal trooper, the "citizens had them cleaned out 21 hours before wee got there." Any civilians who remained on the border this late in the war had effectively turned from being victims to being combatants. Taylor's men, meeting intense resistance from groups of civilians and local militia, did what nearly every irregular force did in such a situation: they fled.[31]

The Third Wisconsin followed the guerrillas' trail out of town the next morning. After a hard thirty-mile ride, the cavalrymen entered a densely wooded area and were surprised by Taylor's rear guard. The guerrillas poured a heavy fire into their ranks, but the Wisconsin horsemen pressed forward and returned the fire. The rebels again fled. This time, to the Federals' consternation, the partisans "took to the Mountains and got Clear."[32]

The cavalrymen soon found the house where the guerrillas had stayed. An elderly woman, a young woman, and four small children had housed and fed Taylor's force the previous night. After a brief interrogation, the Federals found that the "old woman" was an avowed Confederate sympathizer and then went to work. "Wee wair ordard to fead our horses and take what wee wanted for our own use," one trooper reported, "and then set fiar to the rest of the house and stables and evrything." The women and children, with no shelter, were left with only bedding and some food. Vengeance was exacting.[33]

Before riding back to Fort Scott, the Union cavalrymen further questioned the older woman. Her responses were blunt and forceful. "The old woman told the boys that her husband and 2 sons was in the army under Prise and that her husband was killed," Hugh Sloan reported to his wife, "and her sones was in Talors command bushwhacking, and that she was a braiv woman and paid 2000 dolars a year to the suthering Confedericy and she cheard for Jef Davis." The woman brazenly continued, explaining to the Federals, "This was the 3 time [for her] to be burned out and that she did not cair, for her sones could make it up in a short time out of the Yankay sons of biches."[34] Clearly invested in the conflict, this southwest Missouri woman was not afraid of the Union cavalry. She and her grandchildren went physically unharmed only because they were female. Frustrated by their failed attempt to catch Taylor's guerrillas, the Third Wisconsin burned six more structures on its way back to Fort Scott.

Feeling guilty for his participation, if only by association, in burning out civilians and seizing their food and supplies, Sloan assured his wife that he had little control over the destruction. "I had no hand in burning the house or property but I did take corn a nuf to fead my horse and bakin a nuf for 2 days [rations]." He made clear to her, "it may look hard to you for mee to doe so but that is going to be oure buisnes for this summer and I must doe what I am toald." For the Third Wisconsin Cavalry, what had occurred outside Lamar had been nothing out of the ordinary. Indeed, by the latter half of the war, such units were designed and maintained for counterguerrilla operations. With some exceptions, Union cavalry along the western Trans-Mississippi border rarely participated in "regular" battles. Instead, they were guerrilla hunters, and a vital part of that job was bringing the war to those civilians suspected of having supported rebel irregulars.[35]

The old woman and children were certainly not alone. At seventeen years old, Priscilla Hunter was desperate for the war to let up in southwest Missouri. Writing to relatives in Illinois, she worried, "If times don't get any better by Fall, I think most of the [remaining] families will leave here but I do not know where they will go." Her mother further explained the situation: "We are blessed with good health but not with peace. Our country is in bad condition. . . . I will try and not fear the wicked. If they take all I have and burn my house, perhaps I will be able to walk off." The very thought of what irregular warfare might bring, then, played a seminal role in shaping the lives (and fears) of people like the Hunters. They had become victims in an anarchic society.[36]

While the Hunters wondered how long they could hold out at their home, Martha Clark was attacked by a band of guerrillas. Knowing that her husband, who had been gunned down just weeks before, had been a devout Unionist, the irregulars tore through Clark's house, stealing what valuables they could find. They threatened to torch the place if she did not give them everything they requested, so she acquiesced.[37]

Then the guerrillas spotted Clark's twelve-year-old son. Resting on the very edge of manhood, for the guerrillas he represented a budding Unionist. They turned on young Clark with every intention of killing him until his mother "grabbed his arm pleading for [his] life." The boy's age did not deter the guerrillas. As they jerked him from his screaming mother, one of them exclaimed, "He's old enough to fire a gun, and he's old enough to kill." At this the boy managed to rip himself free of their grasp, bolting from the house and hiding outside until the frustrated guerrillas left the premises. Surprisingly, they left without torching the house but nevertheless inflicted terror on the woman and her son. No longer could Clark live without the fear of losing her twelve-year-old boy, whose only fault was that he was old enough to pull a trigger.[38]

In the late summer of 1864, a group of Enrolled Missouri Militia in the southwest part of the state was surprised by guerrillas. The militiamen had been stationed in Carthage when, just outside of town, they were caught off guard and quickly shot down by a much larger group of irregulars. Immediately after the brief engagement, wounded soldiers who could not escape were shot on the spot until dead. Even men who had clearly died in the ambush were shot again. One Union soldier, Lee Blake, had been shot in the hip and lay on the field unable to escape. Bleeding and in excruciating pain, Blake had the forethought to play dead. He took slow, shallow breaths as the guerrillas debated what course to take. In the end they were not satisfied with the bloodied, seemingly lifeless bodies of the unfortunate militiamen. Blake could hear them walk to each corpse, cock their revolvers, and fire into his comrades' heads. Amid the intense and terrifying scene, one guerrilla questioned the efficacy of wasting ammunition on what seemed already to be corpses. As they debated the situation, another who had overheard the conversation insisted that "dead men tell no tales." He then rode up to Blake's seemingly lifeless body, cocked the hammer on his musket, and shot him in the face. Remarkably, the militiaman survived to tell the tale.[39]

The engagement had been particularly trying for Martha Clark and Elizabeth Baker. Their husbands were killed by the guerrillas, and being so close to home, the two women witnessed much of the fight. In court testimony after the war, Clark claimed that the rebels had "inflicted three mortal wounds" on her husband. After his death, she told the court, she had "the sole duty of supporting, nursing, clothing, and educating her orphan children."[40] As for Elizabeth Baker, her husband had been shot down when he attempted to escape. In gruesome detail she reported that a guerrilla's bullet went into his body ten inches deep and left an entry wound of a half-inch in his back. The brutal murder had caused her "great distress of mind," and her husband's killing had left her alone to support their children.[41]

In addition to guerrilla actions plaguing the region, Union soldiers, hardened by years of irregular warfare and all its uncertainties and frustrations, increasingly vented their anger against residents. In August, as Confederate forces organized an invasion of Missouri, Federal cavalrymen had become "beastly drunk" just outside of Van Buren. Christian Isely of the Second Kansas Cavalry reported that members of the Sixth Kansas Cavalry "most shamefully abused some poor old citizens, an old man and woman and several boys who met us in the road going peacefully along." The troopers had gotten out of hand, and the officer in charge was "so drunk that he did not know what he was doing." Angered by such conduct, Isley told the lieutenant that, although he would "obey and follow an Officer as long as there is one of us left, [he refused] to obey Whiskey any further." The sober portion of the counterguerrilla patrol wrested control of the mission from the drunken troopers and, until the lieutenant sobered, placed a "whole souled" sergeant in command.[42]

Besides hurting innocent civilians, Isely was troubled by his comrades' conduct in an area where "bushwhackers were reported thick." Noisily abusing an elderly couple and young boys presented ideal bait for attracting guerrillas. Isely and his fellow Kansans were spared any such attacks on this outing, but the event made a distinct impression. The old and young, trying to survive in a region largely abandoned, could trust no one. Not only did guerrillas plague the area, but regular Union cavalry, under the command of a drunken lieutenant, roamed the roadways. Such disorderly conduct reflected the constant stress and frustration that underscored the civilians' plight on the border.[43]

Just weeks later another detachment of Kansas troops happened upon a house full of guerrillas not far from Van Buren. Capt. Marion N. Beeler was doubtlessly surprised at his good fortune of finding over twenty "bushwhackers" trapped in the building, which his troops quickly surrounded. Although Beeler's men urged him to wait until morning before attacking, he was impatient and excited. The captain gave the order to charge. In the ensuing chaos, with few able to clearly see what was happening, the guerrillas sprang from the structure and fired as they ran for their lives. Most made their escape. In the aftermath the Kansans found Beeler with a fatal bullet wound in the stomach. He lingered the rest of the night and died the next morning.[44]

Farther north in Fayetteville, Col. M. La Rue Harrison, charged with operating the Federal post there, realized that antiguerrilla patrols alone had little effect. Instead, in late summer Harrison launched a campaign to destroy the food sources used by irregular forces. Pleased with the short-term success of his strategy, the colonel reported that "the disabling of mills causes more writhing among bushwhackers than any other mode of attack." Hurting as they were from the loss of Walter's Mill, Brown's Mill, and Dutch Mill, all within a two-county radius of Fayetteville, the guerrillas threatened "to stay and fight [Harrison] on boiled acorns." Try as he may, Harrison could not stop trees from producing acorns, and although frustrating local irregulars, including the guerrilla owner of one of the mills, the policy had hurt local civilians and the Federal soldiers as much as anyone. If wartime production equaled prewar production figures, the mill closures deprived the local economy of approximately forty-five thousand dollars annually.[45]

Although acorn-fed guerrillas often worked alone, one of the best markers of irregular and regular Confederate cooperation occurred in the early fall of 1864, when Lt. Gen. Edmund Kirby Smith ordered Sterling Price to gather the strongest remaining forces in Arkansas and launch what turned out to be the Confederate army's last major offensive in the Trans-Mississippi theater. Smith's orders were straightforward: conquer Missouri by raising a large force of new recruits from that state, of which he was confident there were thousands, and return with them to Arkansas to retake the Trans-Mississippi. Such a successful campaign in Price's home state would alter the course of the war, both west and east of the Mississippi River, and relieve pressure on Southern armies in the East by compelling the redeployment of more Federal troops across the Mississippi. A successful invasion would lead to the capture of Saint Louis and, therefore, nominal control of the river. Taking that city would also help rally the remainder of Missouri, demoralize Federal troops there, and equip Price's command for further conquest. If such a venture failed, warned Smith, Price's troops should "retreat through Kansas and Indian Territory, sweeping that country of its mules, horses, cattle, and military supplies of all kinds."[46]

Not coincidentally, Price's campaign coincided with national and state elections in 1864. For the rebel general, even if his army did not end Federal control in Missouri, a good showing might make a significant difference in the elections that fall and winter, perhaps tipping the balance against President Lincoln himself. To this effect, General Curtis remarked that the Confederates' timing found "the whole country engaged in the great National and State political campaign, the very crisis of which seemed to culminate with Price's progress through Missouri. Motives, measures, and men were all distrusted." Price's Raid, as it became known, proved a significant Confederate effort, if ultimately faltering, to change the course of the war regionally and nationally.[47]

The failed foray into Missouri nevertheless incited a higher than usual volume of guerrilla attacks along the western Trans-Mississippi border. The results, however, proved largely unhelpful for the Southern cause and injurious to civilians. To be sure, most bands had never been terribly concerned with official Confederate war strategy (even if it might help "Old Pap"), and for the most part, Confederate commanders were displeased with such efforts to supposedly aid them. After his failed Missouri raid, Price lamented that the irregulars he had once counted on had botched the endeavor miserably. The general thenceforth discounted their utility as a military force. Useful or not in a battlefield sense, irregulars were exceedingly adept at wreaking havoc on the civilian population. And if they did nothing more than that during Price's Raid, they certainly played a critical role in furthering social and physical devastation throughout the region.[48]

Not surprisingly then, already struggling towns and rural areas suffered dearly in the fall of 1864. Carthage, a small town in southwest Missouri that had witnessed one of the first fights of the Civil War, was hit especially hard by the increased irregular activity. Well protected earlier that year by a Federal cavalry contingent that had since been ordered away, the town was now ungarrisoned. Noting this, General Sanborn ordered a unit of the Enrolled Missouri Militia to fill the vacant post. The troubled and often untrustworthy militia was slow to respond to Sanborn's order, though, and Carthage was left dangerously exposed.[49]

On the cool morning of September 22, while Price's columns closed in on Pilot Knob in southeast Missouri, young Carthage resident D. L. Wheeler and his fourteen-year-old sister were finishing their chores. Their mother was not at home, and their father was away looking for a place to relocate the family. Suddenly, Wheeler saw several armed men in civilian clothes, known to him as "bushwhackers or guerrillas," riding into town. From their vantage point just off the town square, he and his sister saw townspeople carrying their things into the street as "several columns of rising smoke showed the buildings to be fired."[50]

A guerrilla rode up and told the terrified children that they must leave, for "the building was to be burned." As the man set fire to a pile of cotton in the corner of the house, Wheeler's sister begged him to stop. At first acquiescing, he changed his mind and "lighted it again, saying that if he did not burn the place, the other boys would." After more pleading by the teenaged girl, the guerrilla finally put out the fire and left. The reprieve did not last long. Soon, as the first had warned, other partisans came in and told Wheeler and his sister "to get whatever they wanted to save out into the street . . . , [helping them] with the things that were too heavy." Here were children fighting to save their property. Their battle was not about nationalism or strategy, but about preserving their livelihood. Thanks to the strained benevolence of their adversaries, they succeeded in preserving some of their property, but the seemingly thoughtful guerrillas went ahead and torched the house. Two more children had become homeless refugees.[51]

Sara Ann Smith and her two children were also present when Carthage was burned. "I saw a crowd of bushwhackers riding into town from the west," Smith remembered. "You could always tell bushwhackers because they wore feathers, bunches of ribbon, etc., in their hats." As they did with the young Wheelers, the guerrillas offered to assist Smith and her children by carrying belongings out of the house before setting it ablaze. "We carried out such stuff as we wanted," stated Smith, "but a good deal of our property we left because we had nowhere to take it anyhow."[52] Indeed, she was not alone in being destitute with nowhere to go after the torching of Carthage. Many homeless residents gathered in barns and in the few remaining houses outside of town until they were able to leave the area for good.

Col. Charles Blair at Fort Scott soon received reports of the calamity. "Two of my scouts were on a hill in sight and saw some houses burning and about fifteen men running in town," Blair stated. In addition to painstakingly clearing and burning civilian homes and businesses, the guerrillas made short work igniting the county jail, public seminary, public records building, and what was left of the courthouse. Blair's men "supposed it to be a small force of . . . local bushwhackers," but he knew well that Price's bold move into southeastern Missouri had been the instigator.[53]

Unionist civilians also understood that this escalation in guerrilla activity was due in large part to Price's raid. "We hear old Price is within forty miles of Springfield with ten thousand men," wrote Priscilla Hunter from southwestern Missouri; "we don't know when they will be here." Although the general's troops were not nearly so close as she and her neighbors had feared, confusion and fear permeated most households as reports and rumors poured in. Moreover, the largest town in the immediate area had just been burned. Hunter explained the situation to her sister: "The bushwhackers burnt Carthage a few days ago. The [Union] Malitia was called off from there. We are looking for a raid all of the time."[54]

As Price and his beleaguered army finally passed through the western Trans-Mississippi border on their way to safety in northern Texas, they let loose their frustrations on any hapless Unionist civilians they encountered. These Confederates "did give us but one robbing," claimed Elizabeth Hunter, "and that was a pretty severe one." She explained: "They took two or three blankets, one thick comforter, two sheets and burnt another, stript all my pillows, Palmyras shoes, twelve or fourteen pounds soda, all my spice, Richards old yellow hat, Mag's saddle, and a lot of other things too tedious to mention."[55]

In addition to robbing the Hunter women of almost all they had, soldiers set fire to the ladies' straw beds in order to ignite their house. They then moved on, satisfied with their minor victory of theft and arson. As the last bed became engulfed in flames, threatening to spread throughout the house, Hunter carefully picked up the burning mattress and tossed it outside. "The straw smoke was so thick and strong I would work a little while then have to run [to] the door to get my breath," she wrote. Contemplating the ordeal afterward, she concluded that the Confederates would have ensured the house's destruction had they not been "afraid the feds were pursuing."[56]

Fort Scott citizens feared a similar fate. People in the town were in an uproar as Price's troops continued south. Hundreds of people fled in fear that the Confederates might veer west and destroy the fort. "Women, children, and a few cowardly men were flying in all directions," reported one newspaper editor, "and the little handful of heroes here, had nerved themselves for a death struggle against seven thousand rebels." The bulk of the Union forces in the region, pursuing Price from behind, had little chance to help Fort Scott from impending attack. And the town, as the editor continued, "could . . . have been bought for a very small consideration." In the end, however, Price bypassed Fort Scott to the east by about five miles. No attack materialized, and dozens of townswomen worked overnight to prepare food for the pursing Union soldiers who would soon appear.[57]

The core of the defeated Confederate army moved quickly along the border, then into Indian Territory, while according to one Union officer, a "mob of bushwhackers, recruits, deserters, and camp-followers . . . plundered from one end to the other." What had just weeks before resembled regular, if downtrodden, Southern units had become the very thing that had for so long plagued the region. Guerrillas who had worked in tandem with Price's troops now "moved off in other directions in search of innocent and defenceless victims whom they could rob and murder." While these irregulars certainly proved particularly destructive in the wake of Price's failed foray into Missouri, Union troops also took their toll on the countryside.[58]

From the Southern perspective, however, the desolate country they passed through along the Trans-Mississippi border was entirely the Yankees' work. William M. McPheeters, a surgeon for the Confederate army, had participated in the failed campaign into Missouri. He was shocked by the war-torn landscape as the beleaguered troops approached southwest Missouri and northeast Indian Territory. After a seventeen-hour march, McPheeters entered Carthage, or as he confided in his diary, "what it once was, for it had been destroyed by the Yankees." After leaving what was left of that town behind, McPheeters and the rapidly retreating Confederates entered another county seat at Pineville—"a complete mess of ruin. . . . [T]he whole country through which we have passed for days has been desolated by the Yankees—a commentary on Yankee civilization." Finally, Price's men reached the very heart of the lower Trans-Mississippi border where, as the surgeon noted, "Ark., Mo., and the Indian Nation come together." McPheeters elaborated: "the country through which we passed yesterday and today has been desolated and almost depopulated by the Yankees. . . . [C]onsequently, we got no forage for the horses last night and none tonight."[59]

When the majority of Price's frazzled soldiers turned west to avoid the rugged Boston Mountains and the Federal stronghold at Fort Smith, most of the Union pursuers pulled back. They had effectively expelled the Confederates from Missouri and had devastated their ranks. But the theft and violence surrounding the failed raid was far from over. Indeed, although much of what McPheeters had so persistently blamed on the Yankees represented half the truth, severe depredations by frustrated Federals did occur in the wake of the fleeing army.

Segments of the Union army proved as destructive as had Price's minions. Most notably, Col. Charles Jennison's Seventh Kansas Cavalry refocused its efforts from chasing Price to raiding civilians. "Where he passed," one Union commander complained bitterly, "the people are almost ruined, as their houses were robbed of the beds and bedding." Jennison's exploits, in addition to those of many of the Seventh Kansas's fellow regiments, were every bit as destructive as guerrilla raids. "In many cases," one Union captain wrote, "every blanket and quilt were taken; also their clothing and every valuable that could be found." Kansas troops left little behind.[60]

What these residents had been able to accumulate for survival, especially for the coming winter, was taken or destroyed by Jennison's men. "All the horses, stock, cattle, sheep, oxen and wagons were driven off," continued the disgusted captain, "what the people are to do is difficult to see." For Federal soldiers, such wide-scale destruction was nothing new by late 1864, but Jennison's men took even this to the extreme. Their wagon train, laden with stolen goods and followed by herds of livestock, crossed into Kansas. The scene must have seemed as strange as it was brutal. Jennison's "warriors" doubtlessly rode proud as they pushed "as many as 200 sheep, 40 or 50 yoke of work oxen, 20 or 30 wagons, and a large number of horses, jacks and jennets, say 100, as they were leading their broken down horses and riding fresh ones." The Union captain reported to General Sanborn, "Threatening to burn houses in order to get money is the[ir] common practice." Jennison's men, he concluded, "acted worse than guerrillas." Along the western Trans-Mississippi border, no harsher insult existed among Union forces.[61]

The path of Union theft and violence against Confederate civilians continued south even with Price out of the picture. In northwest Arkansas soldiers incited even more destruction in an area already largely obliterated. According to one Confederate Arkansan, Union troops "came down the Arkansas and Indian Territory line, covering the country for five miles in width, robbing and then burning a great many homes." There certainly were not many remaining residences to rob or burn after years of warfare, yet some remained, and if their owners had any suspected Confederate connection, they were destroyed.[62]

A small group of soldiers from Jennison's Kansas Brigade went even further by "robbing and cursing the women" and capturing boys and old men. In one case this little band captured an elderly man and his fourteen-year-old son. They told the old man's wife and younger children as they rode away that they intended to kill both of them soon. "They passed a blackberry patch on the way," remembered one local, "and the boy dodged into it and escaped." The teen's father was not so fortunate. The Kansans quickly found a sturdy tree and lynched him while his son remained concealed.[63]

But the Federal spree of destruction had not ended with the old man's hanging. Nearby, according to another local, the Kansans "killed one of Price's sick soldiers at Jim Moore's home, searched his daughter for jewelry, and then burned his house and contents." The roving band moved on to destroy a significant amount of property at Cane Hill and "hanged three men who were innocent of any crime, and of them was a Union man." Three local women who suffered theft by Jennison's men had been forced to subsist for well over a week on potatoes. They also shared the responsibility of cleaning up the mess left in the marauders' wake. One of the women, fueled only by "Irish potatoes," "helped to cut down and bury old man Crozier, seventy five years old." According to neighbors, "his only crime [was] that he was a Southern man with sons in the Confederate army."[64]

Confederate guerrillas reasserted themselves in the region soon after Price's Raid. One local band in southwest Missouri confronted two Unionist men who had not yet left the region. As the guerrillas approached, wrote a neighbor, "Dr. Beck and Linz started to run. Linz jumped the yard fence, his father could not get over." Linz attempted to help his father get over the fence as the guerrillas closed in on horseback. Struggling, Beck pleaded with his son to run while he had the chance. Meanwhile, "old Rusk came up and shot the old man, and Linz [who was apparently armed] shot [Rusk] in the neck and run." Seeing this spectacle take place, Beck's wife ran to the fence and pleaded with the guerrillas not to harm her husband further. They did not listen and shot him repeatedly. Meanwhile, Linz tried to heed his murdered father's advice and save himself. Yet he was no match for the mounted assailants, who quickly chased him down, stripped him of his clothes, and stabbed him to death with their swords. Not satisfied with merely killing Mrs. Beck's husband and son, Rusk's guerrillas "burnt Dr. Beck's house and everything they had, money, medicine, and all."[65]

To neighbor Elizabeth Hunter's chagrin, the group's leader did not die of his wounds: "I suppose Rusk got over the wound Linz gave him. Pitty it did not go through his heart." She soon had good reason to wish the bullet had finished him. For nearly a week after the attack on the Beck home, Rusk and his band targeted Hunter and her children. "We saw them coming on the hill," she recalled. "I told Amy to run but she said she thought they was feds." Amy was wrong. Rusk and his men "came in the house and about the first thing [they wanted] was my greenback or they would burn my house. I told them they would have to burn it, for I had none." In the ensuing melee, the guerrillas "searcht everywhere [and] took all they wanted." Then to Hunter's chagrin, "they cut a hole in [the] straw bed and lit a match in it." In desperation and defiance, Hunter put out the fire, but the marauders would not be denied. They took the mattress off of the frame and set fire to it for good. The guerrillas then set another bed on fire and left the house, thinking that was all it would take to set the house ablaze. Elizabeth and her children were able to put out the fire, though, before it got out of hand. This was the second time in a matter of months that the Hunters had faced a guerrilla attack and prevented their home from burning down.[66]

Even after this, Elizabeth Hunter continued to struggle with the decision of whether to leave the region. After having been repeatedly robbed and threatened by guerrillas, she still wanted to hang on. But as winter approached in late 1864, she knew there would be little chance to survive if she and her family remained. "I think we will leave here in a few weeks," Elizabeth confessed to her daughter in Illinois, "I can't stay here this winter." Her other daughter, Priscilla, also felt mixed emotions about leaving her home. "I hate to live in such a place," she told her sister, "and I hate to leave it when I think of the good home we had in it. The horrid rebel is cause of it all."[67]

No longer could what was left of the region's shattered families remain. Up to the very last days before they departed, the Hunters had been worried that they were going to lose "the few little rags that the secesh left" them. In a last letter to her sister, Priscilla captured the complexity and uncertainty of the time. She had become accustomed to hiding and protecting as the most common of routines. Hunter told her sister that she had refused to weave clothing as winter neared because "we will not let the rebs have the pleasure of getting it." Hiding and surviving led to severe hardships, fear, and loneliness on the western border. The terror and almost constant uncertainty of day-to-day existence took a tremendous toll on the Hunters and countless others. "I almost dread for Sunday to come," Priscilla concluded her letter; "it don't appear like there ever could be anymore preaching here." The Hunters, like most other families who remained in the region, soon moved away.[68]

Families were broken by the deaths of husbands and sons, houses were burned, and the entire antebellum way of life had ceased to exist. The war had reached its peak in the area, and everyone felt it. In Fort Smith thousands of refugees crowded into the undersupplied town—so many that the Federal command ordered nearly 1,500 of them north to Fort Scott. Many had lived in the area since before the war, but overcrowding and harsh conditions made the move imperative. "Among those leaving are many leading Union men who enjoyed the confidence and esteem of loyal men," admonished a local editor, "who, with the wreck of their former competence, are compelled to start life among strangers." The refugees and enough supplies to get them to Fort Scott were loaded on nearly two hundred wagons for the journey. Federal cavalry escorted them to Kansas.[69]

On January 19, 1865, east of Fort Smith, a small Confederate force disabled and destroyed two Union steamboats on the Arkansas River. The vessels had been transporting supplies, soldiers, and civilian refugees from Fort Smith to Little Rock. From the dense underbrush, thick enough even in January to conceal a large force, rebels surprised the *Chippewa* with a barrage of musketry and shells from one cannon, raking it from "stern to stern." Those on board the boat had little choice but to surrender. The Confederates paroled the white civilian passengers, but African Americans were "taken off" and Union soldiers were placed under guard.[70]

Federal troops on the other steamer, the *Annie Jacobs*, returned fire to little avail. They were soon driven into a sandbar on the opposite side of the river. Although some escaped into the river weeds, many women and children, fearing the steamer might explode under the galling Confederate fire, "jumped overboard and were drowned." The attackers killed nearly thirty Union soldiers and took over eighty prisoners. For the Unionist paper in Fort Smith, this surprise attack on steamers laden with civilian refugees was unforgivable. The area where the attack had occurred east of the fort, one editor made clear, had been a "favorite resort" for irregulars. "We doubt not the latter will be speedily attended to," he concluded.[71] Nevertheless, violence persisted on the Trans-Mississippi border into 1865. Just months before the end of the war, civilians still suffered and died.

One hundred and fifty miles to the north in southwest Missouri, progress against insurgency had been imperceptible. Charged with catching livestock and feral stock in the region for the Union army, Nathan Bray reported complete failure. "The Bushwhackers [have] become so numerous," Bray wrote to General Sanborn, "that I could do nothing in Jasper County in slaughtering hogs." The guerrillas had frustrated his efforts and killed one of his hands, who left behind "a large and helpless family." As for Bray, he narrowly escaped harm during the attack, having received "five bullet holes in [his] clothing" and losing two horses, supplies, and weapons.[72]

Those civilians who had remained in Federal strongholds hoping to avoid situations like Bray had found himself in, nevertheless faced appalling conditions during the war's final months. Frustration, boredom, and fear intermingled to contribute to a harsh environment throughout the countryside as well as in towns and forts. Discipline had long since disappeared, and apathy bred dangerous conditions in these crowded havens along the border. "In almost every street and alley, in holes and under houses may be seen numerous carcasses of horses, mules, [and] cows," complained a Fort Smith editor in January, "the sight is extremely disgusting and the smell, even at this time of the year . . . is anything but agreeable." Knowing well the potential problems dead and rotting animals might bring, he warned: "Unless the evil is speedily removed, sickness and death among towns people and troops will be the inevitable consequence."[73]

Just north of Fort Smith, Crawford County residents complained directly to Arkansas governor Isaac Murphy about the "deplorable condition of the country." Through much of 1864 and into 1865, they had dealt with two enemies: Confederate guerrillas and raucous Union soldiers. At any given time they could not discern whom to fear more, but they hoped Murphy might at least constrain the latter. Federal troops stationed in Fort Smith and Van Buren had stolen "everything of value." It was "impossible to keep a horse, a cow, an ox, a piece of meat, or a bushel of meal, unless so far hidden to defy their search." Worse than theft, they regularly abused locals. At times, claimed the petitioners, soldiers would "knock down and maim" civilians and carry out further "indignities." These same men visited "unheard of atrocities" upon civilians' at night, and with "perfect impunity" they abused loyal citizens "in the broad light of day." If residents complained to local authorities about these transgressions, their lives were threatened. In sum, the petitioners told the governor, Union troops sent to protect local civilians and wage war against Confederate guerrillas had instead brought "terror" to the people.[74]

In some cases soldiers went well beyond the typical crimes for which they were often accused. In February at least six Union soldiers, including an army chaplain, attacked four "respectable ladies" east of Fort Smith. The women were suspected of having had a great deal of money, but the attack went well beyond theft. As the women refused to give up the location of their valuables—if they really had any at all—the soldiers tortured them "over a slow fire till they were horribly mutilated about their heads, shoulders and feet . . . , from the effects of which one died and others were made cripples for life." According to the local newspaper, one soldier went even further and stood accused of "additional crimes upon the body of one of the victims which pen would shudder to record." If this were not enough, the Federals torched the women's houses when they left. The men stood accused of murder, torture, theft, and perhaps rape. Although newspapers were not known for their careful objectivity or thorough investigations, for a Union paper in Fort Smith to publish such a story was shocking. Regardless of what *exactly* happened to the women in question, it is clear that they were brutalized, resulting in the death of one. And although this extent of direct physical violence toward women was rare, it sent shockwaves through the community. Furthermore, another editor lamented, the crimes committed against these "highly respectable widow ladies" by Federal soldiers could only make matters worse in terms of Confederate reprisal. "It is useless to conceal that the burning, abusing and robbing of those unfortunate women will be made a pretext by the rebel guerrilla bands hovering in this part of the state," he wrote, "for severe retaliatory measures, and many a brave soldier, or staunch Union man, will be made to suffer." For civilian readers, such stories could only have intensified their desperation. For many, politics and military strategy no longer mattered. Their war was not about Unionism or Southern nationalism, and it certainly had little to do with sweeping military campaigns in Virginia or Tennessee. As it had been since the beginning, their war was about survival.[75]

Hundreds, perhaps thousands, of civilians fled north to escape this abuse, and the people who remained sought permission to build a fortified colony, one that might protect them from both "rebel marauders" and the "wickedness of these soldiers." They proposed to arm and sustain themselves in the fertile lowlands of the Arkansas River valley. Last holdouts in an emaciated society, these civilians were now willing to take matters of security into their own hands.[76]

Residents south of the river in Fort Smith fared little better. Just five days after Crawford County citizens voiced their complaints to Murphy, Union civilians in Fort Smith asked President Lincoln for relief. "The loyal people of this city and vicinity," they attested, "are now, and have been for some time past, to a considerable degree destitute of the necessaries of life." The reasons were numerous. Union soldiers had requisitioned the majority of supplies for themselves, and there existed little reliable "protection against guerrillas and other lawless persons in carrying on farming operations." The signees requested supplies earmarked for civilian consumption, and urged the government to act fast, for the river was notably unpredictable most of the year. The nearest railroad spur was hundreds of miles away, and only heavy spring rains ensured water high enough for steamboat traffic. "Thousands are awaiting your decision with the greatest anxiety," they concluded, "and will have to leave and abandon their all if not succored in time."[77]

It was February 1865, and there existed no discernible change in the region's situation. All anyone could do along the western Trans-Mississippi border was to hold out as refugees or perhaps band together to take care of one another. Rural homesteads were now relics of the past. Both Confederate guerrillas and Union soldiers had ravaged the countryside, and few civilians attempted to remain. For one newspaper editor, residents in Arkansas's western counties had borne the brunt of the conflict. "All have been plundered, and robbed, and left destitute," he declared, "and many have been driven from their homes." Even pro-Union Arkansans suspected Federal forces and their commanders of having systematically emptied the countryside of all vestiges of civilization. Such a policy of vacating the land, the editor continued, had persisted "until the country is depopulated, and thousands of starving women and children" turned into refugees. By one estimate, Union forces had pushed to Kansas "25,000 head of cattle . . . , four-fifths [of] which have been stolen from the people [and] thousands of horses, mules and carriages." Although Union commanders had thousands of refugees to feed both in Arkansas and Kansas, such excesses in relocating livestock and other goods encouraged a good deal of justified suspicion. Regular soldiers, the editor feared, had "become lost to all discipline or restraint, and [devastated] the country, pillaging and plundering until there was nothing left." Regardless of how accurate these charges were, the atmosphere of violence and terror was very real, even in areas perceived to have been safe havens for civilians and refugees.[78]

Throughout March 1865, Union troops in the Cherokee Nation continued to chase guerrillas. Those areas outside the immediate oversight of the garrison at Fort Gibson had turned into a dangerous wartime wilderness. As they had for much of the war, the guerrilla hunters had to contend as much with the environment as they did with their elusive foe. A portion of the Third Indian Regiment left Fort Gibson in mid-March to search for enemy irregulars in the region. Spotting a small band across the rain-swollen Deep Fork of the North Canadian River, they determined to cross at all costs. According to one officer, the largely Native American Union patrol traversed "over Deep Fork partly on a raft, partly on driftwood, and partly by swimming." The determined Federals could not find the fleeing enemy, who had used the flooded river to their advantage, but the frustrated troops did find "considerable quantities of cattle" on their way back to Fort Gibson. Reflecting on the war-torn nature of the region through which they patrolled, a captain remarked that "there are no citizens now living in that part of the country. . . . I was unable to find any grain." The terrain was rough, abandoned by noncombatants, and full of Confederate guerrillas and roaming cattle.[79]

In the last year of the war, troops wrangled cattle in Indian Territory as much as they hunted guerrillas. The river-swimming Federals near Fort Gibson found nearly 110 "average beef-cattle" and pushed them through the thickets and flooded creeks back toward their post. Along the way, these Union cowboys added nearly 100 more head to the herd. The troops successfully moved the animals to a pen that had been built on the banks of the Arkansas River. Native American refugees soon gathered for a chance at the beef. Union scout Charles O. Davis, who had played a big role in moving the herd, complained that these Indians "were crowding every pat and corner where they thought they might [have a] chance to get a beef." Chaos quickly followed as some of the hungry civilians hastily fired into the herd. The cattle stampeded and "scattered in every direction." An exasperated and tired Davis reluctantly followed orders to regather the herd, only a portion of which they were able to find.[80]

Davis's wartime cattle drive reflects the nature of the war in its final months on the Trans-Mississippi frontier. The conflict hinged on controlling the environment—terrain and animals alike. Free-ranging wild cattle had taken over the dense thickets and river bottoms throughout much of the Cherokee Nation and Indian Territory generally. They served as a critical food supply for guerrillas, Federals, and civilians alike. In this case Davis and his comrades successfully wrested them from the wilderness only to have many of them stampede back where they came from due to overzealous and famished civilians. This cattle drive further reflects the complexity of the war on the border. The war for the Federals had become far more than hunting irregulars in the woods. They now were responsible for finding not only a large portion of their own food but also that for the civilian refugees who were rapidly filtering back into Federal strongholds. For Yankee patrols, a typical scouting mission might consist of brutal fighting, cattle wrangling, and more generally a persistent struggle to maintain control over the environment.

From the first year of the war, Union commanders and soldiers had been continually frustrated in their attempts to control the guerrilla problem. Using a largely pro-Confederate population base, the environment, and perfected hit-and-run tactics, irregulars had mostly bested their better-supplied foes. Yet in their increasingly harsh attempts to crack down on guerrillas and their foundations of civilian support, the Union army had effectively wrought a war against everyone in the region. Precision attacks against specific irregular bands simply proved ineffective. Civilians had therefore become critical components in the Union counterinsurgency strategy. They had also become victims of violent excesses by both sides.

By March, the Federal commander at Fort Smith acknowledged the kind of civilian war that raged throughout the region. Brig. Gen. Cyrus Bussey pledged to act. Civilians had suffered for well over a year at the hands of Union soldiers, and as Bussey admitted, they "had nearly all been robbed of everything they had by the troops of this command, and are now left destitute and compelled to leave their homes to avoid starvation." He continued that "in most instances" livestock and supplies had "been taken and no receipts given, the people turned out to starve, and their effects loaded into trains and sent to Kansas." Equally troubling for the general, many civilians, especially women and children, were relatives of Federal soldiers in the district. The brutality of the situation became embarrassingly clear for Bussey and other Union commanders as those civilians who refused to flee organized into armed colonies, like the one proposed for Crawford County. Although Federal forces had never been able to protect loyal civilians completely, the last months of the war proved particularly trying. Law and order within the army itself, much less in the countryside, had slipped to an unprecedented low point. Bussey, however, had gained guarded support from many locals. "Gen. Bussey's moral character is without a blemish," wrote one newspaper editor; "the Augean stable will be cleaned, and discipline restored."[81]

Civilian efforts at self-preservation led to a short-lived but radical defensive mechanism through much of the western Arkansas in late 1864 and 1865: military farms, or fortified colonies. Able-bodied men in each colony formed into armed "Home Guard" companies and elected officers. They then chose a site close to both fresh water and fertile prairies for crops and livestock. Once an adequate location had been determined, the armed "colonists" built a stockade and storehouse. By March, each colony had close to one hundred men who worked together for their collective security. These communities were initiated to protect civilians, alleviate the need for continual military protection of civilians, stimulate agricultural production to feed both residents and Union soldiers, and deny irregulars the ability to live off the land. Concerning the all-important third objective, one editor declared, "No crops will be raised, except under [the colonist's] direction, and if the 'bushwhackers' wish to live off the country, they will have to purchase their board at a generous expenditure of powder and lead."[82]

No sooner had the plan been implemented, Maj. Gen. Joseph Reynolds ordered the evacuation of Union forces from western Arkansas. Mass protests followed. M. La Rue Harrison mounted an eloquent defense in favor of maintaining his forces in northwest Arkansas. "In the name and for the sake of the . . . families who will be left to the tender mercies of assassins and robbers," the colonel pleaded to his superior, "in the name of humanity, I beseech you to try and have the order countermanded." Harrison further explained that his forces had finally gained a modicum of control in certain fortified areas on the border, effectively shutting out guerrillas. Such a withdrawal as Reynolds ordered would prove disastrous so late in the war. If the army remained, at least in small numbers, the colonies would certainly harvest a bumper crop the next year. Although cavalry detachments helped protect the colonies, most of the outposts had been designed for self-sufficiency, Harrison noted, so only minimal numbers of Union troops would be needed. The pleas worked. President Lincoln countermanded Reynolds and ordered that a Federal force be maintained in the region for the remainder of the conflict.[83]

Thanks to Lincoln, the military farms spread throughout northwest Arkansas to approximately fourteen locations, each one boasting a population of over one hundred people. Citizens living within ten miles of a colony were forced either to join it or leave the region, but most, accepting the sense (and reality) of the security offered by these militarized agriculture collectives, joined willingly. Certainly, pro-Union civilians viewed the farm colonies as a benefit. The Unionist newspaper in Fort Smith, greeting Harrison's experiment with enthusiasm, predicted that it would be "an entire success and must result in much good." In a rare bit of clarity, the generally politically motivated paper admitted that civilians throughout western Arkansas suffered from brutal policies carried out by both Confederate and Union forces. "Since the outbreak of the rebellion," the editor confessed, "the people here have lived an isolated life, without any adequate protection, and have been a prey, not only to rebel armies and bushwhackers, but to straggling soldiers from our own army, until many have been reduced to absolute want."[84]

Some post colonies went beyond simple collective farming and passive defense, for armed farmers and Federal cavalry worked together to take the war to rebel guerrillas. In one instance colonists in northwest Arkansas, in tandem with cavalry forces, killed guerrilla William "Buck" Brown, who had plagued Unionists in the region for at least two years. Even if civilians did not always play an active role in pursuing irregulars, their ability to sustain themselves within individual collectives proved helpful to antiguerrilla patrols. Relieved from worrying about these residents, Union forces could focus more intently on catching and destroying the enemy. Moreover, with fewer civilians living outside Union protection, there was less opportunity for guerrillas to plunder and live off the land. For the army, which had also counted on civilians for supplies, the fortified colonies served as supply depots.[85]

Yet problems also materialized as civilians attempted to renew their residence in the war-torn region. In March Bussey warned Harrison that he should consider closing colonies that could not achieve self-sufficiency. For the general and other authorities in the region, these communities represented an anomaly with no proven track record. "I fear your colonies at Bentonville and elsewhere outside Fayetteville cannot be maintained," Bussey told Harrison. If the colonel had any doubts about their efficacy, he clarified, "they had better be broken up before the crops are planted."[86]

The colony experiment did not just suffer from Federal uneasiness. Native Americans from Indian Territory had persistently stolen colony livestock. "Complaints are made to me that Indians cross the line and drive off cattle and other stock," Harrison complained to Col. W. A. Phillips. "I would respectfully suggest that you give such orders to prevent these raids, as all the stock this side of the line will be absolutely required to sustain the Union people who belong to the colonies." Phillips could not possibly comply. His forces based in Fort Gibson had been largely without horses for some time, and he found it difficult enough to protect the immediate vicinity of his post, much less the border between the Cherokee Nation and Arkansas. "No part of the command here is mounted," complained Phillips in February, "I have not even horsemen for picket duty."[87]

Phillips had other problems too. Since 1864 he had been orchestrating efforts both to destroy guerrillas and to maintain thousands of Unionist Native American refugees. By early spring, the colonel was responsible for nearly 10,000 civilians, many of whom had been homeless and suffering since the outset of hostilities. Thousands more who lived well away from Fort Gibson remained in need of the army's protection and provisions. After yet another long winter, the refugees continued to suffer, and Union commanders grew increasingly frustrated. They had hoped to foster a larger version of Arkansas's post colonies by encouraging local civilians and refugees to grow food, but as Phillips made clear, it was "impossible for . . . a force of footmen to defend the refugees while raising a crop." The few horses available were given to scouts for small-scale cattle drives, but not even all these soldiers-turned-cowboys had mounts. In addition to the few cattle his troops could rustle from the countryside, Phillips implored authorities for seeds before the planting season arrived. "If a boat load of seed corn and potatoes could be shipped here within the next two weeks," he pleaded, "its advantages would be incalculable."[88]

By April, the colonel's hopes had been partially realized, at least to the extent of saving the "refugees from starvation." Crops began to grow throughout the area surrounding Fort Gibson. Union soldiers, mostly Native Americans, helped civilians plant corn. Even at the fort they grew "regimental gardens" and labored at creating a "government farm." In relative isolation from ready supplies, Fort Gibson helped refugees and locals harness the environment in order to survive and start to rebuild, however slowly.[89]

As refugees took to the fields that spring, the war was finally coming to a close. By summer, all Confederate armies had surrendered, and the irregular bands mostly stopped fighting. Thousands of civilians and former soldiers drifted back to their homes, though often only to find them in ruins. The conflict had wrought widespread economic and social destruction. By the summer of 1865, peace had finally returned, but civilians who had survived the war found mostly a wilderness on the western Trans-Mississippi border.

# Conclusion

I wish to God the woods had been thicker during the war," one Arkansas woman told famed hunter and traveler Frederick Gerstaecker in 1867, "we might have saved ourselves a few cows." Her comment is as perceptive as it is darkly humorous. Civilians and fighters on both sides had endured a style of warfare that enhanced the harsh environment with brutal, often racially fueled warfare. Cows, hogs, "woods," and a host of other environmental factors perpetuated the conflict as much as complicated it. The often unpredictable environment served as a lifeline, defense, and weapon, and it wrought unparalleled hardship on thousands of civilians and soldiers through intense droughts and unusually frigid winters. Indeed, the fight on the frontier became a protracted struggle fought over, and with, the natural world. The four years of intense fighting reached across gender and age and directly affected everyone living on the border. The social and physical landscape of Missouri, Arkansas, Kansas, and Indian Territory, save for a handful of outposts, had been rendered desolate. Thousands had been violently dispossessed of their homes, land, and livelihoods. And all of this happened within a region defined by the same racial and ethnic diversity that had underscored antebellum racial violence, intensified with the outbreak of war. Black slaves and freedmen in Missouri and Kansas were among the first to join Union ranks in 1862, and Cherokee, Creek, and Choctaw people from Indian Territory jumped headlong into the conflict from the beginning. Here was a war not only in the western margins of the Trans-Mississippi theater but also in the brutal margins of a society at war with itself.

The Civil War on the western Trans-Mississippi frontier rapidly devolved into an all-encompassing conflict in which fighting dramatically and directly affected not just soldiers and armies but entire communities. It was a war that shattered soldiers aligned in battle lines as well as citizens residing in their homes. Hundreds of Southern communities experienced this type of warfare to some extent, yet few experienced the degree of devastation endured by people on the western Trans-Mississippi border. Every facet of combat was exhibited in the region and dramatically affected every aspect of society. Political and legal structures at all levels—local and state—either ceased to exist entirely or no longer held any real semblance of authority by late 1861. The economy became dormant, farmers and workers ran away or were killed, and the hardy families who remained were brutalized by both Confederate guerrillas and the Union army and militia. By mid-war, no families, whether Union or Confederate, lived with any certainty of safety. Working in the fields, walking to a neighbor's house, or eating dinner, men, women, and children suffered constant threats from roving guerrilla bands and soldiers.

Historians have long debated to what extent the war was won or lost on the battlefield. Big battles in every theater of war doubtless shaped the course of the conflict and played a significant role in Confederate defeat. Yet the *other* battles—those in which civilians, mostly women and children, fought to preserve their property, livelihoods, and at times their lives—cannot be overlooked. Here was a war within the wider war, one that directly involved thousands of civilians engaged in their own battles for survival. Women and children fought for hogs, corn, and their belongings. They risked everything to maintain at least a semblance of normality. In the end, thanks in large part to Union occupation due to a dogged guerrilla war, most civilians lost everything. They became refugees or worse. Indeed, the home front was their war, not a distant battlefield. They had not the luxury to revel in victory or defeat elsewhere—they were far too busy fighting in their own front yards.

It is difficult to quantify the amount of destruction wrought along the western Trans-Mississippi frontier. Some detailed sources for social and economic loss do exist for parts of Arkansas, however, and such data is useful in gauging the broader ramifications of the conflict. Through much of the Ozark region, including Washington and Benton Counties, over 50 percent of the male population had either fled or died during the war, a sobering statistic that only includes people who had been on the tax rolls in 1860. In the Arkansas River valley near Fort Smith, that percentage jumps to well over 70 percent. Livestock losses had been even more extreme for western Arkansas. In the region around Fort Smith, virtually no animals survived, and few remained throughout the Ozarks. Losses were likely as pronounced in Indian Territory, southeast Kansas, and southwest Missouri.[1]

After repeated attacks at the hands of guerrillas and soldiers alike, often with the loss of their homes and belongings, most civilians had little choice but to abandon the Trans-Mississippi frontier. Indeed, a community in the midst of war had no means of rebuilding. Those relatively fortunate residents who had not lost their houses could rarely maintain enough essential goods to survive. Most suffered from theft rather than death, although there clearly had been enough killing to go around. With certain significant exceptions, civilians did not experience large battles in their neighborhoods, but they did endure innumerable, persistent skirmishes. Not knowing whom to trust or when their property might be destroyed, civilians also bore the emotional strain of the conflict. War in the region had been defined by terror, accompanied by bouts of death and physical destruction. Everyone on the western Trans-Mississippi border had been affected. Writing in the last year of the war, former Fayetteville resident William Baxter reflected on this. "The tier of border counties was almost depopulated," he lamented, "and it was sad, most sad, to see families who . . . expected to lay their bones in the family graveyard, abandoning homes once most delightful." Like Baxter, one soldier returning home to the region was shocked at the state of things on the border. "Our country is devastated and almost entirely depopulated," he wrote, "the inhabitants of the country . . . indiscriminately robbed of everything valuable . . . , [and] now our mothers, sisters and daughters . . . have been reduced to want, misery and degradation." For this veteran, the "reign of terror" that had inundated the region for four years had forced the last remaining women and children into poverty as refugees. Those who slowly trickled back found something resembling a wilderness. The world of 1860 had been turned upside down.[2]

War had replaced corn and wheat fields with overgrown meadows of grass and weeds. Cattle and other livestock had long since been consumed or removed. Feral hogs, unwittingly set free by the destruction, had thrived. Once flourishing lead mines had been silenced and major towns burned. In the late summer of 1866, over a year after hostilities had officially ceased, a reporter traveling through northwest Arkansas saw "wasted farms, deserted cabins, and lone chimneys marking the sites where dwellings have been destroyed by fire." Waxing eloquent in an otherwise depressing situation, the observer got to the core of the environmental and physical devastation by remarking that "yards, gardens and fields [were] overgrown with weeds and bushes are everywhere within view. The traveler soon ceases to wonder when he sees the charred remains of burnt buildings, and wonders rather when he beholds a house yet standing that it also did not disappear in the general conflagration. Such was the terrible intensity of the recent civil war."[3]

To the west in Indian Territory, William P. Ross remarked in the last months of the conflict that "everything has been much changed by the destroying hand of War." The region's transformation shocked him. "Nearly all the farms are growing up in bushes and briars, houses abandoned or burnt," Chief John Ross's nephew continued, and "livestock of all kinds has become very scarce. . . . We have not a horse, cow or hog left that I know of." In place of domesticated animals, wildlife reemerged as further proof of the war-induced wilderness. "The wolves howl dismally over the land and the panther's scream is often heard," Ross wrote, noting that even "bears have been seen . . . within ten miles of here."[4]

Four years of intense warfare proved especially destructive along Indian Territory's eastern edge. According to a Bureau of Ethnology report, the Cherokee Nation suffered "more desolation and ruin than perhaps any other community." Regular and irregular warfare perpetuated by both Union and Confederate forces had reduced the countryside to a "blackened and desolate waste" where civilians suffered from "want, misery, and the elements." Indeed, the Cherokees alone lost nearly 7,000 people, while most of the remaining 14,000 members had become refugees. Houses had been destroyed and livestock killed or dispersed. Eastern Indian Territory, continued the report, "was distinguishable from the virgin prairie only by the scorched and blackened chimneys and the plowed by now neglected fields." According to historian Clarissa Confer, much of Cherokee society had "suffered almost total destruction, . . . and the entire social fabric had disintegrated."[5]

With depopulation and destruction came the final fall of slavery in much of the border region. Even toward the end, slaveholders scrambled to preserve their investments by fleeing south. "Though slaves had become a very uncertain kind of property," one Arkansas Unionist noted during the war, "men would abandon home, kindred, friends, every thing, in fact, to save their negroes." Hundreds of slaveholders left for Texas or Louisiana as the Union army became increasingly established in the state. But most new freedmen had been left behind and, like thousands of white civilians, took refuge in Federal outposts or fled the region altogether. As historian Jim Downs has recently shown, their new liberty was often celebrated in name only, for they suffered disproportionally from sickness, malnourishment, and exposure. Free blacks on the border suffered alongside thousands of Native American and white refugees, who themselves struggled to survive.[6]

Those masters who remained farther north worried about what they interpreted as increasing insolence among their slaves. In the last year of the conflict, border resident and slaveholder Robert W. Mecklin noted: "I strongly suspect they have a notion of leaving us," which, he makes clear, would make things "more pleasant [because] they do not pay for their board by their services and their impudence is not bearable." Mecklin's predictions came true just days later. "I was right in my opinion of our darkies," he wrote. A full year after the Emancipation Proclamation had taken effect, a slave woman named Net had liberated herself and left for Fayetteville, where she found work as a cook in return for a place she and her children could stay as well as two dollars per week. Reflecting on the loss of his slave and her children, Mecklin confessed, with not a little bitterness, that Net "had been trying for a long while by every act of disobedience to provoke [us] to driver her off. But at last had to leave us all cheerful and pleased to get her away." Actually, Net had taken control of the situation. Undoubtedly encouraged by the strong Union presence in the region, she secured her freedom and that of her children.[7]

As for Mecklin, he only "hoped that Abe's abolition minions" would not influence other slaves who still remained. An underlying if misguided notion of labor appears in Mecklin's letters to his friends and family. For him, as for many slaveholders, his "servants" worked not for free as slaves so much as they worked "to pay for [their] board." Such a distinction became even more important in the last year of the war as slaveholders grappled with the inevitability of emancipation. Mecklin was confident that any slaves who left would soon realize how good they had been treated. His slaves, Mecklin rationalized, enjoyed "more freedom, ease, and comfort than any of those darkies who went off with the Federals." Net and her children freeing themselves belies such notions as do the thousands of freedmen who left Arkansas and Missouri for Kansas and points north. Their actions, as historian Steven Hahn has made clear, were just as political and significant as any legislation.[8]

In addition to depopulation, destruction, and emancipation, the environment contributed an important element to the war along the western Trans-Mississippi border. Civilians relied on the most fundamental aspects of nature for survival. Furthermore, Union and Confederate soldiers as well as irregulars sustained themselves and their animals from the bounty of the land, though too often at the expense of local farmers. Terrain served as a trusty ally to guerrillas, who used the rugged hills and hollows to surprise and evade enemy soldiers and noncombatants. Intensely cold, oppressively hot, and irritatingly wet weather had also shaped regular and irregular warfare, striking with equal fury against soldiers, guerrillas, and civilians.

More than just a series of depressing vignettes that illustrate the brutality of war, the evidence emphasizes failure for all sides, at least in terms of destruction and hardship inflicted. While guerrillas held and maintained a physical and emotional monopoly over the residents of the region, their activity brought an increased Federal presence. Such strong Union counterinsurgency in a traditionally pro-Confederate region proved counterproductive for the rebels. As historian Daniel E. Sutherland has shown throughout the South, guerrilla warfare yielded only a higher level of Union occupation. On the Trans-Mississippi border, the intensity of Federal activities, if not the number of troops, had increased throughout the war. Civilians had become immediate suspects as aiding and abetting the irregulars if they had not already become refugees. Union occupation *because* of guerrilla warfare helped degrade the foundations of the Confederacy—at least on the western margins of the Trans-Mississippi.

A large share of Confederate irregulars who operated along the western border sought personal gain before any cohesive patriotic endeavor to help the Southern cause. Their actions were fueled by hate and personal profit, and although they often worked with revenge in mind, their primary objective remained the same: gain as much as possible—economically and psychologically—with the least amount of risk. Unlike William Clarke Quantrill's band and other large guerrilla forces, the majority of irregulars rarely strayed far from their communities. For Union officials, these were the most frustrating foes, for they acted like combatants but appeared to be peaceable citizens. Such men waged irregular warfare within miles of their homes, knew the best local hideouts, and easily melted back into the populace. The brutality of this localized contest increased as the conflict dragged on. Some of the most villainous irregular bands shifted their attacks from known Unionists to anyone in their path. By midwar if not before, the border had devolved into a region defined by lawless anarchy. Random acts of violence and theft occurred in the name of one side or the other. One band of thieves in northwest Arkansas tortured a husband and wife by burning the soles of their feet in order to make them give up their hidden gold. Other families who tried to hold out suffered random theft, threats, and violence by groups of men who were hardly affiliated with any official military outfit.[9]

Others, such as Quantrill, believed that the guerrilla style of warfare was essential to the Confederate war effort, that they were sincerely aiding the South by warring against Union soldiers and civilians behind the lines of battle. Yet even these most genuine irregulars played no small role in Confederate defeat. Indeed, as Sutherland has shown, the general perpetuation of irregular terror led directly and forcefully to extreme antiguerrilla measures by the Union army. To use modern military terminology, these "counterinsurgency" efforts wreaked havoc on the civilian population (whether Union or Confederate supporters), further demoralizing the rebel spirit and thereby their war effort. Even pro-Confederate civilians in the region recognized the counterintuitive role guerrillas played in the war effort. According to one Arkansan, guerrilla warfare by 1864 had "done ten times more harm than good, and only makes the Feds worse: both sides emulate each other in robbing, killing, and destroying." The man, writing to his son in the Confederate army, continued, "whatever you do, my son, do not come home: your safest place is in the regular army."[10]

But guerrillas were not strategically invincible. Although they did often elude Union troops, they did far more harm than good for their cause. Not only did they sometimes attack Confederate sympathizers, their constant harassment of Union troops and civilians generally led directly to an increasingly harsh Federal presence in the South. Within the first year of the war, Union commanders let loose a series of general orders aimed at reining in the guerrilla menace, and Confederate civilians were invariably targets of this retribution. Reflected by Brig. Gen. Thomas Ewing's Order No. 11, calling for all civilians within three Missouri border counties to be forcefully removed, and Brig. Gen. John McNeil's published order near Fort Smith warning that the nearest pro-Confederate dwelling to any guerrilla activity would be torched, residents became both objects and victims of Federal frustration. Constantly worried about their safety and livelihood, rebel noncombatants on the border could hardly provide any significant support to the Confederate war effort. In the end, although guerrillas occasionally proved helpful to Southern strategy in very specific situations, the irregular war perpetrated against Union soldiers and civilians of all persuasions proved to be terrorizing, brutal, and strategically ineffective. Residents on the western Trans-Mississippi frontier focused most of their attention on self-preservation and as a result had little room left to worry about the Confederate experiment.[11]

In the end, Federal counterguerrilla policies proved nearly as dubious. By 1865, the army had only slightly more control over the region than it had enjoyed four years earlier. Union soldiers waged a constant, frustrating, and largely hopeless war against irregulars and their civilian supporters. They added to the brutality of war by implementing harsh measures that destroyed civilian morale and will to fight while simultaneously failing to gain any significant control over the guerrillas themselves. Yet the constant pressure wrought by Union authorities had been fueled by guerrilla activity. Although rebel irregulars on the whole eluded Federal troops until the very end, they provided the reason to occupy the border for the entire war, which in turn crippled the Confederate home front in the region.

The Confederacy rejected the option of full-scale guerrilla war as a means of survival in 1865. The growing frustration among Federal officers led to an ever-increasing disenchantment among the antiguerrilla fighters. Their attempts at various modes of control, what later generations of American soldiers would term "search and destroy," "defoliation," and "reconcentration," hardly proved fruitful against irregulars, but their strategies perpetuated a bitter and protracted war that ruined the region.

In the end, the conflict on the western Trans-Mississippi border underscored the reality of what might be usefully defined as localized total war. In the parts of the South that witnessed large battles with conventional armies passing through their communities, anxiety and fear had been occasional. Civilians on the border suffered constant strain from a war in which they all participated. This was something more than "hard" war. It was a conflict that permeated every aspect of society.

# NOTES

## INTRODUCTION

1. U.S. War Department, *War of the Rebellion*, ser. 1, 34:605 (hereinafter cited as OR; all references are to series 1).

2. *Thomas Alexander v. Rice and Hugh Challas*, Aug. 30, 1865, box 23, file 128, Circuit Court Records, Jasper County Records Center, Carthage, Mo. It remains unknown whether damages, or how much, were allowed for the lawsuit or if any further legal action had been carried out against Rice and Hugh Challas. See "Thomas Alexander vs. Rice and Hugh Challas, 1865," Community & Conflict: The Impact of the Civil War in the Ozarks, Springfield–Greene County Library District, http://www.ozarkscivilwar.org/archives/5287.

3. Most scholarly studies of the "border" focus squarely on that region between Lawrence, Kansas, and Jackson County, Missouri. See especially Earle and Burke, *Bleeding Kansas, Bleeding Missouri*; and Neely, *Border between Them*. Jeremy Neely explores the social, political, and economic history of the central Missouri-Kansas border before, during, and after the Civil War.

4. U.S. Bureau of the Census, Population Schedules, Arkansas, Kansas, and Missouri, 1860; Hauptman, *Between Two Fires*, 45; Thornton, *Cherokees*, 82, 92.

5. Michael Fellman, "At the Nihilist Edge: Reflections on Guerrilla Warfare during the American Civil War," in *Views from the Dark Side of American History*. For state studies, see, for example, Daniel E. Sutherland, "Guerrillas: The Real War in Arkansas," in Bailey and Sutherland, *Civil War Arkansas*, 133–53; Fellman, *Inside War*; Fisher, *War at Every Door*; and Inscoe and McKinney, *Heart of Confederate Appalachia*.

6. Shea, "War We Have Lost," 101, 105–6.

7. Civil War environmental history has become a valuable and flourishing subfield. See especially, Drake, *Blue, the Gray, and the Green*. Also see Kirby, "American Civil War"; Brady, "From Battlefield to Fertile Ground," 320–21; Stith, "'Deplorable Condition of the Country,'" 322–47; Brady, *War upon the Land*; Nelson, *Ruin Nation*; Downs, *Sick from Freedom*;

Yael A. Sternhell, *Routes of War: The World of Movement in the Confederate South* (Cambridge, Mass.: Harvard University Press, 2012); Meier, *Nature's Civil War*; Nelson, "Looking at Landscapes of War," 439–49; and Ted Widmer, "The Civil War's Environmental Impact," "Disunion," *New York Times*, Nov. 15, 2014.

8. Fellman, "At the Nihilist Edge," 59. For an excellent discussion of warfare amid a cultural milieu of distrust and hatred, see James D. Drake, *King Philip's War: Civil War in New England, 1675–1676* (Amherst: University of Massachusetts Press, 1999), 6–7.

9. For the most recent scholarship on the Civil War in Indian Territory, see Warde, *When the Wolf Came*; Confer, *Cherokee Nation in the Civil War*; White and White, *Now the Wolf Has Come*; Crowe, "War in the Nations"; and Lause, *Race and Radicalism*, 4–5.

10. Gallagher, *Confederate War*, 11; See also Gallagher, "Disaffection, Persistence, and Nation: Some Directions in Recent Scholarship on the Confederacy," *Civil War History* 55 (Sept. 2009): 329–53; and James M. McPherson, *This Mighty Scourge: Perspectives on the Civil War* (New York: Oxford University Press, 2007), 43–50.

11. Sutherland, *Savage Conflict*, x.

12. McKnight, *Contested Borderland*, 6; Barton A. Myers, *Executing Daniel Bright: Race, Loyalty, and Guerrilla Violence in a Coastal Carolina Community, 1861–1865* (Baton Rouge: Louisiana State University Press, 2009), 3. See also Brian D. McKnight, *Confederate Outlaw: Champ Ferguson and the Civil War in Appalachia* (Baton Rouge: Louisiana State University Press, 2011); Fisher, *War at Every Door*; and Inscoe and McKinney, *Heart of Confederate Appalachia*.

13. J. David Hacker, "A Census-Based Count of the Civil War Dead," *Civil War History* 57 (Dec. 2011): 328; Fellman, "At the Nihilist Edge," 60; Mark W. Geiger, "Indebtedness and the Origins of Guerrilla Violence in Civil War Missouri," *Journal of Southern History* 75 (Feb. 2009): 49; Moneyhon, *Impact of the Civil War and Reconstruction on Arkansas*, 178; Lause, *Race and Radicalism*, 129; Confer, *Cherokee Nation in the Civil War*, 145. For the depopulation of the Ozarks, see Bradbury, "Buckwheat Cake Philanthropy," 234–35.

14. For an explanation of the broad contours of guerrilla-war historiography, see Sutherland, "Sideshow No Longer," 5–23; and Mackey, *Uncivil War*, 15–20. For important early work in the field, see Jones, *Gray Ghosts and Rebel Raiders*; Monaghan, *Civil War on the Western Border*; Brownlee, *Gray Ghosts of the Confederacy*; and Castel, *Frontier State at War*. For concern over the West's inability to wage effective counterinsurgency operations in the face of increased irregular warfare, see Ney, "Guerrilla War and Modern Strategy."

15. Paludan, *Victims*. For scholarly biographies and general studies using guerrilla leaders and larger events as vehicles to better understand society at war, see Ramage, *Rebel Raider*; Ramage, *Gray Ghost*; Ash, *When the Yankees Came*; Grimsley, *Hard Hand of War*; and Storey, *Loyalty and Loss*.

16. Fellman, *Inside War*.

17. Mackey, *Uncivil War*; McKnight, *Contested Borderland*; Fisher, *War at Every Door*; Sarris, *Separate Civil War*; Neely, *Border between Them*; Mountcastle, *Punitive War*; Sutherland, *Savage Conflict*, x. Neely's research does not extend to the lower Trans-Mississippi frontier.

18. Boot, *Invisible Armies*, 212–13. For a discussion of guerrilla warfare and Southern identity, see Beringer et al., *Why the South Lost the Civil War*, 438–39.

19. Gary W. Gallagher and Kathryn Shively Meier, "Coming to Terms with Civil War Military History," *Journal of the Civil War Era* 4 (Dec. 2014), 492–93.

20. Shea, "War We Have Lost," 106.

21. There is a thriving discussion concerning frontiers, borderlands, and "middle-grounds" in American history. Most work, however, deals primarily with colonial and revolutionary-era America, not extending into the nineteenth century. The Civil War on the Trans-Mississippi border encompasses the same general themes that appeared among the French, British, and American Indians in the Great Lakes region—what Richard White made famous in his *The Middle Ground: Indians, Empires, and Republics in the Great Lakes Region, 1650–1815*. For more of the ever-budding debate on the topic, see especially Pekka Hämäläinen and Samuel Truett, "On Borderlands," *Journal of American History* 98 (Sept. 2011): 338–61; Jeremy Adelman and Stephen Aron, "From Borderlands to Borders: Empires, Nation-States, and the Peoples in between in North American History," *American Historical Review* 104 (June 1999): 814–41; Daniel K. Richter, *Facing East from Indian Country: A Native History of Early America* (Cambridge, Mass.: Harvard University Press, 2001); and Derek R. Everett, "Frontiers Within: State Boundaries and Borderlands in the American West" (Ph.D. diss., University of Arkansas, 2008).

22. See Castel, *Frontier State at War*; Fellman, *Inside War*; Sutherland, "Guerrillas"; Confer, *Cherokee Nation in the Civil War*; and Goodrich, *Black Flag*. Helpful local studies concerning civilian warfare in specific regions along the border Trans-Mississippi include Wood, *Civil War on the Lower Kansas-Missouri Border*. For studies at the county or local level along the southern frontier Trans-Mississippi, see Prier, "Under the Black Flag"; and Stith, "At the Heart of Total War," 1–27.

23. *Kansas Daily Tribune*, May 10, 1864, quoted in Cheatham, "'Desperate Characters,'" 148; *Memphis Daily Bulletin*, May 2, 1863, quoted in Huff, "Guerrillas, Jayhawkers, and Bushwhackers in Northern Arkansas," 128.

24. George T. Maddox, *Hard Trials and Tribulations of an Old Confederate Soldier* (Van Buren, Ark.: Argus, 1897), 11; Joseph M. Bailey, "The Story of a Confederate Soldier, 1861–1865," Special Collections, University of Arkansas Libraries, Fayetteville, 34–35; Sutherland, "Guerrillas," 136; Prier, "Under the Black Flag," 7.

25. Sutherland, *Savage Conflict*, xi–xii. See also Noe, "Who Were the Bushwhackers?," 5–31; and Mark W. Geiger, *Financial Fraud and Guerrilla Violence in Missouri's Civil War, 1861–1865* (New Haven, Conn.: Yale University Press, 2010).

26. Fellman, Gordon, and Sutherland, *This Terrible War*, 196–97; Fellman, *Inside War*, 176–92.

27. Fellman, "At the Nihilist Edge," 60–61. No reliable figures for civilian deaths during the Civil War exist, much less for those in the Trans-Mississippi. One historian estimates that 50,000 civilians died directly due to the war, but this hardly accounts for the untold thousands who perished as an indirect result due to malnourishment, exposure, and

disease. See Faust, *This Republic of Suffering*, xii. Yet some historians play down the amount of destruction in the South. For such an interpretation, see Paul E. Paskoff, "Measures of War: A Quantitative Examination of the Civil War's Destructiveness in the Confederacy," *Civil War History* 54 (Mar. 2008): 35–62.

28. For an excellent discussion of the "mythical ambience" created by guerrillas in Kansas and along the border, see Cheatham, "'Desperate Characters,'" 146.

29. Carl von Clausewitz, *On War*, ed. and trans. Michael Howard and Peter Paret (Princeton, N.J.: Princeton University Press, 1976).

30. For a discussion of Union policy toward suspected rebel sympathizers, see Fellman, *Inside War*, 126–27.

31. See especially Whites, "Forty Shirts and a Wagonload of Wheat," 56–78; Harvell, "Cope, Cooperate, and Combat"; Michael Fellman, "Women and Guerrilla Warfare," in Clinton and Silber, *Divided Houses*, 150–51; and Donna Krug, "Women and War in the Confederacy," in Forster and Nagler, *On the Road to Total War*, 413, 448.

32. Fellman, "Women and Guerrilla Warfare," 147–48. For women's dilemma during the war throughout the South, see Faust, *Mothers of Invention*.

33. John Fabian Witt, *Lincoln's Code: The Laws of War in American History* (New York: Free Press, 2012), 4, 187–96. See also Scheipers, *Unlawful Combatants*, 69–104.

34. Sutherland, *Savage Conflict*, 126–27; Fellman, "At the Nihilist Edge," 61–62; Moneyhon, *Impact of the Civil War and Reconstruction on Arkansas*, 132. For an examination of how Lieber's code of laws applied to the Civil War, see Mancini, "Francis Lieber, Slavery, and the 'Genesis' of the Laws of War," 325–48.

35. For increasingly harsh Union reprisals, see especially Fellman, *Inside War*, 132–92; and Mountcastle, *Punitive War*.

36. For the best study on Union impressions of the border, see William L. Shea, "A Semi-Savage State: The Image of Arkansas in the Civil War," in Bailey and Sutherland, *Civil War Arkansas*, 85–99.

37. For the ongoing debate on how to define the level of violence during Civil War in whole or in part, see Hsieh, "Total War and the American Civil War Reconsidered," 394. See also Andrew F. Lang, "The Garrison War: Culture, Race, and the Problem of Military Occupation during the American Civil War Era" (Ph.D. diss., Rice University, 2013), 97; and Imlay, "Total War," esp. 550–55. For more on the thriving and at times contentious historiographical debate, see Mark E. Neely Jr., *The Civil War and the Limits of Destruction* (Cambridge, Mass.: Harvard University Press, 2007), 198–207. See also Sutherland, "Abraham Lincoln, John Pope, and the Origins of Total War," 567–86; Neely, "Was the Civil War a Total War?," 434–58; James M. McPherson, "From Limited to Total War: Missouri and the Nation, 1861–1865," in Forster and Nagler, *On the Road to Total War*, 295–309; Janda, "Shutting the Gates of Mercy," 7–26; Grimsley, *Hard Hand of War*; Ash, *When the Yankees Came*; Neely, *Border between Them*; Faust, *This Republic of Suffering*, xi–xiii; Newton, "What Kind of War?," 16–25; and Lause, *Race and Radicalism*, 4. Jeremy Neely argues that not only

was the war here "total" but it was also "the worst guerrilla fighting ever witnessed on American soil." Neely, *Border between Them*, 2, 99.

38. Historian Wendell Beall has aptly called the war in the region "a grinding, no-holds-barred . . . war of attrition." See Beall, "Wildwood Skirmishers," 5–6. For a useful measure of the extent of destruction in the South, see Paskoff, "Measures of War," 35–62.

## CHAPTER 1

1. For scholarship regarding the prewar border, see especially Neely, *Border between Them*, 60–95; Earle and Burke, *Bleeding Kansas, Bleeding Missouri*; S. Charles Bolton, *Arkansas, 1800–1860: Remote and Restless* (Fayetteville: University of Arkansas Press, 1998), 167–86; and Warde, *When the Wolf Came*, 3–40. Chapter title from *OR*, 22(1):497.

2. See Gambone, "Economic Relief in Territorial Kansas," 149–74; Gambone, "Starving Kansas," 30–35; Sweeney, "Thirsting for War, Hungering for Peace," 71–78; and Sweeney, "Twixt Scylla and Charybdis," 72–93.

3. For population studies along the Trans-Mississippi frontier prior to the Civil War, see Gerlach, "Population Origins in Rural Missouri," 1–21 (esp. 11–13); Thornton, *Cherokees*, 82; and Castel, *Civil War Kansas*, 2–7. See also Gerlach, *Immigrants in the Ozarks*, and *Settlement Patterns in Missouri*.

4. See Fellman, *Inside War*, 8–9. For useful analyses of upcountry socioeconomic evolution in the mid-nineteenth century, see Hahn, *Roots of Southern Populism*; and Blevins, *Hill Folks*, 14–31. For the economic growth of antebellum Arkansas, see Moneyhon, *Impact of the Civil War and Reconstruction on Arkansas*, 13–15, 19–21. For Arkansas's role as Southern progenitor of the gold rush, see Priscilla McArthur, *Arkansas in the Gold Rush* (Little Rock: August House, 1986).

5. See Foreman, *Fort Gibson*, 22–24; Goins and Goble, *Historical Atlas of Oklahoma*, 5, 12, 80, 86; Hanson and Moneyhon, *Historical Atlas of Arkansas*, 2, 5, 8, 33, 35, 36, 41–42; Socolofsky and Self, *Historical Atlas of Kansas*, 3, 4, 5, 28; and Rafferty, *Historical Atlas of Missouri*, 9, 42, 57, 58, 79.

6. U.S. Bureau of the Census, *Agriculture of the United States in 1860*, 6–9; U.S. Bureau of the Census, *Manufactures of the United States in 1860*, 15–19; Goins and Goble, *Historical Atlas of Oklahoma*, 5, 12, 80, 86; Hanson and Moneyhon, *Historical Atlas of Arkansas*, 2, 5, 8, 33, 35, 36, 41–42; Socolofsky and Self, *Historical Atlas of Kansas*, 3, 4, 5, 28; Rafferty, *Historical Atlas of Missouri*, 9, 42, 57, 58, 79. See also Michael A. Hughes, "Wartime Gristmill Destruction in Northwest Arkansas and Military Farm Colonies," in Bailey and Sutherland, *Civil War Arkansas*, 31–32.

7. *Van Buren (Ark.) Intelligencer*, Nov. 3, 1849. See also C. Fred Williams, "The Bear State Image: Arkansas in the Nineteenth Century," *Arkansas Historical Quarterly* 34 (Summer 1980): 99, 104–5; and Blevins, *Arkansas/Arkansaw*. For views of Arkansas and the Ozarks before the war, see Frederick Gerstaecker, *Wild Sports in the Far West* (London, 1855); Charles Fenton Mercer

Noland, *Cavorting on the Devil's Fork: The Pete Whetstone Letters of C. F. M. Noland*, ed. Leonard Williams (Fayetteville: University of Arkansas Press, 2006); and Thomas Bangs Thorpe, *The Big Bear of Arkansas and Other Sketches, Illustrative of Characters and Incidents in the South and Southwest* (Philadelphia, 1845).

8. Creek [Col. Albert C. Ellithorpe], "From the Army on the Western Frontier," *Chicago Evening Journal*, Dec. 1, 1862.

9. Ibid.; E. G. Ross to his wife, Nov. 30, 1862, Edmund G. Ross Letters, Kansas Historical Society; Noble et al., *Thirteenth Regiment of Illinois Volunteer Infantry*, 170; Marshall, *Army Life*, 93; *Cincinnati Daily Gazette*, Mar. 18, 1862. See also William L. Shea, "A Semi-Savage State: The Image of Arkansas in the Civil War," in Bailey and Sutherland, *Civil War Arkansas*, 86–91.

10. Britton, *Pioneer Life*, 330.

11. Confer, *Cherokee Nation in the Civil War*, 35–41. The nearest railroad spur to the Cherokee Nation during the Civil War, and the frontier Trans-Mississippi generally, was located at Rolla, Missouri.

12. OR, 13(1):491.

13. Britton, *Pioneer Life*, 35–37.

14. J. T. Livingston, *History of Jasper County, Missouri*, 1:35–37.

15. Ibid., 39.

16. See J. T. Livingston, *History of Jasper County*, 1:197; *History of Jasper County, Missouri* (Des Moines: Mills, 1883), 35–36; Fellman, Gordon, and Sutherland, *This Terrible War*, 74; and *Liberty (Mo.) Tribune*, Dec. 14, 1860.

17. Neely, *Border between Them*, 100–101. See also Phillip T. Tucker, "'Ho, for Kansas': The Southwest Expedition of 1860," *Missouri Historical Review* 86 (Spring 1991): 22–36.

18. U.S. Office of Indian Affairs, *Report of the Commissioner of Indian Affairs, for the Year 1864*, 232 (first quote); Thornton, *Cherokees*, 90; OR, 13(1):490; Confer, *Cherokee Nation in the Civil War*, 42–43; Gary E. Moulton, *John Ross: Cherokee Chief* (Athens: University of Georgia Press, 1978), 167–68.

19. OR, 13(1):492; Confer, *Cherokee Nation in the Civil War*, 35.

20. Goins and Goble, *Historical Atlas of Oklahoma*, 5, 12.

21. OR, 1(1):683–84.

22. OR, 13(1):497; John Ross, "Proclamation," May 17, 1861, in Ross, *Papers*, 469–70.

23. See especially Sweeney, "Twixt Scylla and Charybdis," 88–89.

24. Leopard and Shoemaker, *Messages and Proclamations of the Governors of the State of Missouri*, 376–77.

25. Gov. Claiborne Fox Jackson to David Walker, Apr. 28, 1861, Governor's Papers, box 1, folder 3, RG 003, MSA.

26. Christopher Phillips, *Missouri's Confederate: Claiborne Fox Jackson and the Creation of Southern Identity in the Border West* (Columbia: University of Missouri Press, 2000), 255–62.

27. Leopard and Shoemaker, *Messages and Proclamations of the Governors of the State of Missouri*, 385–86.

28. Phillips, *Missouri's Confederate*, 255–62; Neely, *Border between Them*, 101–2.

29. Leopard and Shoemaker, *Messages and Proclamations of the Governors of the State of Missouri*, 411–14 (quote on 413).

30. *Arkansas Gazette*, Dec. 22, 1860; OR, 1(1):639. See also Moneyhon, *Impact of the Civil War and Reconstruction on Arkansas*, 95–98; and Moneyhon, "1861: 'The Die is Cast,'" in Christ, *Rugged and Sublime*, 4–6.

31. Moneyhon, "1861," 7–8.

32. Baxter, *Pea Ridge and Prairie Grove*, 17–18.

33. Fellman, *Inside War*, xvii.

## CHAPTER 2

Epigraph. Gov. Hamilton R. Gamble, Message to Fourth Session of State Convention, June 2, 1862, in Leopard and Shoemaker, *Messages and Proclamations of the Governors of the State of Missouri*, 419.

1. Hinze and Farnham, *Battle of Carthage*, 100–101 (quote on 101). See also Burchett, *Battle of Carthage*.

2. Hinze and Farnham, *Battle of Carthage*, 100; OR, 3(1):38.

3. *Fort Scott Democrat*, July 13, 1861. Fort Scott was not reincorporated as an official Federal fort until January 17, 1863. Until then, it played a key role as a temporary Union supply depot and base of operations. See Erwin N. Thompson, *Fort Scott, Kansas: Site Identification and Evaluation* (Washington, D.C.: Division of History, U.S. Department of the Interior, 1967), 124. Crowding to watch a battle was nothing new this early in the war. Union civilians gathered to picnic and to watch the fight at the First Battle of Bull Run just weeks later in Virginia. See McPherson, *Battle Cry of Freedom*, 347–50.

4. Britton, *Civil War on the Border*, 1:67–68.

5. Ibid.

6. *Fort Scott Democrat*, Aug. 24, 1861.

7. Augustus Wattles to W. P. Dole, Sept. 1861, Letters Received by the Office of Indian Affairs, 1824–81, Neosho Agency, RG 75, National Archives and Records Administration, Washington, D.C. (hereinafter NARA), M234, roll 532, 560 (first quote); James G. Blunt, "General Blunt's Account of His Civil War Experiences," *Kansas Historical Quarterly* 1 (May 1932), 214 (second quote).

8. Cheatham, "'If the Union Wins,'" 172–74; Castel, *Civil War Kansas*, 54.

9. Sarah A. Cox statement, n.d., F1158, Records of the Provost Marshal, RG 109, Missouri State Archives, Jefferson City (hereinafter cited as RPM-MSA).

10. Ibid.

11. Ibid.

12. Ibid.

13. Ibid.

14. H. E. Palmer, "The Black-Flag Character of War on the Border," *Transactions of the Kansas State Historical Society, 1905–1906* (Topeka: State Printing Office, 1906), 459–60.

15. Joseph H. Trego to his wife, Sept. 5, 1861, Joseph Harrington Trego Papers, 1850–89, Collection 523, Kansas State Historical Society, Topeka (hereinafter KSHS).

16. *Fort Scott Democrat*, Sept. 21, 1861.

17. James H. Lane, *Leavenworth (Kans.) Daily Conservative*, Sept. 26, 1861. See also Wood, *Civil War on the Lower Kansas-Missouri Border*, 36.

18. See Benedict, *Jayhawkers*; Wendell Holmes Stephenson, *The Political Career of General James H. Lane* (Topeka, 1930); Albert Castel, "Jim Lane of Kansas," *Civil War Times Illustrated* 12, no. 1 (1973): 22–29; Eric Ethier, "The Wild World of Jim Lane," *Civil War Times* 46, no. 8 (2007): 48–53; and Robert Collins, *Jim Lane: Scoundrel, Statesman, Kansan* (Gretna, La: Pelican, 2007).

19. "Civil War Experiences of Sarah Ellis Yeater," *Flashback* 3 (Aug. 1966), 14–15.

20. OR, 3(1):196 (first quote); Kansas Brigade correspondent, in Goodrich, *Black Flag*, 18 (second quote); Langsdorf, "Letters of Joseph H. Trego," 298 (third quote).

21. Kansas Brigade correspondent, in Goodrich, *Black Flag*, 18.

22. Ibid.; "Civil War Experiences of Sarah Ellis Yeater," *Flashback* 3 (Aug. 1966), 15.

23. "Civil War Experiences of Sarah Ellis Yeater," 17.

24. Lee, *Wartime Washington*, 77.

25. Etcheson, *Bleeding Kansas*, 225–26; and McPherson, *Battle Cry of Freedom*, 352–54.

26. OR, 3(1):516.

27. Ibid.

28. "Civil War Experiences of Sarah Ellis Yeater," 16.

29. Unnamed reporter, *New York Daily Times*, in Goodrich, *Black Flag*, 18–19. Lane's Osceola raid is reinterpreted by Bryce Benedict, who argues that its destructiveness has been exaggerated by historians who have relied too literally on biased sources. See Benedict, *Jayhawkers*, 98–103.

30. OR, 8(1):381.

31. Joseph H. Trego to his wife, Sept. 6, 1861, Joseph Harrington Trego Papers, 1850–89, Collection 523, KSHS.

32. Interview with Lucy [Bryant] Blakely, n.d., in Schrantz, *Jasper County*, 55–56.

33. Crowe, "War in the Nations," 72–73; Opothleyahola and Ouktahnaserharjo to Pres. Abraham Lincoln, Aug. 15, 1861, cited in ibid., 73; John Ross, "Address to the Cherokees," Aug. 21, 1861, in Ross, *Papers*, 480–81. The refugees included Creeks, Seminoles, Yuchis, Cherokees, Chickasaws, and African Americans. Crowe, "War in the Nations," 74. For an excellent discussion of Opothleyahola's trek to Kansas and its larger ramifications, see Lause, *Race and Radicalism*, 57–62. See also White and White, *Now the Wolf Has Come*, 40–76.

34. George L. Griscom, *Fighting with Ross' Texas Cavalry C.S.A.: The Diary of George L. Griscom, Adjutant, 9th Texas Cavalry Regiment*, ed. Homer L. Kerr (Hillsboro, Tex.: Hill Junior College Press, 1976), 4–5; Julie Renee Courtwright, "Taming the Red Buffalo: Prairie Fire on the Great Plains" (Ph.D. diss., University of Arkansas, 2007), 39–40.

35. *OR*, 8(1):5; Bates, *Texas Cavalry Officer's Civil War*, 22. See also W. Edwards, "*Prairie Was on Fire*," 3–14.

36. Confer, *Cherokee Nation in the Civil War*, 61.

37. Britton, *Civil War on the Border*, 1:173; James M. McIntosh, report, Dec. 26, 1861, in Hewett et al., *Supplement to the Official Records*, 1(1):538; Lause, *Race and Radicalism*, 60; Confer, *Cherokee Nation in the Civil War*, 65–66.

38. George A. Cutler to William G. Coffin, Sept. 30, 1862, U.S. Office of Indian Affairs, *Report of the Commissioner of Indian Affairs, for the Year 1862*, 139; A. B. Campbell to Joseph B. Barnes, Feb. 5, 1862, in ibid., 151–52; William G. Coffin to William P. Dole, Feb. 13, 1862, in ibid., 156; Britton, *Civil War on the Border*, 1:174. See also Banks, "Civil War Refugees from Indian Territory," 287–90.

39. Blow and Kennett Firm report, Aug. 26, 1862, F1584, RPM-MSA.

40. *OR*, 3(1):718.

41. Schrantz, *Jasper County*, 51–52.

## CHAPTER 3

1. Davis, *Papers*, 8:310; Hamilton R. Gamble, Message to Fourth Session of State Convention, June 2, 1862, in Leopard and Shoemaker, *Messages and Proclamations of the Governors of the State of Missouri*, 419.

2. For the most thorough examination of the Pea Ridge Campaign, see Shea and Hess, *Pea Ridge*.

3. Interview with Lucy [Bryant] Blakely, n.d., in Schrantz, *Jasper County*, 61–62.

4. Ibid., 63–64.

5. Banks, "Refugees from Indian Territory," 290–91.

6. Ibid., 291–92; George W. Collamore to William P. Dole, Apr. 21, 1862, in U.S. Office of Indian Affairs, *Report of the Commissioner of Indian Affairs*, 1862, 156–57.

7. "Civil War Experiences of Sarah Ellis Yeater," *Flashback* 16 (Aug. 1966), 19.

8. Baxter, *Pea Ridge and Prairie Grove*, 47–48; I. V. Smith Memoirs, State Historical Society of Missouri Research Center—Columbia; Lt. George Taylor, Mar. 3, 1862, Rebecca Stirman Davidson Papers, Special Collections, University of Arkansas, Fayetteville. See also Shea and Hess, *Pea Ridge*, 48–49.

9. Marian Tebbetts Banes, *Journal of Marian Tebbetts Banes* (Fayetteville, AR: Washington County Historical Society, n. d.), 91. See also Prier, "Under the Black Flag," 15–16.

10. George Taylor, Mar. 3, 1862, Stirman Davidson Papers; Washington L. Gammage, *The Camp, the Bivouac, and the Battle Field. Being a History of the Fourth Arkansas Regiment, from Its First Organization down to the Present Day* (Selma, Ala., 1864), 23. See also Shea and Hess, *Pea Ridge*, 49.

11. OR, 8(1):69.

12. Bek, "Civil War Diary of John T. Buegel," 319; Shea and Hess, *Pea Ridge*, 51.

13. *Aurora (Ill.) Beacon*, June 12, 1862. See also William L. Shea, "A Semi-Savage State: The Image of Arkansas in the Civil War," in Bailey and Sutherland, *Civil War Arkansas*, 96–97.

14. Shea and Hess, *Pea Ridge*, 270–71.

15. McIntyre, *Federals on the Frontier*, 42. McIntyre writes in early November that "many ball and quantities of small shot was picked up in our camp." A month later his regiment (the Nineteenth Iowa) saw significant action at the Battle of Prairie Grove. For the best treatment of Civil War ruins, physical and otherwise, see Nelson, *Ruin Nation*.

16. Donat, "Diary of Joseph Sanders," 7; Watson, *Life in the Confederate Army*, 319–21.

17. OR, 8(1):640; McMahan, "Campaigning through Missouri . . . Part 1," 148.

18. Smith Crim Military Commission Trial, Aug. 28, 1862, RPM-MSA. Crim was tried for murder and "Violations of the Laws of War" for aiding and abetting a guerrilla.

19. *Susan Stemmons v. Simon Burns et al.*, Cave Springs, 1865, box 22, file 131, Circuit Court Records, Jasper County Records Center, Carthage, Mo.; J. B. Stemmons interview, n.d., in Schrantz, *Jasper County*, 93–94.

20. Shrantz, *Jasper County*, 94.

21. *Stemmons v. Burns et al.*

22. *Miles Overton v. Simon P. Burns et al.*, Cave Springs, 1865, box 22, file 131, Circuit Court Records, Jasper County Records Center.

23. *Miles Overton v. William Warren et al.*, 1865, box 22, file 75, ibid.

24. Haas, "This Day We Marched Again," 24–25.

25. See Confer, *Cherokee Nation in the Civil War*, 76–81; Warde, *When the Wolf Came*, 104–11; and Banasik, *Embattled Arkansas*, 86–111.

26. George Falconer and Albert C. Ellithorpe Diary, July 14, 1862 (Ellithorpe), Wilson's Creek National Battlefield, Mo. For a general overview of the Indian Expedition of 1862, see Confer, *Cherokee Nation in the Civil War*, 76–82.

27. White Papers, 1862, Pearce Civil War Collection, 2005.055, Narvarro College, Corsicana, Tex. See also Ozarks Civil War, Springfield–Greene County Library District, http://www.ozarkscivilwar.org/archives/3551.

28. Theodore Gardner, "The First Kansas Battery," *Collections of the Kansas State Historical Society* 14 (1915–18), 241; Luman Harris Tenny, *War Diary of Luman Harris Tenny, 1861–65* (Cleveland, 1914), 21. See also Banasik, *Embattled Arkansas*, 94–96.

29. James G. Blunt to William Weer, July 12, 1862, entry 3154, pt. 2, RG 393, NARA; OR, 13(1):162.

30. McMahan, *Reluctant Cannoneer*, 43–48 (Oct. 23, 1862).

31. OR, 13(1):860–61.

32. Frederick Salomon to the Commanders comprising the Indian Expedition, July 18, 1862, entry 3154, pt. 2, RG 393, NARA; Confer, *Cherokee Nation in the Civil War*, 76–80.

33. Gause, *Four Years with Five Armies*, 96–97. Also see Banasik, *Embattled Arkansas*, 107.

34. Unknown to John Ross, Jan. 8, 1863, in Ross, *Papers*, 2:528.

35. *Fort Scott Bulletin*, Nov. 29, 1862; Ross, *Papers*, 2:539. Most fighting-age men among these refugees enlisted in the First, Second, and Third Indian Regiments.

36. *Freedom's Champion* (Atchison, Kans.), July 26, 1862. For the best treatment of Governor Gamble, see Boman, *Lincoln's Resolute Unionist*.

37. Louis Gerteis, *The Civil War in Missouri: A Military History* (Columbia: University of Missouri Press, 2012), 147 (quote), 149. Also see D. Connelly, *John M. Schofield and the Politics of Generalship*, 74–77.

38. *Fort Scott Bulletin*, July 26, 1862.

39. *Elizabeth James v. John Zachra et al.*, box 22, file 69, Circuit Court Records, Jasper County Records Center, Carthage, Mo.; Hamilton R. Gamble, First Biennial Message, Dec. 30, 1861, in Leopard and Shoemaker, *Messages and Proclamations of the Governors of the State of Missouri*, 431.

40. OR, 13(1):420.

41. Ibid.

42. *Daily Times* (Leavenworth, Kans.), Oct. 30, 1862.

43. Hicks, "Diary," 7–9.

44. McMahan, *Reluctant Cannoneer*, 69 (Oct. 23, 1862).

45. Ibid.

46. McIntyre, *Federals on the Frontier*, 27–28.

47. Ibid., 36.

48. Thompson, *Civil War Letters*, 26. Also see Beall, "Wildwood Skirmishers," 68.

49. Baxter, *Pea Ridge and Prairie Grove*, 175.

50. Falconer and Ellithorpe Diary, Oct. 28, 1862 (Ellithorpe).

51. Ibid., Nov. 3, 1862.

52. Greene, "Campaigning in the Army of the Frontier," 293–94.

53. OR, 53(1):456–57. For the best treatment of the engagement at Island Mound and the First Kansas Colored generally, see Spurgeon, *Soldiers in the Army of Freedom*, 80–97. See also Nichols, *Guerrilla Warfare in Civil War Missouri*, 1:178–79.

54. OR, 53(1):457.

55. Ibid., 457–58.

56. Falconer and Ellithorpe Diary, Nov. 5–6, 1862 (Ellithorpe).

57. OR, 13(1):445, 461, 761, 776; Falconer and Ellithorpe Diary, Nov. 5–6, 1862 (Ellithorpe).

58. Falconer and Ellithorpe Diary, Nov. 26, 1862 (Ellithorpe).

59. Greene, "Campaigning in the Army of the Frontier," 295.

60. Bishop, *Loyalty on the Frontier*, 102. For a detailed discussion of Wilhite's role in the region, see Prier, "Under the Black Flag," 145–50.

61. Thompson, *Civil War Letters*, 48; Beall, "Wildwood Skirmishers," 69. For an excellent study of the First Arkansas Cavalry (U.S.), see Beall, "Wildwood Skirmishers."

62. Edmund G. Ross to his wife, Nov. 30, 1862, Edmund G. Ross Letters, KSHS.

63. OR, 22(1):75; Banasik, *Embattled Arkansas*; DeBlack, *With Fire and Sword*, 67–72; Don Montgomery, ed., *The Battle of Prairie Grove* (Prairie Grove, Ark.: Prairie Grove Battlefield Historic State Park, 1996). The most thorough study of the Prairie Grove Campaign is Shea, *Fields of Blood*.

64. Greene, "Campaigning in the Army of the Frontier," 300.

65. Margaret Mock to Martha Meier, Apr. 18, 1921, Prairie Grove Files, Prairie Grove Battlefield State Park; Staples, "Personal Recollections," 37.

66. Caledonia Ann (Borden) Brandenburg Memoir, Prairie Grove Battlefield State Park. See also DeBlack, *With Fire and Sword*, 71–72.

67. Baxter, *Pea Ridge and Prairie Grove*, 91.

68. "W. H. Rhea . . . Totals His Losses," 17–18. See also Michael A. Hughes, "Wartime Gristmill Destruction in Northwest Arkansas and Military Farm Colonies," in Bailey and Sutherland, *Civil War Arkansas*, 36–37. According to Hughes, Rhea's Mill changed hands no less than seven times in late 1862.

69. Staples, "Personal Recollections," 37–38.

70. Ibid.

71. *James McFarland v. David Hamley et al.*, box 45, file 141, 1867, Circuit Court Records, Jasper County Records Center.

72. *Martha P. Hood v. David Rusk et al.*, June 19, 1865, box 4, file 40, ibid. David Rusk was second in command under Thomas Livingston. For a description of Livingston's death, see Wood, *Civil War on the Lower Kansas-Missouri Border*, 110–11.

73. "Reminiscences of Major T. S. Chandler," in Missouri Division, United Daughters of the Confederacy, *Reminiscences of the Women of Missouri during the Sixties* (reprint, Dayton, Ohio: Morningside House, 1988), 199–200.

74. Greene, "Campaigning in the Army of the Frontier," 301–2.

75. Ibid., 301–2; Britton, *Civil War on the Border*, 1:433–39; Robert F. Braden, "Selected Letters of Robert F. Braden, 1861–1863," *Indiana History Bulletin* 41 (1964): 120. The captured Confederate steamboats were the *Rose Douglas*, *Notre*, and *Key West*. Britton, *Civil War on the Border*, 1:437.

76. Greene, "Campaigning in the Army of the Frontier," 305.

77. Ibid., 307. See also Britton, *Memoirs of the Rebellion on the Border*, 65–70.

## CHAPTER 4

1. Charges and Specification against Leroy Crain, Jan. 11, 1863, F1243, RPM-MSA. Chapter title from Mecklin, *Letters*, 30.

2. George Falconer and Albert C. Ellithorpe Diary, Jan. 18–19, 1863 (Ellithorpe), Wilson's Creek National Battlefield, Mo.

3. Springer, *Preacher's Tale*, 23–24.

4. Ibid., 25.

5. For a broader treatment of increasing Federal frustration toward the Confederacy, see Grimsley, *Hard Hand of War*, 67–68, 142–44; and Sutherland, "Abraham Lincoln, John Pope, and the Origins of Total War," 568.

6. Interview of Mrs. James Brummett, n.d., in Schrantz, *Jasper County* 197. The Union militia group was Company D, Seventh Provisional Militia.

7. Interview of D. L. Wheeler, n.d., in Schrantz, *Jasper County*, 198–99.

8. "Miss Barrington's Bravery," in United Confederate Veterans, Arkansas Division, *Confederate Women of Arkansas*, 73–74.

9. Baxter, *Pea Ridge and Prairie Grove*, 110–11. See also Prier, "Under the Black Flag," 23–24.

10. Baxter, *Pea Ridge and Prairie Grove*, 110–11.

11. Springer, *Preacher's Tale*, 16–17.

12. Nathan Bray to John Schofield, Feb. 1, 1863, F1282, RPM-MSA.

13. McMahan, *Reluctant Cannoneer*, 128 (Mar. 16, 1863).

14. OR, 22(1):234–35.

15. Ibid.

16. Ibid., 238.

17. Ibid.

18. Ibid. With some exceptions, scouting parties were not prepared to embark on extended chases at the irregulars' whim.

19. Britton, *Memoirs of the Rebellion on the Border*, 193.

20. Hugh L. Thompson, "Baxter Springs as a Military Post," n.d., KSHS, 11–12. Thompson, a member of Company C, Third Wisconsin Regiment, wrote this memoir sometime after the war.

21. James M. Williams to Thomas R. Livingston, May 11, 1863, Regimental Orders and Letter Book, 79th USCT, Records of the Adjutant General's Office, RG 94, NARA.

22. *Official Military History of Kansas Regiments*, 409; Tom Growell and Eliza Jameson interviews, in William N. Pearson, "Sherwood: The Forgotten Village," 1978, R750, State Historical Society of Missouri Research Center—Rolla (hereinafter cited as SHSMRC-Rolla), 198.

23. Thompson, "Baxter Springs as a Military Post," 11–12; OR, 22(1):321–22.

24. Thompson, "Baxter Springs as a Military Post," 14–15. Thomas R. Livingston began his "military" career as a major in the First Missouri Cavalry (C.S.). His tenure in any *official* capacity ended early in the war, and he thenceforth became a guerrilla leader in southwest Missouri. For a study of the man (written by a descendent) with a decidedly pro-Livingston tone, see J. C. Livingston, *Such a Foe as Livingston*.

25. *Official Military History of Kansas Regiments*, 409; OR, 22(1):321–22, 22(2):849. Union reports for lost supplies are exactly the same as Livingston's, a rarity in battle reports. See John Graton to his wife, May 22, 1863, R750, SHSMRC-Rolla.

26. *Official Military History of Kansas Regiments*, 410.

27. John Graton to his wife, May 22, 1863, R750, SHSMRC-Rolla; Thompson, "Baxter Springs as a Military Post," 18. See also Pearsons, "Sherwood."

28. *Official Military History of Kansas Regiments*, 410. The First Kansas Colored Regiment went on to fight in several heated engagements, including the Battles of Honey Springs and Cabin Creek in Indian Territory and, most notably, the Battle of Poison Spring in Arkansas. See Cornish, *Sable Arm*, 146, 152–56; Anne J. Bailey, "Was There a Massacre at Poison Spring?," *Military History of the Southwest* 20 (Fall 1990): 157–68; Gregory J. W. Urwin, "'We Cannot Treat Negroes . . . as Prisoners of War': Racial Atrocities and Reprisals in Civil War Arkansas," in Bailey and Sutherland, *Civil War Arkansas*, 213–29.

29. Thomas R. Livingston to James M. Williams, May 20, 1863, Regimental Orders and Letter Book, 79th USCT, RG 94, NARA.

30. James M. Williams to Thomas R. Livingston, May 21, 1863, ibid.

31. James M. Williams to Thomas R. Livingston, May 26, 1863, ibid.; Thomas R. Livingston to James M. Williams, May 27, 1863, ibid.

32. Williams Collection, Kansas History Center, Topeka. See also Spurgeon, *Soldiers in the Army of Freedom*, 142.

33. OR, 22(1):329.

34. Ibid., 22(2):849.

35. The guerrilla band was surprised in the town square of Stockton, Missouri. Wounded, Livingston fell from his horse within easy reach of Union soldiers. As he tried to escape, the Federals began beat him and later shot him to death. Wood, "Life and Death of Civil War Guerrilla Tom Livingston," 34; Schrantz, *Jasper County*, 189.

36. Clayton Abbott, *Historical Sketches of Cedar County, Missouri* (Greenfield, Mo.: Vedette, 1967), 91–94 (quote on 92).

37. Ibid., 92; J. B. Johnson, *History of Vernon County, Missouri: Past and Present*, vol. 1 (Chicago: C. F. Cooper, 1911), 316. On August 25, 1863, Thomas Ewing ordered most civilians living in the west-central Missouri counties to "remove from their present places of residence within fifteen days." OR, 22(2):473.

38. Dwight D. Hitchcock to "friend," Feb. 11, 1863, Anna August Robertson Moore Papers, Oklahoma Historical Society, Oklahoma City; Warde, "Now the Wolf Has Come," 77–78.

39. U.S. Office of Indian Affairs, *Report of the Commissioner of Indian Affairs 1863*, 179. See also Crowe, "War in the Nations," 210–11.

40. Warde, *When the Wolf Came*, 156–61, 171–75.

41. Springer, *Preacher's Tale*, 73–74.

42. OR, 34(1):602; Bearss and Gibson, *Fort Smith*, 268–69; Springer, *Preacher's Tale*, 72; Crawford, *Kansas in the Sixties*, 101. Also see Thomas A. DeBlack, "1863: 'We Must Stand or Fall Alone,'" in Christ, *Rugged and Sublime*, 88.

43. Bearss and Gibson, *Fort Smith*, 268–70; Springer, *Preacher's Tale*, 86–87.

44. OR, 34(1):603; Bearss and Gibson, *Fort Smith*, 270.

45. Thomas and Sarah Miller to their children, July 24, 1863, Levina Miller Letters, Fort Scott National Historic Site.

46. Mecklin, *Letters*, 20.

47. Ibid., 7, 30.

48. Fellman, *Inside War*, 201. Fellman argues that soldiers and guerrillas maintained a sliver of civility by not directly or purposefully harming white women or young children.

49. Mecklin, *Letters*, 25.

50. Quoted in Banks, "Civil War Refugees from Indian Territory," 294.

51. Larry C. Rampp, "Incident at Baxter Springs on October 6, 1863," *Kansas Historical Quarterly* 2 (Summer 1970): 185–87. For the best historical analysis of the Baxter Springs massacre, see Lindberg and Matthews, "It Haunts Me Night and Day," 42–53.

52. *OR*, 22(1):689, 701; Lindberg and Matthews, "It Haunts Me Day and Night," 50.

53. Lindberg and Matthews, "It Haunts Me Day and Night," 51.

54. Ibid.

55. *OR*, 22(1):697.

56. Lindberg and Matthews, "It Haunts Me Day and Night," 48.

57. Ibid.

58. Blunt, "General Blunt," 248.

59. Charles E. Beecham to his mother, July 15, 1862, Charles E. Beecham Letters, Wisconsin State Historical Society, Madison; Fellman, *Inside War*, 164.

60. "Arrival of General Blunt," *Fort Smith New Era*, Nov. 14, 1863, 2. The *New Era* began operations after the Federal takeover of Fort Smith in early September 1863.

61. *Fort Smith New Era*, Nov. 14, 1863.

62. Springer, *Preacher's Tale*, 93–94.

63. *Fort Smith New Era*, Nov. 21, 1863; Langsdorf, "Letters of Joseph H. Trego," 384.

64. *Fort Smith New Era*, Nov. 28, 1863.

65. Crawford, *Kansas in the Sixties*, 104.

66. Strong, "Rough Introduction," 14–15.

67. Ibid., 16–17.

68. Mecklin, *Letters*, 30.

69. Ibid., 30.

70. Ibid. For work on Vietnam-era counterinsurgency measures, especially the destruction of the forests to rid the enemy of cover, see Robert Schulzinger, *A Time for War: The United States and Vietnam, 1941–1975* (New York: Oxford University Press, 1997), 193. Although both Daniel E. Sutherland and Robert R. Mackey argue against any attempt to draw parallels between Civil War–era guerrilla warfare and twentieth-century models, specific comparisons are helpful in understanding broader implications of irregular warfare through history. See Sutherland, *Savage Conflict*; and Mackey, *Uncivil War*, 23.

71. Fred H. Wines to John B. Sanborn, Dec. 3, 1863, entry 3421, pt. 2, RG 393, NARA.

72. Ibid.

73. Britton, *Memoirs of the Rebellion on the Border*, 127; Schrantz, *Jasper County*, 240.

74. Mecklin, *Letters*, 29; *Fort Smith New Era*, Dec. 26, 1863, 3. Locally, Federal victories at Little Rock and Helena provided an optimistic tone for Unionist civilians on the southern Trans-Mississippi frontier. For an adroit analysis of the battle of Helena, July 3, 1863, and its larger ramifications for warfare in the Trans-Mississippi theater, see Schieffler, "Too Little, Too Late to Save Vicksburg."

## CHAPTER 5

1. *Fort Smith New Era*, Jan. 9, 1864, 4; Strong, "Rough Introduction," 19; Porter, *In the Devil's Dominion*, 121.

2. Mecklin, *Letters*, 32.

3. *OR*, 34(2):24.

4. *OR*, 34(1):925; Moneyhon, *Impact of the Civil War and Reconstruction on Arkansas*, 131.

5. *OR*, 34(1):86–87. See also Moneyhon, *Impact of the Civil War and Reconstruction on Arkansas*, 133.

6. *Fort Smith New Era*, Jan. 9, 1864, 6.

7. Strong, "Rough Introduction," 21, 25.

8. John A. Mitchell to his family, Feb. 21, Mar. 9, 1864, John A. Mitchell Civil War Letters, MSS 07-18, Butler Center for Arkansas Studies, Arkansas Studies Institute.

9. *Fort Smith New Era*, Jan. 30, Mar. 18, 1864.

10. Bradbury, "Buckwheat Cake Philanthropy," 243–44.

11. Strong, "Rough Introduction," 22.

12. *Fort Smith New Era*, Feb. 20, 1864, 3.

13. Mecklin, *Letters*, 35, 37, 39. For a broad discussion of food's prominent role in the Civil War, see Steinberg, *Down to Earth*, 89–98.

14. Interview of Mrs. Hazelwood (John Onstott's daughter), n.d., in Schrantz, *Jasper County*, 202.

15. Ozias Ruark Diary, Feb. 27, 1864, C2651, SHSMRC-Columbia; *OR*, 34(1):605. See also "Thomas Alexander vs. Rice and Hugh Challas, 1865," Community & Conflict: The Impact of the Civil War in the Ozarks, Springfield–Greene County Library District, http://www.ozarkscivilwar.org/archives/1265.

16. *OR*, 34(2):443–44.

17. Ibid.

18. Beckenbaugh, "War of Politics," 115–16.

19. *OR*, 34(2):504, 527. See also Beckenbaugh, "War of Politics," 115–16.

20. *OR*, 34(2):775–77.

21. Ibid., 776.

22. Ibid., 34(1):925. See also Moneyhon, *Impact of the Civil War and Reconstruction on Arkansas*, 131. Moneyhon shows that most semblances of civil and military authority in northern Arkansas had broken down by 1864, if not earlier.

23. *Fort Smith New Era*, Mar. 26, 1864.

24. Thomas Moonlight, Circular of Instruction, Apr. 5, 1864, entry 3362, RG393, NARA.

25. Ibid.

26. *Fort Smith New Era*, July 29, 1864.

27. Springer, *Preacher's Tale*, 113–14, 119, 122; *Fort Smith New Era*, July 29, 1864. The letters by each guerrilla prisoner are published in Appendix A of Springer, *Preacher's Tale*, 114–26.

28. *Freedoms Champion* (Atchison, Kans.), May 5, 1864; *Fort Smith New Era*, May 28, 1864.

29. *Fort Smith New Era*, May 28, 1864.

30. OR, 34(4):84. For the best treatment of the refugee problem in the region, see Bradbury, "Buckwheat Cake Philanthropy." See also Bearss and Gibson, *Fort Smith*, 290–91.

31. Hugh Sloan to his wife, May 20, 1864, Hugh Sloan Letters, Vertical File, Fort Scott National Historic Site, Kans.; OR, 34(1):942.

32. Sloan to his wife, May 20, 1864.

33. Ibid.

34. Ibid.

35. Ibid.

36. Priscilla Hunter to Margaret Newberry, July 1864, Hunter Family Letters, SHSMRC-Rolla.

37. Burt Stemmons, "Antebellum House in Poor Repair Is Only Monument to Orange Clark, Union Soldier Killed Here in 1864," *Carthage Press*, Oct. 22, 1962; U.S. Bureau of the Census, Population Schedules, Missouri, 1860.

38. Stemmons, "Antebellum House." Martha Clark's neighbor had heard about her ordeal and wrote to her family in Illinois about the encounter. The guerrilla band "came to Mrs. Clark's and cut up a terrible rate [and] made her give them what money she had and took a good many things." Priscilla Hunter to Margaret Newberry, Sept. 25, 1864, Hunter Family Letters, SHSMRC-Rolla.

39. Schrantz, *Jasper County*, 191.

40. *Martha Clark v. David Rusk, et al*, Oct. 20, 1865, box 4, file 40, Circuit Court Records, Jasper County Records Center, Carthage, Mo.

41. *Elizabeth Baker v. David Rusk et al.*, 1865, box 11, file 91, ibid.

42. Christian H. Isely to his wife, Aug. 22, 1864, Isely Family Papers, Special Collections and University Archives, Wichita State University, Kansas.

43. Ibid.

44. *Freedom's Champion* (Atchison, Kans.), Sept. 15, 1864.

45. OR, 41(1):267–68; Michael A. Hughes, "Wartime Gristmill Destruction in Northwest Arkansas and Military Farm Colonies," in Bailey and Sutherland, *Civil War Arkansas*, 37–38.

Infamous northwest Arkansas guerrilla William "Buck" Brown had owned Brown's Mill in Washington County before the war.

46. OR, 41(1):729. See also Castel, *General Sterling Price and the Civil War in the West*, 200–202.

47. OR, 41(1):465; Sutherland, *Savage Conflict*, 201–4. For the best overview of Price's Raid, see Lause, *Price's Lost Campaign*.

48. Fellman, *Inside War*, 110–11.

49. John Sanborn to L. J. Mitchell, Sept. 20, 1864, in Schrantz, *Jasper County*, 210–11.

50. D. L. Wheeler interview, n.d., in ibid., 213–14.

51. Ibid.

52. Sara Ann Smith interview, n.d., in ibid., 215.

53. *Jasper County v. John B. Chenault et al.*, 1867, box 23, file 117, Circuit Court Records, Jasper County Records Center; Charles Blair to Samuel Curtis, Sept. 24, 1864, in Schrantz, *Jasper County*, 211–12.

54. Priscilla Hunter to Margaret Newberry, 25 Sept. 1864, Hunter Family Letters, SHSMRC-Rolla. Hunter was fairly accurate concerning the number of men in Price's army, though by the time he came back south through Jasper County toward Arkansas, he had far fewer than 10,000 men. Raids did come—and quite frequently—after Hunter wrote to her sister. Price, having failed in his attempt to recruit 75,000 Confederate sympathizers, led his army through Jasper County in the beginning of October. He did so quickly, for he wished to return to the relative safety of Arkansas and the Indian Territory. See Fellman, *Inside War*, 108.

55. Elizabeth Hunter to "My dear children," Nov. 1, 1864, Hunter Family Letters, SHSMRC-Rolla.

56. Ibid.

57. *Union Monitor* (Fort Scott, Kans.), Oct. 17, 1864.

58. Crawford, *Kansas in the Sixties*, 170.

59. McPheeters, "I Acted from Principle," 238–39 (Oct. 26, 29, 31, 1864).

60. Green Stotts to John Sanborn, n.d., in Schrantz, *Jasper County*, 229.

61. Ibid.

62. J. Mont. Wilson, "Barbarities in Northwest Arkansas," *Confederate Veteran* 14 (Feb. 1911): 74.

63. Ibid.

64. Ibid.

65. Elizabeth Hunter to Margaret Newberry, Jan. 10, 1865, Hunter Family Letters, SHSMRC-Rolla.

66. Ibid.

67. Ibid.

68. Priscilla Hunter to her sister, Nov. 1, 1864, ibid.

69. *Fort Smith New Era*, Aug. 13, 1864; Bearss and Gibson, *Fort Smith*, 292.

70. Strong, "Rough Introduction," 74.

71. *Fort Smith New Era*, Jan. 21, 1865, 2 (first, third quotes); Strong, "*Rough Introduction*," 74 (second quote); OR, 48(2):16–17.

72. Nathan Bray to John B. Sanborn, Feb. 22, 1865, pt. 2, entry 3421, RG393, NARA.

73. *Fort Smith New Era*, Jan. 21, 1865, 2.

74. OR, 48(1):741–43.

75. *Fort Smith New Era*, Feb. 11, 1865; *National Democrat* (Little Rock), Feb. 25, 1865. The accused include soldiers from the Fourteenth and Sixth Kansas Cavalry.

76. OR, 48(1):741–43.

77. Ibid., 790–91.

78. *National Democrat* (Little Rock), Apr. 1, 1865.

79. OR, 48(1):142–43.

80. Ibid., 144–45.

81. Ibid., 1120–21; *National Democrat* (Little Rock), Apr. 1, 1865. See also Hughes, "Wartime Gristmill Destruction," 38–39.

82. *Fort Smith New Era*, Mar. 25, 1865. By March, "post colonies" had been established at Union Valley, Walnut Grove, Mountain Prairie, West Fork, Middle Fork, Mount Comfort, Elm Spring, Bentonville, Pea Ridge, Osage, Huntsville, War Eagle, Richland, and Brush Creek. Ibid.

83. OR, 41(4):917; Carl Moneyhon, "1865: 'A State of Perfect Anarchy,'" in Christ, *Rugged and Sublime*, 148; Hughes, "Wartime Gristmill Destruction," 40–41; Mackey, *Uncivil War*, 69; Daniel E. Sutherland, "Guerrillas: The Real War in Arkansas," in Bailey and Sutherland, *Civil War Arkansas*, 151–53.

84. *Fort Smith New Era*, Mar. 25, 1865; Hughes, "Wartime Gristmill Destruction," 40–41; Mackey, *Uncivil War*, 69.

85. Hughes, "Wartime Gristmill Destruction," 41; Mackey, *Uncivil War*, 68–70.

86. OR, 48(1):1179.

87. Ibid., 789–90, 1179.

88. Ibid.; W. A. Phillips to Cyrus Bussey, Mar. 7, 1865, Fort Gibson Letterbook, vol. 93, Department of Arkansas, Letters and Orders, RG 393, NARA. See also Crowe, "War in the Nations," 326–27.

89. Ibid.

## CONCLUSION

1. Anita Bukey and Evan Burr Bukey, eds., "Arkansas after the War: From the Journal of Frederick Gerstaecker," *Arkansas Historical Quarterly* 32 (Autumn 1973): 268; Moneyhon, *Impact of the Civil War and Reconstruction on Arkansas*, 134–35. Moneyhon uses the *Biennial Report of the Auditor of Public Accounts of the State of Arkansas, for 1859 and 1860* (Little Rock, 1860), Table H; and *Biennial Report of the Auditor of Public Accounts for the State of Arkansas for 1864, 1865, and 1866* (Little Rock, 1866), Table 9. See also DeBlack, *With Fire and Sword*, 143–45.

2. Baxter, *Pea Ridge and Prairie Grove*, 64; Fort Smith New Era, Apr. 1, 1865.

3. *Daily Arkansas Gazette*, Aug. 15, 1866, quoted in Huff, "Guerrillas, Jayhawkers, and Bushwhackers in Northern Arkansas," 148.

4. Hicks, "Diary," 22.

5. *Annual Report of the Bureau of Ethnology to the Secretary of the Smithsonian Institution, 1880* (Washington, D.C.: Government Printing Office, 1887), 376; Confer, *Cherokee Nation in the Civil War*, 145. See also Minges, *Slavery in the Cherokee Nation*, 160; and Lause, *Race and Radicalism*, 129. For population, see especially Thornton, *Cherokees*.

6. Baxter, *Pea Ridge and Prairie Grove*, 64; Downs, *Sick from Freedom*. See also Bradbury, "Buckwheat Cake Philanthropy," 235–36.

7. Mecklin, *Letters*, 37–38.

8. Ibid., 16, 37–38; Hahn, *Nation under Our Feet*, 82–83.

9. See Fellman, *Inside War*, 176–92; and Moneyhon, *Impact of the Civil War and Reconstruction on Arkansas*, 133.

10. Sutherland, *Savage Conflict*, x; Unconditional Union, Apr. 8, 1864, quoted in Huff, "Guerrillas, Jayhawkers, and Bushwhackers in Northern Arkansas," 144.

11. OR, (22):473; Fort Smith New Era, Nov. 14, 1863. Daniel E. Sutherland makes a similar argument in regard to the South as a whole, concluding that the general guerrilla war effort played a "decisive" and direct role in Confederate defeat. See *Savage Conflict*, xiii.

# BIBLIOGRAPHY

## MANUSCRIPT SOURCES

**Arkansas History Commission, Little Rock**
Civil War Letters and Papers of Jonathan W. Callaway, CSA

**Briscoe Center for American History, The University of Texas, Austin**
Capt. A. B. Blocker Memoir
Stand Watie Papers

**Butler Center for Arkansas Studies, Little Rock**
David E. Ballard Civil War Letters
John A. Mitchell Civil War Letters
John Reed Civil War Letters

**Fort Scott National Historic Site, Kansas**
Levina Miller Letters
Hugh Sloan Letters, Vertical Files

**Jasper County Records Center, Carthage, Missouri**
Circuit Court Records, 1865–76

**Kansas City Public Library, Kansas City, Missouri**
James J. Akard Papers

**Kansas History Center, Topeka**
Williams Collection

**Kansas State Historical Society, Topeka**
Albert C. Ellithorpe Collection
Edmund G. Ross Letters
Hugh L. Thompson, "Baxter Springs as a Military Post," n.d.
Joseph Harrington Trego Papers, 1850–89, Collection 523
Kansas State Auditor, "Record of Claims Allowed for Losses by Guerillas and
    Marauders during 1861–1865"

**Missouri Historical Society, Saint Louis**
Civil War Collection
George Richardson Cruzen, "The Story of My Life"
Hamilton R. Gamble Collection
Gert Goebel, "The Development of Missouri"

**Missouri State Archives, Jefferson City**
Record Group 003, Office of the Governor
    Claiborne Fox Jackson
    Hamilton R. Gamble
    Willard P. Hall
    Thomas C. Fletcher
Record Group 005, Office of the Secretary of State
Record Group 109, Records of the Provost Marshal
Record Group 133, Office of the Adjutant General of Missouri
Record Group 403, Civil War Centennial of Missouri

**National Archives and Record Administration, Washington, D.C.**
Record Group 75, Correspondence of the Office of Indian Affairs
Record Group 94, Records of the Adjutant General's Office
Record Group 107, Office of the Secretary of War
Record Group 109, War Department Collection of Captured Confederate Records
Record Group 110, Provost Marshal General's Bureau
Record Group 153, Office of the Judge Advocate General (Army), 1692–1981
Record Group 393, Records of U.S. Army Continental Commands, 1821–1920

**Oklahoma Historical Society, Oklahoma City**
John Harrah Collection, 1865
George Fine Collections, 1862
Anna August Robertson Moore Papers

Kenneth N. Phillips Collection
John Ross Letters Collection
George L. Washington Papers, 1863
Stand Watie Collection, 1846–84

**Prairie Grove Battlefield State Park, Prairie Grove, Arkansas**
Caledonia Ann (Borden) Brandenburg Memoir
Prairie Grove Files

**Rare Book, Manuscript, and Special Collections, Duke University, Durham, North Carolina**
S. S. Marrett Papers, 1862–83
Missouri Militia Records, 1861–65
Reports of the Adjutant-General of the State of Missouri
J. H. Rhea Diary, 1857–66
Phillip D. Riggs Letters, 1862–70
Abby E. Stafford Papers, 1859–66
Shadrach Ward Papers, 1854–71
James H. Wiswell Letters, 1861–67

**Shiloh Museum of Ozark History, Springdale, Arkansas**
Rhea's Mill Ledger

**Southern Historical Collection, University of North Carolina Library, Chapel Hill**
Richard Caswell Gatlin Papers
Kenton Harper Papers
Henry Champlin Lay Papers
John R. Peacock Papers
Trusten Polk Papers
W. H. Stewart Reminiscence, 1894
M. Jeff Thompson Papers
Isabella Ann Roberts Woodruff Papers

**Special Collections, University of Arkansas, Fayetteville**
Clinton Owen Bates Memoir
Jonathan W. Callaway Letters and Papers, 1861–64, film 322
Rebecca Stirman Davidson Papers, 1860–1958
Sarah Jane Smith Collection

**Special Collections, University of Iowa, Ames**
Lot Abraham Papers, 1841–1921

**Special Collections and University Archives, Wichita State University, Kansas**
Isely Family Papers

**State Historical Society of Missouri Research Center—Columbia**
Ozias Ruark Collection
I. V. Smith Memoirs

**State Historical Society of Missouri Research Center—Rolla**
Lyman Gibson Bennett Collection
Franklin S. Denny Diary, 1862–64
John Graton Papers
Hunter-Hagler Collection
Thomas Murray Collection
Ozias Ruark Collection

**Wichita State University Special Collections and University Archives**
Isley Family Papers

**Wilson's Creek National Battlefield, Republic, Missouri**
George Falconer and Albert C. Ellithorpe Diary
John W. Fisher Diary
John S. Phelps Papers

**Wisconsin Historical Society, Madison**
Charles E. Beecham Letters
Quiner Scrapbooks, Correspondence of the Wisconsin Volunteers, 1861–65, vols. 1–10

## GOVERNMENT DOCUMENTS

Hewett, Janet B., et al., eds. *Supplement to the Official Records of the Union and Confederate Armies.* 100 vols. in 3 pts. plus index. Wilmington, N.C.: Broadfoot, 1994–2001.
Leopard, Buel, and Floyd C. Shoemaker, eds. *The Messages and Proclamations of the Governors of the State of Missouri.* Columbia: State Historical Society of Missouri, 1922.

*Official Military History of Kansas Regiments during the War for the Suppression of the Great Rebellion.* Leavenworth, KS: W.S. Burke, 1870.

U.S. Bureau of the Census. Agriculture Schedules. Arkansas, Kansas, and Missouri. 1860.

———. *Agriculture of the United States in 1860, Compiled from the Original Returns of the Eighth Census.* Washington, D.C., 1867.

———. *Manufactures of the United States in 1860, Compiled from the Original Returns of the Eighth Census.* Washington, D.C., 1867.

———. Population Schedules. Missouri and Arkansas. 1860, 1870.

———. Products of Industry. Arkansas and Missouri. 1860.

———. Slave Schedules. Arkansas and Missouri. 1860.

———. Social Statistics. Arkansas and Missouri. 1860.

U.S. Office of Indian Affairs. *Report of the Commissioner of Indian Affairs, for the Year 1862.* Washington, D.C.: Government Printing Office, 1863.

U.S. Office of Indian Affairs. *Report of the Commissioner of Indian Affairs, for the Year 1863.* Washington, D.C.: Government Printing Office, 1864.

U.S. Office of Indian Affairs. *Report of the Commissioner of Indian Affairs, for the Year 1864.* Washington, D.C.: Government Printing Office, 1865.

U.S. War Department. *War of the Rebellion: A Compilation of the Official Records of the Union and Confederate Armies.* 70 vols. in 128 parts. Washington, D.C.: Government Printing Office, 1880–1901.

## NEWSPAPERS

*Arkansas Gazette* (Little Rock)

*Border Star* (Kansas City, Mo.)

*Buck & Ball* (Cane Hill, Ark.)

*Chicago Evening Journal*

*Cincinnati (Ohio) Daily Gazette*

*Daily Missouri Democrat* (Saint Louis)

*Daily Times* (Leavenworth, Kans.)

*Fort Scott Bulletin*

*Fort Scott Daily Monitor*

*Fort Smith New Era*

*Fort Smith Times and Herald*

*Freedom's Champion* (Atchison, Kans.)

Kansas Daily Tribune (Lawrence)
Kansas Weekly Tribune (Lawrence)
Lawrence (Kans.) Republican
Leavenworth (Kans.) Daily Conservative
Liberty (Mo.) Tribune
New York Times

## PUBLISHED PRIMARY SOURCES

Armitage, Katie H., ed. "Elizabeth 'Bettie' Duncan: Diary of Daily Life, 1864." *Kansas History* 10 (Winter 1987–88): 275–89.

Badger, David W. "Civil War Letters of Corporal David W. Badger." *Flashback* 47 (February 1997): 24–30.

Bailey, Joseph M. *Confederate Guerrilla: The Civil War Memoir of Joseph M. Bailey.* Edited by T. Lindsey Baker. Fayetteville: University of Arkansas Press, 2007.

Baird, W. David., ed. *A Creek Warrior for the Confederacy: The Autobiography of Chief G. W. Grayson.* Norman: University of Oklahoma Press, 1988.

Banasik, Michael, ed. *Missouri Brothers in Gray: The Reminiscences and Letters of William J. Bull and John P. Bull.* Iowa City: Camp Pope Bookshop, 1998.

Barry, Louise, ed. "With the First U.S. Cavalry in Indian Country, 1859–1861, Concluded." *Kansas Historical Quarterly* 24 (Winter 1958): 399–425.

Bartels, Carolyn, ed. *Iowa Boy Makes Good: Dr. Seymour Carpenter, His Memoirs.* Shawnee Mission, Kans.: Two Trails, 1996.

Barton, O. S. *Three Years with Quantrill: A True Story Told by His Scout John McCorkle.* 1914. Reprint, Norman: University of Oklahoma Press, 1992.

Bates, James C. *A Texas Cavalry Officer's Civil War: The Diary and Letters of James C. Bates.* Edited by Richard Lowe. Baton Rouge: Louisiana State University Press, 1999.

Baxter, William. *Pea Ridge and Prairie Grove; Or, Scenes and Incidents of the War in Arkansas.* Cincinnati: Poe and Hitchcock, 1864.

Bek, William G., ed. "The Civil War Diary of John T. Buegel." *Missouri Historical Review* 40 (1946): 307–29.

Bender, Robert Patrick, ed. *Worthy of the Cause for Which They Fight: The Civil War Diary of Brigadier General Daniel Harris Reynolds, 1861–1865.* Fayetteville: University of Arkansas Press, 2011.

Bishop, A. W. *Loyalty on the Frontier, or Sketches of Union Men of the South-West, with Incidents and Adventures in Rebellion on the Border.* Edited by Kim Allen Scott. Fayetteville: University of Arkansas Press, 2003.

Blunt, James G. "General Blunt's Account of His Civil War Experiences." *Kansas Historical Quarterly* 1 (May 1932): 211–65.

Bock, H. Riley, ed. "Confederate Col. A. C. Riley: His Reports and Letters: Part I." *Missouri Historical Review* 85 (January 1991): 158–81.

Britton, Wiley. *The Civil War on the Border.* 2 vols. New York: Putnam's Sons, 1891.

————. *Memoirs of the Rebellion on the Border, 1863.* 1882. Reprint, Lincoln: University of Nebraska Press, 1993.

————. *Pioneer Life in Southwest Missouri.* Kansas City, Mo.: Smith-Grieves, 1929.

————. *The Union Indian Brigade in the Civil War.* Kansas City, Mo.: Franklin Hudson, 1922.

Christ, Mark K., and Patrick G. Williams, eds. *I Do Wish This Cruel War Was Over: First-Person Accounts of Civil War Arkansas from the Arkansas Historical Quarterly.* Fayetteville: University of Arkansas Press, 2014.

"A Confederate Soldier Writes Home." *Flashback* 24 (November 1974): 27–29.

Crawford, Samuel J. *Kansas in the Sixties.* A. C. McLurg, 1911. Reprint, Ottawa: Kansas Heritage, 1994.

Darling, Earnest F. "Lincoln's Message to Indian Territory." *Chronicles of Oklahoma* 63 (June 1985): 186–91.

Davis, Jefferson. *The Papers of Jefferson Davis.* Edited by Lynda Liswell Crist. 10 vols. Baton Rouge: Louisiana State University Press, 1995.

Demuth, Albert. *The Civil War Letters of Albert Demuth and the Roster Eighth Missouri Cavalry [U.S.].* Edited by Leo E. Huff. Springfield, Mo.: Greene County Historical Society, 1997.

Dobak, William A., ed. "Civil War on the Kansas-Missouri Border: The Narrative of Former Slave Andrew Williams." *Kansas History* 6 (Winter 1983–84): 237–42.

Donat, Pat, ed. "Diary of Joseph Sanders." *Flashback* 34 (August 1984): 1–11.

Dryden, John G. *With Plow and Pen: The Diary of John G. Dryden, 1856–1883.* Edited by Patrick Brophy. Nevada, Mo.: Vernon County Historical Society, 2001.

Editors. "The Civil War Diary of John Howard Kitts." *Collections of the Kansas State Historical Society* 14 (1915–16): 318–27.

————. "The Letters of Samuel James Reader, 1861–1863." *Kansas Historical Quarterly* 9 (February 1940): 26–57.

Edwards, John N. *Noted Guerrillas; Or, Warfare of the Border.* St. Louis: Bryan, Brand, 1877.

Edwards, Whit, ed. *The Prairie Was on Fire: Eyewitness Accounts of the Civil War in Indian Territory.* Oklahoma City: Oklahoma Historical Society, 2001.

Estes, Thomas Jerome. *Early Days and War Times in Northern Arkansas.* Lubbock: Dow Printing, 1928.

Evans, Clarence, ed. and trans. "Memoirs, Letters, and Diary Entries of German Settlers in Northwest Arkansas, 1853–1863." *Arkansas Historical Quarterly* 6 (Fall 1947): 225–49.

Frederick, J. V., ed. "War Diary of W. C. Porter." *Arkansas Historical Quarterly* 11 (Winter 1952): 286–314.

Fremont, Jessie Benton. *The Letters of Jessie Benton Fremont.* Edited by Pamela Herr and Mary Jane Spence. Urbana: University of Illinois Press, 1993.

Gause, Isaac. *Four Years with Five Armies.* New York: Neale, 1908.

Glover, Robert W., ed. "The War Letters of a Texas Conscript in Arkansas." *Arkansas Historical Quarterly* 20 (Winter 1961): 355–87.

Greene, Albert R. "Campaigning in the Army of the Frontier." *Collections of the Kansas State Historical Society* 14 (1918): 283–310.

Haas, Jacob. *"This Day We Marched Again": A Union Soldier's Account of War in Arkansas and the Trans-Mississippi.* Edited by Mark K. Christ. Little Rock: Butler Center for Arkansas Studies, 2014.

Haynes, Dennis E. *A Thrilling Narrative: The Memoir of a Southern Unionist.* 1866. Reprint, edited by Arthur W. Bergeron, Jr., Fayetteville: University of Arkansas Press, 2006.

Hemphill, Anne E., ed. "The 1864 Diary of Cpl. Seth Kelly." *Kansas History* 1 (Autumn 1978): 189–210.

Hicks, Hannah. "The Diary of Hannah Hicks." *American Scene* 13, no. 3 (1972): 1–24.

Hinds, M. Dallas Pittman. "A Civil War Journey, Part II." *Flashback* 27 (August 1977): 27–34.

Hinds, W. G. D. "True Stories of the Adventures of the Civil War." Edited by Bill Painter. *Arkansas Historical Quarterly* 13 (Winter 1954): 325–37.

———. "A True Story of the Civil War." *Flashback* 27 (May 1977): 1–8.

King, Wilburn Hill. *With the 18th Texas Infantry: The Autobiography of Wilburn Hill King.* Edited by L. David Norris. Hillsboro, Tex.: Hill College Press, 1996.

Kiper, Richard L., ed. *Dear Catherine, Dear Taylor: The Civil War Letters of a Union Soldier and His Wife.* Lawrence: University Press of Kansas, 2002.

Langsdorf, Edgar, ed. "The Letters of Joseph H. Trego, 1857–1864, Linn County Pioneer." *Kansas Historical Quarterly* 19 (August 1951): 287–309.

Lee, Elizabeth Blair. *Wartime Washington: The Civil War Letters of Elizabeth Blair Lee.* Edited by Virginia Jeans Laas. Urbana: University of Illinois Press, 1989.

Lemke, W. J., ed. "A Civil War Court Martial in Fayetteville." *Flashback* 7 (November 1957): 19–26.

———. "A Kansas Soldier in Northwest Arkansas." *Flashback* 8 (May 1958): 15–18.

———. "A Wartime Diary in Northwest Arkansas." *Flashback* 6 (November 1956): 3–11.

Macha, Jurgen, and Andrea Wolf, ed. *Michael Zimmer's Diary: En Deutsches Tagebuch aus dem Amerikanischen Burgerkrieg*. Frankfurt: Peter Lang, 2001.

Marshall, Albert O. *Army Life; From a Soldier's Journal*. Joliet, Ill., 1884.

McIntyre, Benjamin F. *Federals on the Frontier: The Diary of Benjamin F. McIntyre, 1862–1864*. Edited by Nannie M. Tilley. Austin: University of Texas Press, 1963.

McMahan, Robert T. "Campaigning through Missouri: The Civil War Journal of Robert Todd McMahan: Part 1." Edited by Dennis K. Boman. *Missouri Historical Review* 93 (January 1999): 133–48.

———. "Campaigning through Missouri: The Civil War Journal of Robert Todd Mcmahan, Part 2." Edited by Dennis K. Boman. *Missouri Historical Review* 93 (April 1999): 241–56.

———. *Reluctant Cannoneer: The Diary of Robert T. McMahan of the Twenty-Fifth Independent Ohio Light Artillery*. Edited by Michael E. Banasik. Iowa City: Camp Pope Bookshop, 2000.

McPheeters, William M. *"I Acted from Principle": The Civil War Diary of Dr. William M. McPheeters, Confederate Surgeon in the Trans-Mississippi*. Edited by Cynthia DeHaven Pitcock and Bill J. Gurley. Fayetteville: University of Arkansas Press, 2002.

Mecklin, Robert W. *The Mecklin Letters*. Edited by W. J. Lemke. Fayetteville, Ark.: Washington County Historical Society, 1955.

Monks, William. *A History of Southern Missouri and Northern Arkansas: Being an Account of the Early Settlements, the Civil War, the Ku-Klux, and Times of Peace*. Edited by John F. Bradbury Jr. and Lou Wehmer. Fayetteville: University of Arkansas Press, 2003.

Noble, Henry T., et al. *Military History and Reminiscences of the Thirteenth Regiment of Illinois Volunteer Infantry in the Civil War in the United States, 1861–1865*. Chicago: Women's Temperance Publications, 1892.

Panter, Bill, ed. "True Stories of Adventures of the Civil War." *Arkansas Historical Quarterly* 13 (Winter 1954): 325–37.

Park, Ruie Ann Smith, ed. *"Dear Parents": The Civil War Letters of the Shibley Brothers of Van Buren, Arkansas*. Fayetteville, Ark.: Washington County Historical Society, 1963.

Patrick, Jeffrey L., ed. "'This Regiment Will Make a Mark': Letters from a Member of Jennison's Jayhawkers, 1861–1862." *Kansas History* 20 (Spring 1997): 50–58.

Porter, Charles W. *In the Devil's Dominion: A Union Soldier's Adventures in "Bushwhacker Country."* Edited by Patrick Brophy. Nevada, Mo.: Vernon County Historical Society, 1998.

Quiner, E. B. *The Military History of Wisconsin: A Record of the Civil and Military Patriotism of the State in the War for the Union*. Chicago: Clarke, 1866.

Ross, John. *The Papers of Chief John Ross*. Edited by Gary Moulton. Vol. 2. Norman: University of Oklahoma Press, 1985.

Schrantz, Ward L. *Jasper County, Missouri, in the Civil War*. Carthage, Mo.: Carthage Press, 1923.

Scott, Joe M. *Four Years' Service in the Southern Army*. Fayetteville, Ark.: Washington County Historical Society, 1958.

Scott, S. S., with an introduction by Mark Lea Cantrell. "Condition of the Indians West of Arkansas, 1863." *Chronicles of Oklahoma* 62 (September 1984): 325–33.

Springer, Francis. *The Preacher's Tale: The Civil War Journal of Rev. Francis Springer, Chaplain, U.S. Army of the Frontier*. Edited by William Furry. Fayetteville: University of Arkansas Press, 2001.

Staples, Nancy Morton. "Personal Recollections of the Battle of Prairie Grove and Troubles that Followed." *Flashback* 2 (December 1952): 37–38.

Strong, Henry A. *"A Rough Introduction to This Sunny Land": The Civil War Diary of Private Henry A. Strong, Co. K, Twelfth Kansas Infantry*. Edited by Tom Wing. Little Rock: Butler Center for Arkansas Studies, 2006.

Suderow, Bryce A., ed., "McLain's Battery and Price's 1864 Invasion: A Letter from Lt. Caleb S. Burdsal, Jr." *Kansas History* 6 (Spring 1983): 29–45.

"The Pittman Family in the Civil War." *Flashback* 27 (August 1977): 17–34.

Thompson, Alan, ed. "'Frank and Out Spoken in My Disposition': The Wartime Letters of Confederate General Dandridge McRae." *Arkansas Historical Quarterly* 72 (Winter 2013): 333–65.

Thompson, William G. *The Civil War Letters of Major William G. Thompson of the 20th Iowa Infantry Regiment*. Edited by Edwin C. Bearrs. Fayetteville, Ark.: Washington County Historical Society, 1966.

Turnbo, Silas Claborn. *Turnbo's Tales of the Ozarks: War and Guerrilla Stories*. Edited by Desmond Walls Allen. Conway: Arkansas Research, 1989.

United Confederate Veterans, Arkansas Division. *Confederate Women of Arkansas in the Civil War, 1861–1865: Memorial Reminiscences*. 1907. Reprint, edited by Michael B. Dougan, Fayetteville, Ark.: M&M, 1993.

"W. H. Rhea . . . Totals His Losses." *Flashback* (May 1956): 17–18.

Watson, William. *Life in the Confederate Army, being the Observations and Experiences of an Alien in the South during the American Civil War*. New York: Scribner and Welford, 1888.

Winn, Robert G. "A Civil War Casualty." *Flashback* 27 (February 1977): 1–3.

Wright, John C. *Memoirs of John C. Wright*. Pine Bluff, Ark: Rare Book, 1982.

Yeater, Sarah Ellis. "Civil War Experiences of Sarah Ellis Yeater." *Flashback* 3 (August 1966): 13–35.

## SECONDARY SOURCES: BOOKS

Ash, Stephen V. *When the Yankees Came: Conflict and Chaos in the Occupied South, 1861–1865*. Chapel Hill: University of North Carolina Press, 1995.

Astor, Aaron. *Rebels on the Border: Civil War, Emancipation, and the Reconstruction of Kentucky and Missouri*. Baton Rouge: Louisiana State University Press, 2012.

Bailey, Anne J., and Daniel E. Sutherland, eds. *Civil War Arkansas: Beyond Battles and Leaders*. Fayetteville: University of Arkansas Press, 2000.

Banasik, Michael E. *Embattled Arkansas: The Prairie Grove Campaign of 1862*. Wilmington, N.C.: Broadfoot, 1996.

Bartels, Carolyn M. *Stand Watie and the First Cherokee Regiment, 1861 to 1865*. Shawnee Mission, Kans.: Two Trails, 1995.

Bearss, Edwin C., and Arrell M. Gibson. *Fort Smith: Little Gibraltar on the Arkansas*. 2nd ed. Norman: University of Oklahoma Press, 1979.

Beilein, Joseph M., Jr., and Matthew C. Hulbert, eds. *The Civil War Guerrilla: Unfolding the Black Flag in History, Memory, and Myth*. Lexington: University Press of Kentucky, 2015.

Beringer, Richard E., Herman Hattaway, Archer Jones, and William N. Still Jr. *Why the South Lost the Civil War*. Athens: University of Georgia Press, 1986.

Blevins, Brooks. *Arkansas/Arkansaw: How Bear Hunters, Hillbillies, and Good Ole Boys Defined a State*. Fayetteville: University of Arkansas Press, 2009.

———. *Hill Folks: A History of Arkansas Ozarks and Their Image*. Chapel Hill: University of North Carolina Press, 2002.

Boman, Dennis K. *Lincoln and Citizens' Rights in Civil War Missouri*. Baton Rouge: Louisiana State University Press, 2011.

———. *Lincoln's Resolute Unionist: Hamilton Gamble, Dred Scott Dissenter and Missouri's Civil War Governor*. Baton Rouge: Louisiana State University Press, 2006.

Boot, Max. *Invisible Armies: An Epic History of Guerrilla Warfare from Ancient Times to the Present*. New York: W. W. Norton, 2013.

Brady, Lisa M. *War upon the Land: Military Strategy and the Transformation of Southern Landscapes during the American Civil War*. Athens: University of Georgia Press, 2012.

Brophy, Dixie, comp., and Patrick Brophy, ed. *Vernon County Confederates: Soldiers, Bushwhackers, Sympathizers, Victims, and Veterans of the Southern Cause with Connections to Vernon County, Missouri*. Nevada, Mo.: Bushwhacker Museum, 1991.

Brophy, Patrick. *Bushwhackers on the Border: The Civil War Period in Western Missouri*. Nevada, Mo.: Vernon County Historical Society, 2000.

Brownlee, Richard S. *Gray Ghosts of the Confederacy: Guerrilla Warfare in the West*. Baton Rouge: Louisiana State University Press, 1958.

Burchett, Kenneth E. *The Battle of Carthage: First Trans-Mississippi Conflict of the Civil War*. Jefferson, N.C.: McFarland, 2013.

Cashin, Joan. *A Family Venture: Men and Women on the Southern Frontier*. Baltimore: Johns Hopkins University Press, 1991.

Castel, Albert. *Civil War Kansas: Reaping the Whirlwind*. 1958. Reprint, Lawrence: University Press of Kansas, 1997.

———. *A Frontier State at War: Kansas, 1861–1865*. Ithaca, N.Y.: Cornell University Press, 1958.

———. *General Sterling Price and the Civil War in the West*. Baton Rouge: Louisiana State University Press, 1968.

———. *William Clarke Quantrill: His Life and Times*. New York: F. Fell, 1962.

Catalfano-Serio, Chris. *The Effect of the Civil War on Ozark Culture*. Little Rock: Arkansas Endowment for the Humanities, 1979.

Christ, Mark K. *Civil War Arkansas, 1863: The Battle for a State*. Norman: University of Oklahoma Press, 2010.

———, ed. *The Die Is Cast: Arkansas Goes to War, 1861*. Little Rock: Butler Center Books, 2010.

———, ed. *Rugged and Sublime: The Civil War in Arkansas*. Fayetteville: University of Arkansas Press, 1994.

Clark, Thomas. *The South since Appomattox: A Century of Regional Change*. New York: Oxford University Press, 1967.

Clinton, Catherine, and Nina Silber, eds. *Divided Houses: Gender and the Civil War*. New York: Oxford University Press, 1992.

Closmann, Charles E., ed. *War and the Environment: Military Destruction in the Modern Age*. College Station: Texas A&M University Press, 2009.

Confer, Clarissa W. *The Cherokee Nation in the Civil War*. Norman: University of Oklahoma Press, 2007.

Connelly, Donald B. *John M. Schofield and the Politics of Generalship*. Chapel Hill: University of North Carolina Press, 2006.

Connelly, William E. *Quantrill and the Border Wars*. Cedar Rapids, Iowa: Torch, 1910.

Cooling, Benjamin F. *Fort Donelson's Legacy: War and Society in Kentucky and Tennessee, 1862–1863*. Knoxville: University of Tennessee Press, 1997.

———. *To the Battles of Franklin and Nashville and Beyond*. Nashville: University of Tennessee Press, 2011.

Cornish, Dudley Taylor. *The Sable Arm: Black Troops in the Union Army, 1861–1865*. 1956. Reprint, Lawrence: University Press of Kansas, 1987.

Cross, James E. *Conflict in the Shadows: The Nature and Politics of Guerrilla War*. Berkeley: University of California Press, 1982.

Cunningham, Frank. *General Stand Watie's Confederate Indians*. 1959. Reprint, Norman: University of Oklahoma Press, 1998.

Cutrer, Thomas W. *Ben McCulloch and the Frontier Military Tradition*. Chapel Hill: University of North Carolina Press, 1993.

DeBlack, Thomas A. *With Fire and Sword: Arkansas, 1861–1874*. Fayetteville: University of Arkansas Press, 2003.

Donovan, Timothy P., Willard B. Gatewood Jr., and Jeannie M. Whayne, eds. *The Governors of Arkansas: Essays in Political Biography*. Fayetteville: University of Arkansas Press, 1995.

Dougan, Michael B. *Confederate Arkansas: The People and Policies of a Frontier State in Wartime*. 1976. Reprint, Tuscaloosa: University of Alabama Press, 1991.

Downs, Jim. *Sick from Freedom: African American Illness and Suffering during the Civil War and Reconstruction*. New York: Oxford University Press, 2012.

Drake, Brian Allen, ed. *The Blue, the Gray, and the Green: Toward an Environmental History of the Civil War*. Athens: University of Georgia Press, 2015.

Eakin, Joanne W. C., and Donald R. Hale. *Branded as Rebels: A List of Bushwhackers, Guerrillas, and Partisan Rangers, Confederate and Southern Sympathizers from Missouri during the War Years*. Lee's Summit, Mo.: J. C. Eakin and D. R. Hale, 1993.

Earle, Jonathan, and Diane Mutti Burke, eds. *Bleeding Kansas, Bleeding Missouri: The Long Civil War on the Border*. Lawrence: University Press of Kansas, 2013.

Edwards, John N. *Noted Guerrillas*. St. Louis: Bryan, Brand, 1877.

Etcheson, Nicole. *Bleeding Kansas: Contested Liberty in the Civil War Era*. Lawrence: University Press of Kansas, 2004.

Faragher, John Mack, ed. *Rereading Frederick Jackson Turner: "The Significance of the Frontier in American History" and Other Essays*. New York: Holt, 1994.

Faust, Drew Gilpin. *Mothers of Invention: Women of the Slaveholding South in the American Civil War*. Chapel Hill: University of North Carolina Press, 1996.

———. *This Republic of Suffering: Death and the American Civil War*. New York: Alfred A. Knopf, 2008.

Fellman, Michael. *Inside War: The Guerrilla Conflict in Missouri during the American Civil War*. New York: Oxford University Press, 1989.

———. *Views from the Dark Side of American History*. Baton Rouge: Louisiana State University Press, 2011.

Fellman, Michael, Lesley J. Gordon, and Daniel E. Sutherland. *This Terrible War: The Civil War and Its Aftermath*. New York: Longman, 2003.

Fisher, Noel C. *War at Every Door: Partisan Politics and Guerrilla Violence in East Tennessee*. Chapel Hill: University of North Carolina Press, 1997.

Foreman, Grant. *Fort Gibson: A Brief History*. Muskogee, Okla.: Hoffman-Speed Printing, 1970.

Forster, Stig, and Jeorg Nagler, eds. *On the Road to Total War: The American Civil War and the German Wars of Unification, 1861–1871*. Washington, D.C.: German Historical Institute; New York: Cambridge University Press, 1997.

Gaines, W. Craig. *The Confederate Cherokees: John Drew's Regiment of Mounted Rifles*. Baton Rouge: Louisiana State University Press, 1989.

Gallagher, Gary W. *The Confederate War*. Cambridge, Mass.: Harvard University Press, 1997.

Gastil, Raymond D. *Cultural Regions of the United States*. Seattle: University of Washington Press, 1975.

Gerlach, Russel L. *Immigrants in the Ozarks: A Study in Ethnic Geography*. Columbia: University of Missouri Press, 1976.

———. *Settlement Patterns in Missouri: A Study of Population Origins*. Columbia: University of Missouri Press, 1986.

Goins, Charles R., and Danney Goble. *Historical Atlas of Oklahoma*. Norman: University of Oklahoma Press, 2006.

Goodrich, Thomas. *Black Flag: Guerrilla Warfare on the Western Border, 1861–1865*. Bloomington: Indiana University Press, 1995.

———. *Bloody Dawn: The Story of the Lawrence Massacre*. Kent, Ohio: Kent State University Press, 1991.

Grimsley, Mark. *The Hard Hand of War: Union Military Policy toward Southern Civilians, 1861–1865*. New York: Cambridge University Press, 1995.

Hahn, Steven. *A Nation under Our Feet: Black Political Struggles in the Rural South from Slavery to the Great Migration*. Cambridge: Harvard University Press, 2003.

———. *The Roots of Southern Populism: Yeoman Farmers and the Transformation of the Georgia Upcountry, 1850–1890*. New York: Oxford University Press, 1983.

Hale, Donald R. *Branded as Rebels, Vol. II*. Lee's Summit, Mo.: Donald R. Hale, 2003.

Hanson, Gerald T., and Carl. H. Moneyhon. *The Historical Atlas of Arkansas*. Norman: University of Oklahoma Press, 1989.

Harper, Kimberly. *White Man's Heaven: The Lynching and Expulsion of Blacks in the Southern Ozarks, 1894–1909*. Fayetteville: University of Arkansas Press, 2010.

Hauptman, Laurence M. *Between Two Fires: American Indians in the Civil War*. New York: Free Press, 1996.

Hinze, David C., and Karen Farnham. *The Battle of Carthage: Border War in Southwest Missouri, July 5, 1861*. Campbell, Calif.: Savas, 1997.

History of Newton, Lawrence, Barry, and McDonald Counties, Missouri, Pt.1. Chicago: Goodspeed, 1888.

History of Vernon County, Missouri. 1887. Reprint, Clinton, Mo.: Printery, 1974.

Ingenthron, Elmo. Borderland Rebellion: A History of the Civil War on the Arkansas-Missouri Border. Branson, Mo.: Ozarks Mountaineer, 1980.

Inscoe, John, and Gordon McKinney. The Heart of Confederate Appalachia: Western North Carolina in the Civil War. Chapel Hill: University of North Carolina Press, 2000.

Johnston, Carolyn Ross. Cherokee Women in Crisis: Trail of Tears, Civil War, and Allotment, 1838–1907. Tuscaloosa: University of Alabama Press, 2003.

Jones, Virgil C. Gray Ghosts and Rebel Raiders: The Daring Exploits of the Confederate Guerrillas. New York: Henry Holt, 1956.

Josephy, Alvin M., Jr. The Civil War in the American West. New York: Alfred A. Knopf, 1991.

Kerby, Robert L. Kirby Smith's Confederacy: The Trans-Mississippi South, 1863–1865. New York: Columbia University Press, 1972.

Knight, Wifred. Red Fox: Stand Watie and the Confederate Indian Nations during the Civil War Years in Indian Territory. Glendale, Calif.: Arthur H. Clark, 1988.

Lause, Mark A. Price's Lost Campaign: The 1864 Invasion of Missouri. Columbia: University of Missouri Press, 2011.

————. Race and Radicalism in the Union Army. Urbana: University of Illinois Press, 2009.

Leslie, Edward E. The Devil Knows How to Ride: The True Story of William Clark Quantrill and His Confederate Raiders. New York: Random House, 1976.

Livingston, Joel T. A History of Jasper County, Missouri, and Its People. 2 vols. New York: Lewis, 1912.

Livingston, John C., Jr. Such a Foe as Livingston: The Campaign of Confederate Major Thomas R. Livingston's First Missouri Cavalry Battalion of Southwest Missouri. Wyandotte, Okla: Gregarth, 2004.

Mackey, Robert R. . The Uncivil War: Irregular Warfare in the Upper South, 1861–1865. Norman: University of Oklahoma Press, 2004.

McBride, Lela J. Opothleyahola and the Loyal Muskogee: Their Flight to Kansas in the Civil War. Jefferson, N.C.: McFarland, 2000.

McKnight, Brian D. Contested Borderland: The Civil War in Appalachian Kentucky and Virginia. Lexington: University Press of Kentucky, 2006.

McPherson, James. The Battle Cry of Freedom: The Civil War Era. New York: Oxford University Press, 1988.

———. *Drawn with the Sword: Reflections on the American Civil War.* New York: Oxford University Press, 1996.

Meier, Kathryn Shively. *Nature's Civil War: Common Soldiers and the Environment in 1862 Virginia.* Chapel Hill: University of North Carolina Press, 2013.

Minges, Patrick. *Slavery in the Cherokee Nation: The Keetowah Society and the Defining of a People, 1855–1867.* New York: Routledge, 2003.

Monaghan, Jay. *Civil War on the Western Border, 1854–1865.* Boston: Little, Brown, 1955.

Moneyhon, Carl H. *The Impact of the Civil War and Reconstruction on Arkansas: Persistence in the Midst of Ruin.* Baton Rouge: Louisiana State University Press, 1994.

Mountcastle, Clay. *Punitive War: Confederate Guerrillas and Union Reprisals.* Lawrence: University Press of Kansas, 2009.

Neely, Jeremy. *The Border between Them: Violence and Reconciliation on the Kansas-Missouri Line.* Columbia: University of Missouri Press, 2007.

Nelson, Megan Kate. *Ruin Nation: Destruction and the American Civil War.* Athens: University of Georgia Press, 2012.

Nichols, Bruce. *Guerrilla Warfare in Civil War Missouri.* Vol. 1, *1862.* Jefferson, N.C.: McFarland, 2004.

———. *Guerrilla Warfare in Civil War Missouri.* Vol. 2, *1864.* Jefferson, N.C.: McFarland, 2007.

Noe, Kenneth W., and Shannon H. Wilson, eds. *The Civil War in Appalachia: Collected Essays.* Knoxville: University of Tennessee Press, 1997.

Otto, John S. *Southern Agriculture during the Civil War Era, 1860–1880.* Westport, Conn.: Greenwood, 1994.

Ouchley, Kelby. *Flora and Fauna of the Civil War: An Environmental Reference Guide.* Baton Rouge: Louisiana State University Press, 2010.

Paludan, Philip S. *Victims: A True Story of the Civil War.* Knoxville: University of Tennessee Press, 1981.

Parrish, William E. *Frank Blair: Lincoln's Conservative.* Columbia: University of Missouri Press, 1998.

———. *Turbulent Partnership: Missouri and the Union, 1861–1865.* Columbia: University of Missouri Press, 1963.

Parrish, William E., and William E. Foley. *A History of Missouri.* Columbia: University of Missouri Press, 1971.

Prushankin, Jeffrey S. *A Crisis in Confederate Command: Edmund Kirby Smith, Richard Taylor, and the Army of the Trans-Mississippi.* Baton Rouge: Louisiana State University, 2005.

Rafferty, Milton D. *Historical Atlas of Missouri.* Norman: University of Oklahoma Press, 1981.

Ramage, James A. *Gray Ghost: The Life of Col. John Singleton Mosby*. Lexington: University Press of Kentucky, 1999.

———. *Rebel Raider: The Life of General John Hunt Morgan*. Lexington: University Press of Kentucky, 1986.

Roberts, Bobby, and Carl H. Moneyhon. *Portraits of Conflict: A Photographic History of Arkansas in the Civil War*. Fayetteville: University of Arkansas Press, 1987.

Sarris, Jonathan Dean. *A Separate Civil War: Communities in Conflict in the Mountain South*. Charlottesville: University of Virginia Press, 2006.

Scheipers, Sibylle. *Unlawful Combatants: A Genealogy of the Irregular Fighter*. London: Oxford University Press, 2015.

Shalhope, Robert E. *Sterling Price: Portrait of a Southerner*. Columbia: University of Missouri Press, 1971.

Shea, William L. *Fields of Blood: The Prairie Grove Campaign*. Chapel Hill: University of North Carolina Press, 2009.

———. *War in the West: Pea Ridge and Prairie Grove*. Fort Worth, Tex.: Ryan Place, 1996.

Shea, William L., and Earl J. Hess. *Pea Ridge: Civil War Campaign in the West*. Chapel Hill: University of North Carolina Press, 1992.

Slover, James Anderson. *Minister to the Cherokees: A Civil War Autobiography*. Lincoln: University of Nebraska Press, 2001.

Smith, Andrew F. *Starving the South: How the North Won the Civil War*. New York: St. Martin's, 2011.

Smith, John I. *The Courage of a Southern Unionist: A Biography of Isaac Murphy, Governor of Arkansas, 1864–1868*. Little Rock: Rose, 1979.

Socolofsky, Homer E., and Huber Self. *Historical Atlas of Kansas*. Norman: University of Oklahoma Press, 1988.

Spurgeon, Ian Michael. *Soldiers in the Army of Freedom: The 1st Kansas Colored, the Civil War's First African American Combat Unit*. Norman: University of Oklahoma Press, 2014.

Steinberg, Ted. *Down to Earth: Nature's Role in American History*. New York: Oxford University Press, 2002.

Storey, Margaret M. *Loyalty and Loss: Alabama's Unionists in the Civil War and Reconstruction*. Baton Rouge: Louisiana State University Press, 2004.

Stout, Harry S. *Upon the Altar of the Nation: A Moral History of the Civil War*. New York: Penguin, 2006.

Sutherland, Daniel E. *The Emergence of Total War*. Fort Worth, Tex.: Ryan Place, 1996.

———, ed. *Guerrillas, Unionists, and Violence on the Confederate Home Front*. Fayetteville: University of Arkansas Press, 1999.

———. *A Savage Conflict: The Decisive Role of Guerrillas in the American Civil War*. Chapel Hill: University of North Carolina Press, 2009.

———. *Seasons of War: The Ordeal of a Confederate Community, 1861–1865*. New York: Free Press, 1995.

Thompson, George H. *Arkansas and Reconstruction: The Influence of Geography, Economics, and Personality*. Port Washington, N.Y.: Kennikat, 1976.

Thornton, Russell, with the assistance of C. Matthew Snipp and Nancy Breen. *The Cherokees: A Population History*. Lincoln: University of Nebraska Press, 1990.

Tucker, Richard, and Edmund Russell, eds. *Natural Enemy, Natural Ally: Toward an Environmental History of Warfare*. Corvallis: Oregon State University Press, 2004.

Warde, Mary Jane. *When the Wolf Came: The Civil War and the Indian Territory*. Fayetteville: University of Arkansas Press, 2013.

White, Christine Schultz, and Benton R. White. *Now the Wolf Has Come: The Creek Nation in the Civil War*. College Station: Texas A&M Press, 1996.

White, Richard. *The Middle Ground: Indians, Empires, and Republics in the Great Lakes Region, 1650–1815*. Cambridge: Cambridge University Press, 1991.

Winters, Harold, et al. *Battling the Elements: Weather and Terrain in the Conduct of War*. Baltimore: Johns Hopkins University Press, 1998.

Wood, Larry E. *The Civil War on the Lower Kansas-Missouri Border*. Joplin, Mo.: Hickory, 2000.

———. *Other Noted Guerrillas of the Civil War in Missouri*. Joplin, Mo.: Hickory, 2007.

Woods, James M. *Rebellion and Realignment: Arkansas' Road to Secession*. Fayetteville: University of Arkansas Press, 1987.

Worster, Donald. *The Wealth of Nature: Environmental History and the Ecological Imagination*. New York: Oxford University Press, 1993.

Zellar, Gary. *African Creeks: Estelvste and the Creek Nation*. Norman: University of Oklahoma Press, 2007.

## SECONDARY SOURCES: ARTICLES AND CHAPTERS

Banks, Dean. "Civil War Refugees from Indian Territory, in the North, 1861–1864." *Chronicles of Oklahoma* 41 (Autumn 1963): 286–88.

Bannon, John F. "Missouri, a Borderland." *Missouri Historical Review* 63 (January 1969): 227–40.

Barry, Louise. "The Fort Leavenworth–Fort Gibson Military Road and the Founding of Fort Scott." *Kansas Historical Quarterly* 11 (1942): 115–29.

Bearrs, Edwin C. "The Federals Capture Fort Smith, 1863." *Arkansas Historical Quarterly* 28 (Summer 1969): 156–90.

———. "The Federals Raid Van Buren and Threaten Fort Smith." *Arkansas Historical Quarterly* 26 (Summer 1967): 123–42.

———. "General Bussey Takes Over at Fort Smith." *Arkansas Historical Quarterly* 24 (Autumn 1965): 220–38.

Beilein, Joseph M., Jr. "The Guerrilla Shirt: A Labor of Love and the Style of Rebellion in Civil War Missouri." *Civil War History* 58 (June 2012): 151–179.

Berlin, Ira. "The Black Military Experience, 1861–1867." In *Slaves No More: Three Essays on Emancipation and the Civil War*, 187–234. New York: Cambridge University Press, 1992.

Bowen, Don R. "Counterrevolutionary Guerrilla War: Missouri, 1861–1865." *Conflict* (1988): 69–78.

———. "Guerrilla War in Western Missouri, 1862–1865: Historical Extensions of the Relative Deprivation Hypothesis." *Comparative Studies in Society and History* 19 (January 1977): 30–51.

———. "Quantrill, James, Younger, et al.: Leadership in a Guerrilla Movement, Missouri, 1861–1865." *Military Affairs* 41 (February 1977): 42–48.

Bradbury, John F., Jr. "'Buckwheat Cake Philanthropy': Refugees and the Union Army in the Ozarks." *Arkansas Historical Quarterly* 57 (Autumn 1998): 233–54.

———. "'Good Water & Ample Wood but the Country Is a Miserable Botch': Flatland Soldiers Confront the Ozarks." *Missouri Historical Review* 90 (January 1996): 166–86.

Brady, Lisa M. "From Battlefield to Fertile Ground." *Civil War History* 58 (September 2012): 305–21.

———. "The Wilderness of War: Nature and Strategy in the American Civil War." *Environmental History* 10 (July 2005): 421–47.

Bunch, Clea Lutz. "Confederate Women in Arkansas Face 'the Fiends in Human Shape.'" *Military History of the West* 27 (Fall 1997): 173–87.

Burch, Paul W. "Kansas: Bushwhackers vs. Jayhawkers." *Journal of the West* 14 (Winter 1975): 83–104.

Cain, Marvin R., and John F. Bradbury Jr. "Union Troops and the Civil War in Southwestern Missouri and Northwestern Arkansas." *Missouri Historical Review* 88 (October 1993): 29–47.

Castel, Albert E. "The Jayhawkers and Copperheads of Kansas." *Civil War History* 5 (September 1959): 283–93.

———. "Order No. 11 and the Civil War on the Border." *Missouri Historical Review* 57 (July 1963): 357–68.

Cheatham, Gary L. "'Desperate Characters': The Development and Impact of the Confederate Guerrillas in Kansas." *Kansas History* 14 (Autumn 1991): 144–61.

———. "Divided Loyalties in Civil War Kansas." *Kansas History* 11 (Summer 1988): 93–107.

———. "'If the Union Wins, We Won't Have Anything Left': The Rise and Fall of the Southern Cherokees of Kansas." *Kansas History* 30 (Autumn 2007): 154–77.

Cunningham, Roger D. "Welcoming 'Pa' on the Kaw: Kansas's 'Colored' Militia and the 1864 Price Raid." *Kansas History* 25 (Summer 2002): 86–101.

Danziger, Edmund J. "The Office of Indian Affairs and the Problem of Civil War Indian Refugees in Kansas." *Kansas Historical Quarterly* 35, no. 3 (1969): 257–75.

Davis, Michael A. "The Legend of Bill Dark: Guerrilla Warfare, Oral History, and the Unmaking of an Arkansas Bushwhacker." *Arkansas Historical Quarterly* 58 (Winter 1999): 414–29.

Demaree, L. S. "Post–Civil War Immigration to Southwest Missouri, 1865–1873." *Missouri Historical Review* 69 (January 1975): 169–90.

Dirck, Brian "By the Hand of God: James Montgomery and Redemptive Violence." *Kansas History* 27 (Spring/Summer 2004): 100–115.

Drees, James David. "The Army and the Horse Thieves." *Kansas History* 11 (Spring 1988): 35–53.

Duffield, Mark. "Total War as Environmental Terror: Linking Liberalism, Resilience, and the Bunker." *South Atlantic Quarterly* 110 (Summer 2011): 757–69.

Eno, Clara B. "Activities of the Women of Arkansas during the War between the States." *Arkansas Historical Quarterly* 3 (Spring 1944): 5–27.

Fellman, Michael, and Mark E. Neely Jr. "How Do You Define Total . . . [and] Total War?" *Civil War Times* 48 (April 2009): 27–29.

Fischer, LeRoy H. "A Civil War Experience of Some Women in Indian Territory." *Chronicles of Oklahoma* 57 (Summer 1979): 137–63.

———. "Confederate Refugees from Indian Territory." *Chronicles of Oklahoma* 57 (December 1979): 451–62.

Fisher, Mike. "The First Kansas Colored: Massacre at Poison Springs." *Kansas History* 2 (Summer 1979): 121–28.

Franzman, Tom L. "'Peculiarly Situated between Rebellion and Loyalty': Civilized Tribes, Savagery, and the American Civil War." *Chronicles of Oklahoma* 76 (Summer 1998): 140–59.

Gambone, Joseph G. "Economic Relief in Territorial Kansas, 1860–1861." *Kansas Historical Quarterly* 36, no. 2 (1970): 149–74.

———. "Starving Kansas: The Great Drought and Famine of 1859–1860." *American West* 6, no. 4 (1971): 30–35.

Gerlach, Russell. "Population Origins in Rural Missouri." *Missouri Historical Review* 71 (October 1976): 1–21.

Gilmore, Donald L. "Total War on the Missouri Border." *Journal of the West* 35 (July 1996): 70–80.

Hamilton, James A. "The Enrolled Missouri Militia: Its Creation and Controversial History." *Missouri Historical Review* 69 (July 1975): 413–32.

Harris, Jason. "A Historiographical Review of the Literature of the Civil War in Indian Territory." *Chronicles of Oklahoma* 89 (Summer 2011): 222–35.

Hatley, Paul B., and Noor Ampssler. "Army General Orders Number 11: Final Valid Option or Wanton Act of Brutality? The Missouri Question in the American Civil War." *Journal of the West* 33 (July 1944): 77–87.

Herklotz, Hildegarde Rose. "Jayhawkers in Missouri, 1858–1863." *Missouri Historical Review* 18 (October 1923): 64–101.

Herring, Joseph B. "The Chippewa and Munsee Indians: Acculturation and Survival in Kansas, 1850s–1870." *Kansas History* 6 (Winter 1983–84): 212–20.

Hsieh, Wayne Wei-Sang. "Total War and the American Civil War Reconsidered: The End of an Outdated 'Master Narrative.'" *Journal of the Civil War Era* 1 (September 2011): 394–408.

Huff, Leo E. "Guerrillas, Jayhawkers, and Bushwhackers in Northern Arkansas during the Civil War." *Arkansas Historical Quarterly* 24 (Summer 1965): 127–28.

Hulbert, Matthew C. "How to Remember 'This Damnable Guerrilla Warfare': Four Vignettes from Civil War Missouri." *Civil War History* 59 (June 2013): 143–68.

Imlay, Talbot. "Total War." *Journal of Strategic Studies* 30 (June 2007): 547–70.

Inscoe, John C. "Guerrilla War and Remembrance." *Appalachian Journal* 34 (Fall 2006): 74–97.

Janda, Lance. "Shutting the Gates of Mercy: The American Origins of Total War, 1860–1880." *Journal of Military History* 59 (January 1995): 7–26.

Johnston, Carolyn Ross. "The Panther's Scream Is Often Heard": Cherokee Women in Indian Territory during the Civil War." *Chronicles of Oklahoma* 78 (Spring 2000): 84–107.

Johnston, James J. "Jayhawker Stories: Historical Lore in the Arkansas Ozarks." *Mid-South Folklore* 4 (Spring 1976): 3–9.

Jones, Trevor. "In Defense of Sovereignty: Cherokee Soldiers, White Officers, and Discipline in the Third Indian Home Guard." *Chronicles of Oklahoma* 82 (Winter 2004): 412–27.

Kelman, Ari. "Deadly Currents: John Ross's Decision of 1861." *Chronicles of Oklahoma* 75 (March 1995): 80–103.

Kirby, Jack Temple. "The American Civil War: An Environmental View." Nature Transformed: The Environment in American History. National Humanities Center, revised July 2001, http://nationalhumanitiescenter.org/tserve/nattrans/ntuseland/essays/amcwar.htm.

Langsdorf, Edgar. "Jim Lane and the Frontier Guard." *Kansas Historical Quarterly* 9 (February 1940): 13–25.

Lemke, W. J. "Civil War Guerrillas." *Flashback* 31 (May 1982): 11–12.

Lewis, Lloyd. "Propaganda and the Kansas-Missouri War." *Missouri Historical Review* 92 (January 1998): 135–48.

Lindberg, Kip, and Matt Matthews. "'Better Off in Hell': The Evolution of the Kansas Red Legs." *North & South* 5 (May 2002): 20–31.

———. "'It Haunts Me Night and Day': The Baxter Springs Massacre." *North & South* 4 (June 2001): 42–53.

Lockyer, Adam. "The Dynamics in Civil War." *Civil Wars* 12 (March 2010): 91–116.

Mancini, Matthew J. "Francis Lieber, Slavery, and the 'Genesis' of the Laws of War." *Journal of Southern History* 77 (May 2011): 325–48.

McConnell, Lloyd. "The Colony at Union Valley." *Flashback* (November 1976): 7–15.

Miller, Chandra. "'A Perfect Institution Belonging to the Regiment': The *Soldier's Letter* and American Identity among Civil War Soldiers in Kansas." *Kansas History* 22 (Winter 1999–2000): 284–97.

Neal, Diane, and Thomas W. Kremm. "An Experiment in Collective Security: The Union Army's use of Armed Colonies in Arkansas." *Military History of the Southwest* 20 (Fall 1990): 169–81.

Neely, Mark E. Jr. "'Unbeknownst' to Lincoln: A Note on Radical Pacification in Missouri during the Civil War." *Civil War History* 44 (September 1998): 212–16.

———. "Was the Civil War a Total War?" *Civil War History* 37 (1991): 5–28.

Nelson, Megan Kate. "Looking at Landscapes of War." *Journal of the Civil War Era* 3 (September 2013): 439–49.

Newton, Steven H. "What Kind of War?" *North & South* 10 (July 2007): 16–25.

Ney, Virgil. "Guerrilla War and Modern Strategy." *Orbis* 2 (Spring 1958): 66–83.

Niepman, Ann D. "General Order No. 11 and Border Warfare during the Civil War." *Missouri Historical Review* 66 (January 1972): 185–210.

Noe, Kenneth W. "Who Were the Bushwhackers? Age, Class, Kin, and Western Virginia's Confederate Guerrillas, 1861–1862." *Civil War History* 49 (March 2003): 5–26.

Phillips, Christopher. "Calculated Confederate: Claiborne Fox Jackson and the Strategy of Secession in Missouri." *Missouri Historical Review* 94 (July 2000): 389–414.

————. "'The Crime against Missouri': Slavery, Kansas, and the Cant of Southernness in the Border West." *Civil War History* 48 (March 2002): 60–81.

Roberts, Bobby L. "General T. C. Hindman and the Trans-Mississippi District." *Arkansas Historical Quarterly* 32 (Winter 1973): 297–311.

Schroeder, Walter A. "The Civil War and Regional Distribution of Wealth in Missouri." *Missouri Geographer* 20 (1974): 33–47.

Scott, Kim Allen. "The Preacher, the Lawyer, and the Spoils of War." *Kansas History* 13 (Winter 1990): 206–17.

SenGupta, Gunja. "Bleeding Kansas." *Kansas History* 24 (Winter 2001–2): 318–41.

Shea, William L. "The War We Have Lost." *Arkansas Historical Quarterly* 70 (Summer 2011): 100–108.

Sheridan, Richard B. "From Slavery in Missouri to Freedom in Kansas: The Influx of Black Fugitives and Contrabands into Kansas, 1854–1865." In *Kansas and the West: New Perspectives*, edited by Rita Napier, 157–80. Lawrence: University Press of Kansas, 2003.

Smith, Robert F. "The Confederate Attempt to Counteract Reunion Propaganda in Arkansas: 1863–1865." *Arkansas Historical Quarterly* 16 (Spring 1957): 54–62.

Smith, W. Wayne. "An Experiment in Counterinsurgency: The Assessment of Confederate Sympathizers in Missouri." *Journal of Southern History* 35 (August 1969): 361–80.

Sternhill, Yael A. "Revisionism Reinvented?: The Antiwar Turn in Civil War Scholarship." *Journal of the Civil War Era* 3 (June 2013): 239–56.

Stith, Matthew M. "At the Heart of Total War: Guerrillas, Civilians, and the Union Response in Jasper County, Missouri, 1861–1865." *Military History of the West* 38 (2008): 1–27.

————. "'The Deplorable Condition of this Country': Nature, Society, and War on the Trans-Mississippi Frontier." *Civil War History* 58 (September 2012): 322–47.

Sutherland, Daniel E. "Abraham Lincoln, John Pope, and the Origins of Total War." *Journal of Military History* 56 (October 1992): 567–86.

————. "Guerrilla Warfare, Democracy, and the Fate of the Confederacy." *Journal of Southern History* 68 (May 2002): 259–92.

————. "Sideshow No Longer: A Historiographical Review of the Guerrilla War." *Civil War History* 46 (March 2000): 5–23.

———. "'Without Mercy, and Without the Blessing of God': Could Guerrilla Warfare Have Been the Key to Confederate Victory?" *North and South* 1 (September 1998): 12–21.

Sweeney, Kevin. "The Desiccated Plain: Comanche and Non-Indian Settler Responses to Drought in the Southern Plains, 1854–1897." *Heritage of the Great Plains* 36 (July 2003): 29–40.

———. "Drought in the Heart of Texas, 1854–1865." *West Texas Association Yearbook* 84 (October 2008): 58–73.

———. "Thirsting for War, Hungering for Peace: Drought, Bison Migrations, and Native Peoples on the Southern Plains, 1845–1859." *Journal of the West* 41 (Summer 2002): 71–78.

———. "Twixt Scylla and Charybdis: Environmental Pressure on the Choctaw to Ally with the Confederacy." *Chronicles of Oklahoma* 85 (Spring 2007): 72–93.

Warde, Mary Jane. "Now the Wolf Has Come: The Civilian Civil War in the Indian Territory." *Chronicles of Oklahoma* 71 (Spring 1993): 64–87.

Whites, LeeAnn. "Forty Shirts and a Wagonload of Wheat: Women, the Domestic Supply Line, and the Civil War on the Western Border." *Journal of the Civil War Era* 1 (March 2011): 56–78.

Windham, William T. "The Problem of Supply in the Trans-Mississippi Confederacy." *Journal of Southern History* 27 (May 1961): 149–68.

Winn, Robert G. "A Civil War Casualty." *Flashback* 27 (February 1977): 1–4.

Wood, Larry E. "The Life and Death of Civil War Guerrilla Tom Livingston." *Ozarks Mountaineer* (April/May 2000): 32–34.

Zellar, Gary. "Occupying the Middle Ground: African Creeks in the First Indian Home Guard, 1862–1865." *Chronicles of Oklahoma* 76 (Spring 1998): 48–71.

## UNPUBLISHED THESES AND DISSERTATIONS

Beall, Wendell P. "Wildwood Skirmishers: The First Federal Arkansas Cavalry." M.A. thesis, University of Arkansas, 1988.

Beckenbaugh, Terry Lee. "The War of Politics: Samuel Ryan Curtis, Race, and the Political/Military Establishment." PhD diss., University of Arkansas, 2001.

Bellas, Joseph R. "The Forgotten Loyalists: Unionism in Arkansas, 1861–1865." M.A. thesis, Ohio State University, 1991.

Butler, William D. "The Ozarks as a Barrier during the Civil War." M.A. thesis, University of Missouri, 1988.

Crowe, Clint. "War in the Nations: The Devastation of a Removed People during the American Civil War." PhD diss., University of Arkansas, 2009.

Davis, Dale E. "Guerrilla Operations in the Civil War: Assessing Compound Warfare during Price's Raid." M.A. thesis, U.S. Army Command and General Staff College, 2004.

Harvell, Elle. "Cope, Cooperate, and Combat: Civilian Responses to Union Occupation in Saline County, Missouri, during the Civil War." M.A. thesis, University of Texas at Tyler, 2012.

Holman, Tommy L. "James Montgomery in Kansas, 1854–1863." M.A. thesis, Pittsburg State University, 1959.

Martin, James Brent. "The Third War: Irregular Warfare on the Western Border, 1861–1865." PhD diss., University of Texas, 1997.

Prier, Jay Anthony. "Under the Black Flag: The Real War in Washington County, Arkansas, 1861–1865." M.A. thesis, University of Arkansas, 1998.

Schieffler, George David. "Too Little, Too Late to Save Vicksburg: The Battle of Helena, Arkansas, July 4, 1863." M.A. thesis, University of Arkansas, 2005.

# INDEX